Many Blessings:

A Tapestry of Accomplished African American Women

Sonnee D. Weedn, Ph.D.

Chispa Publishing

Novato, California

Many Blessings:
A Tapestry of Accomplished African American Women
by Sonnee D. Weedn, Ph.D.

Chispa Publishing
P.O. Box 1723
Novato, CA 94948

Available through:
Amazon.com, BarnesandNoble.com, Ingram and Baker and Taylor.

This book may be purchased for educational, business,
or sales promotional use. For information, please visit
www.chispapublishing.com

Designed by: Lynda Banks Design

ISBN-13: 978-0-9832776-0-6
ISBN-10: 0-9832776-0-5
Library of Congress Control Number: 2011921911

For

Sekyiwa Shakur,

who provided the original inspiration for this project,

and

Robert Weedn,

"heart whole, soul free. The august Father gave to me."

For Bradford,
Thank-you for your
work in the world!
many Blessings on your
journey,
Sonnie Weedn, Ph.D
April 19, 2011

Contents

Introduction

I am the great, great granddaughter of a man who fought for the North in the Civil War. "He was with the Wisconsin Regiment," Grandmother Delight would tell me with great pride. She added a little more to the story by saying that he and his compatriots were without food for many days. They stopped at a farmhouse and asked to be fed. The farmer not only fed them, but also said that they could sleep in the barn, where his wife brought them a provision of grain to take with them. She had packed the grain in several of her long, black woolen stockings; the only containers she was willing to part with.

As a child, growing up in a white, middle-class family, I had only a few encounters with African Americans. As Minnesotans, we were the white subjects of de facto segregation, though my parents wouldn't have understood this or thought about it at all. Blacks, or "colored people," as they were called then, were simply unknown to us. In 1950, when I was four, my father was called up for the Korean War. He was a fighter pilot, and we were sent to the Marine Corps base at Cherry Point, North Carolina, our first experience with the segregated South.

My mother was told by the neighbors that she should hire a "colored girl" to help keep house. And so entered a sweet, silent woman, named Willie Whitehead. I was only four, but I can see her face today: shiny dark skin, and a halo of fluffy hair. She was young, I think. My mother, who was only twenty-six, was told that she must keep a separate set of dishes and silverware for Willie. She didn't really understand the reasoning, but did as she was told, marking each plate and utensil that Willie would use with red fingernail polish on the bottom.

Within weeks my mother decided that the whole idea of these separate dishes was ridiculous. "Willie Whitehead is cleaner than we are," she said. And that was the end of that.

We only stayed in North Carolina for nine months before heading to California, as my father was sent to Korea. But, the red marks on the dishes served as a reminder of Willie Whitehead for all the decades of their use.

In 1956, my family transferred to Cape Canaveral, Florida, where my father was a test pilot. Once again, we were experiencing the segregated South. My parents abhorred it.

Our housekeeper was Doris Rivers, and she was married to James Rivers. Doris was a registered nurse. Her family had sent her north to school somewhere. But, there were no jobs for "colored" nurses in our small town. Nevertheless, various members of her family took turns heading north to school, despite the lack of real opportunity.

Doris would sometimes babysit us children when my parents went out in the evening. My mother would insist that her husband join her at our home for dinner because she didn't think a married man should have to eat his dinner alone. The next-door neighbors called the police and the police came to remind Mr. Rivers that "colored" men were not allowed in our neighborhood after 5 p.m. My parents arrived home soon thereafter, and my mother ran the police off, saying that no one was going to tell her who was going to be a guest in her home. She never spoke to those neighbors again, and even though they were teachers at our elementary school, we children were advised to have nothing to do with such ignorant people.

When I was ten, I was a Girl Scout. We were still in Florida and my mother realized that there were no Girl Scouts at the colored school. She called the national office of The Girl Scouts of America and told them that it was a disgrace that most employed people in our area had money automatically deducted from their paychecks as a donation to The United Way, which supported the Girl Scouts. But, only the white people benefited from this charity. She was informed that if she was willing to start a Girl Scout troop at "that" school, she was welcome to do so. They would fund materials and uniforms.

And so my mother recruited me, and we started the Girl Scout troop with the help of Mrs. Lewis, the teacher at the colored school. It was simply our task to help them get started. We did that by going to the school once a week for a period of time and teaching Girl Scout songs and providing curriculum. They got their uniforms, pins, and handbooks, and they were thrilled. I was only ten, but I remember being struck by the fact that the children were cleaning their own classroom (no custodian), and learning to read from old Life magazines (no textbooks). But, when it came time for the all Girl Scout "Sing" at the local Civic Center, these new Girl Scouts could not come, because the white leaders of the city would not permit it. "We don't have any bathrooms for colored people," they said. "What if one of the little girls has to go to the bathroom?" And so it went.

We left Florida in 1959. My mother begged Doris to come with us to California. But she declined, and after some years we lost touch with her. Through the years, I have thought of these lovely women, Willie Whitehead and Doris Rivers, many times. What became of them? I have searched for Doris with no success.

My life has been lived, since then, mostly in the actuality of de facto segregation. This has not been intentional, really. It just tends to be a common reality of American demographics.

And so, it was quite a surprise and a blessing when a young, urban, African American woman entered my life requesting to be a patient in my psychology practice. She was young, courageous, and brilliant. She could be profane, too, and she made me laugh.

She had called my psychology office requesting to enter psychotherapy. I was well aware that I knew nothing of African American culture. I felt inadequate to treat her and told her so. But, when I expressed my concerns to her, she was adamant in her desire to continue with me and in a therapy group made up of white, upper-middle class women. To say that we all learned a lot is an understatement!

I looked around to see what education I could find for myself on treating diverse populations. At that time, there was little available, but I found a class called "Race Matters" and quickly signed on for a weekend intensive experience. I was the only heterosexual, White Anglo Saxon Protestant in a class of twenty-five or so students. Where were the rest of us, the dominant culture?

What I learned was invaluable! I only wish that every member of the dominant culture, i.e. caucasian heterosexuals, could take a similar class. We discussed the implications of privilege in ways I had never previously considered or realized. I had never thought of myself as terribly privileged. I had started working as a young teenager. And I had worked all through college, unlike many of the young women I considered truly privileged who didn't have to work. My ignorance really showed!

I learned to be the first to extend myself in any encounter with a minority person, even if I risked rebuff. It was up to me to take that risk, because of my privileged status, and it was actually much less physically and emotionally risky for a person from the dominant culture to do this than for a member of a minority group. I learned to try to be sensitive to cultural issues, though I often failed. But, learning to fail gracefully was part of the learning. When I made a mistake, I had to learn to apologize for my ignorance or insensitivity and try harder. There was so much to learn!

I had a Ph.D. and thought of myself as an intelligent person with liberal leanings. I experienced my own ignorance and felt humiliated. At the same time, I was delighted by the opportunity to learn and practice a new way; a way that would bring the richness of increased diversity to my everyday life.

When the class was over, I didn't necessarily know much more about African American culture; but, I had learned more about my own assumptions about life, in general, and how they didn't necessarily apply to everyone, as I had foolishly assumed.

So, back to my patient… She welcomed me into her world, and though there were certainly rocky moments, our affection for one another has continued over the ensuing years. Though she moved to the opposite coast some years ago, we have remained in close contact.

Because of my experience with my African American patient, and my "Race Matters" class, and because of my interest in women's issues, in general, I began to think about how it might be that African American women, usually perceived to be from the bottom rung of the social and economic hierarchy of the United States could rise up to succeed and claim their destiny in such diverse ways. These women often seemed to be invisible, no matter their achievements or the actual circumstances of their backgrounds. I imagined that they must have valuable wisdom to impart and that someone just needed to ask them about themselves. I also thought that the Civil Rights movement and the Women's Rights movement had come about in close proximity time-wise. And, that as a result, the opportunities for African American women's achievements to be recognized were probably more possible now than ever before as the cross-currents of these two social movements converged.

In addition, I believed that African American women born during segregation, and still alive today, would represent a particular segment of U.S. history that would not be repeated. Their stories needed to be told!

So, I set about to interview accomplished (in the broadest sense of the word) African American women. I asked them to tell me their life stories and how they achieved what they had achieved. Thirty-one of them did just that, offering their stories along with their wisdom and advice to others.

How did I find them? How did I choose them? Well, I started by asking my patient. And, then I began cutting out magazine and newspaper articles about African American women and I developed a very thick file of them. I approached women who just looked interesting ("Oh, hello. I'm writing a book. May I interview you?") And, friends and colleagues gave me names and telephone numbers of women they knew and recommended.

I sent letters of introduction and followed up on those who responded, flying all over the United States to interview these generous women. More times than not, I would have to stop the interview midway, as my interviewee and I took time to compose ourselves, before continuing, because the conversations were emotional.

Each interview was wonderful in it's depth and complexity, and I would call my husband after each one to say, "Now, *this* one was really amazing!"

I have abiding respect for these amazing women, who are clearly just the tip of the proverbial iceberg. They have seen to it that people around them are made better just because of knowing them. I am better for having known them!

And, so, this book is the story, not only of thirty-one accomplished African American women, but also of my own journey in meeting and interacting with them. It has been a delightful and enriching experience, which also had its frustrations and challenging moments. But, then overcoming obstacles is part of every woman's story.

My teacher, Albert Sombrero, a Navajo man and Spirit Guide, says that it is time to repair the Sacred Hoop. By this, he means that at this time in history, all races and creeds are meant to come together in peace and understanding for the healing of our world and it's people. He says that his grandfather told him that this turn of events signals the beginning of "The Glittering Time." This book is meant to be a contribution to that goal as we enter The Glittering Time. May it be so.

Sonnee Weedn, Ph.D.

2011

Preface

African American women hold a unique place in the history of the United States of America. The prejudice and discrimination they have experienced has been well documented and need not be reviewed here. Suffice it to say; overcoming the particular obstacles of racism and sexism, sometimes combined with poverty and poor educational opportunities, previously advertised as separate but equal, takes great courage, creativity, perseverance, and strength of character.

What is it within the characters of so many African American women that sets them apart and allows them to claim their destiny, bringing forth their particular gifts and talents in order to support themselves and contribute to their families and communities? There are likely to be many theories about this. However, in this book, I identified seven character strengths that are apparent to me in the development of African American women's ability to thrive despite the challenges they experience as a result of being subject to the unique circumstances that are the historical legacy of all African American women today.

Women typically identify themselves in any number of ways. We are daughters, sisters, wives, mothers, teachers, cooks, nurses, and on and on. The titles and categories are endless. As children, we are full of possibilities and may grow up to embody any number of roles as we form our personalities. In this process of forming our adult identities we, hopefully, begin to see our characteristic strengths, combined with our particular gifts and talents.

Some women have had the good fortune to be able to nurture these strengths in ways that have allowed them to bring them to full fruition. For others, one or two of their strengths have been identified and utilized, while others are less well developed. Some women, though adults, are just beginning the process of self-awareness. Everyone starts somewhere.

This book is meant to honor all women, who despite many forward strides, still face discrimination in the workplace, and make up large numbers of the disenfranchised. However, this book is especially meant to honor and highlight the strengths of African American women, who have usually had to face the double discrimination of being female and black, and thus have had to work harder than their sisters of other ethnicities to rise to their full potential. They have much to offer all of us with their examples of faith and perseverance, as well as their sage advice.

It is my hope that this book provides you, the reader, whether you are African American, or not, the opportunity to think about your own characteristic strengths. In order to do this, I requested the help of the women you will read about in these pages. Each of them was generous with her time and her story, sometimes delving into material she had not previously discussed publicly. I am grateful for their assistance. Some of them have written books of their own, and if you are intrigued by their interviews here, I encourage you to get their books and learn more about them.

In addition, many men have expressed interest in this project. Men have much to learn from the women around them, who, so often have enhanced their lives in some supportive role, whether in the workplace or at home. So, I hope that my male readers are equally inspired by these stories.

The interviewees often had opinions about which of the seven strengths I identified most exemplified them. I often agreed with them. But, mostly I saw that each of them had all the strengths in some measure, and had really utilized them all to achieve their goals. Their wisdom, generosity of spirit, and amazing grace will be quite obvious to you as you review their unique stories and understand their contributions. They do, indeed, provide many blessings to the rest of us!

CHAPTER 1

Faith, Family, Fortitude, and Flexibility

There is an old proverb that says, "Be good to the women, for you will be under their hands at the time of your birth and, again at the time of your death." Because, historically, it was often African American women who were midwives, as well as caretakers of the old and the sick, it is a saying that ought to especially apply to them. However, traditional American culture has not been particularly good to African Americans, in general, or African American women, in particular. And so, when these same marginalized women rise up and make important contributions to the larger community, it is a wonder and a blessing!

As I traveled around the country, talking to African American women of all economic, educational, and social strata, I began to have a deeper understanding of the various factors that had shaped them and allowed them to make the most of their particular gifts, despite overt and covert discrimination, and the despair that comes of internalized racism.

Certainly, every woman is unique. Her life circumstances and history belong to her alone. And yet, I found threads running through each story that wove them together in meaningful ways.

It is important to note that young people today never experienced law-enforced segregation, and have no real understanding of its meaning to those it was meant to hold back. This was so evident when I went to hear Melba Beals, one of the original nine students to integrate Central High School in Little Rock, Arkansas, speak at Dominican University. High school students in the audience responded to some of her stories of racial injustice by commenting that they would just never tolerate that kind of treatment if it happened to them. They seemed not to understand that resisting "that kind of treatment" could mean risking one's life ... or worse.

In addition, most young women I speak with have not experienced the spirit-deflating effects of overt sexist attitudes that barred women from many jobs, especially the higher paying ones, as well as equal treatment in the home and society as a whole.

As we begin the 21st century, these old attitudes of racism and sexism have certainly not been completely eradicated. Though we have come a long way, we have a long way to go.

Four fundamental values or attributes became apparent to me in the interviews and discussions I conducted with thirty-one accomplished African American women. Almost every woman spoke of her family's deep, Christian *faith*. Most had been raised attending church services regularly, singing in the choir, or otherwise participating in a religious community. Bible verses were quoted as themes for many of their lives. Frequently, the women were still active members of congregations, though they may have branched out from the faith of their childhood to embrace other forms of spiritual practice that nourish their souls. Faith communities typically provide children with core values of kindness, compassion, and altruism. Most of the women I interviewed spoke of having been taught these values that are critical to a thriving, humane society. They are actively involved in the generous giving of their time and expertise in a variety of ways.

There is *family*. Not every woman came from a healthy, supportive family, but many did. If they were lucky enough to have this benefit, the family often didn't just mean the immediate, nuclear family, but a patchwork of extended family made up of blood relatives, as well as those designated by mutual agreement as aunties, uncles, and cousins. In other words, they had a community of connection.

For those who had difficult family backgrounds, other forms of "family-style" relationships made the difference. This could be a 12-Step Fellowship, teachers who reached out, employers who empowered, helpers of one sort or another along the way. But, it certainly cannot be over-emphasized that a family who not only cares, but also holds its members accountable is invaluable.

Fortitude was evident in the lives of every woman I encountered. It takes strength and courage to face the hurdles and challenges presented to each of the women interviewed. If a woman came from a secure and educated family, she still faced the obstacles of the prejudice of the dominant culture, not to speak of the internalized racism that gives self-doubt to even the most confident and competent woman.

For those who came from more humble beginnings, the challenges have been even more daunting. But, what is so obvious is that it is some of these challenges, themselves, that have pushed the particular woman to set her intention and strengthen herself by whatever means she could, to rise to the challenges and move forward despite setbacks.

Flexibility is the ability to change course or tolerate changes in plans, even setbacks, without losing faith or ambition. It is also the ability to entertain new ideas without being threatened by them. It was obvious that this flexibility was essential in each of the stories of success. These women learned to take risks that are unimaginable to the average person from the dominant culture. They adjusted to changes in living arrangements, jobs, and personal relationships. They let go of entire careers and security when other possibilities arose, or the necessity of moving on became apparent. They tolerated disappointments and failures without giving in or giving up. They simply changed course, gathered their energy and kept on.

In addition to the core values that shaped these women, seven character strengths seemed to describe them and appeared to characterize African American women, in general. Each of the following chapters features one of these character strengths, and brings forward the stories of distinct women who exemplify this particular strength. The individual stories are meant to affirm and honor the contributions of the particular woman featured, as well as inspire the reader to adopt and nurture the particular strength personified.

What became clear about the thirty-one women interviewed for this book is that each woman could actually fit into every one of the categories I had identified. Each of them had some degree of each of the strengths, as you will see. At the same time, some aspect of their individual stories exemplifies the strength recognized and helps it come alive.

In addition to honoring these amazing women, this book is meant to support you, the reader, in your pursuit of your life's work and your destiny. When you are in need of one of the strengths identified in these pages, go to that chapter and read several of the stories for inspiration. See if you can find the support you are looking for in the stories of these thirty-one women. Then make a plan and take action!

CHAPTER 2

The Survivors

We are survivors and not victims, and we have to take a stand or take a step or make a statement that allows us to move from being the victim of other people's decisions to the architect of our own well being and that of our community and country.

—Lani Guinier

African American women, despite their social or economic status, have been called upon to survive and make their way in a Euro-centric culture that is frequently unwelcoming and often downright disdainful of them. Given the fact that their ancestors survived the Middle Passage, then slavery, with its unspeakable hardships, as well as the intervening years from emancipation through the Civil Rights movement of the 60's, and beyond, it is no surprise that endurance is part of their shared cultural history.

The women represented in this chapter have amazing stories of surviving in the face of obstacles, and perseverance despite roadblocks of every sort. They have moved through the challenges they encountered to live enviable lives of success and service, each in her own way and according to her own gifts. When one considers the challenges that African American women in the United States have faced in previous generations, it becomes obvious that the ability to set one's jaw and push through whatever obstacles are in her path is a birthright, and has become inherent in her character.

Being a Survivor does not mean that a woman should simply endure hardships and endlessly "take it." But, it does mean that this strength can be called upon to move through difficulties a day at a time, with perseverance and determination. She can rely on the memory of her ancestors and their dogged strength and resolve when she falters or feels disheartened.

During the "midnight hour," when it feels as though it is time to give up, this strength can carry a woman through. The question becomes, how to illuminate that darkest hour and follow the light.

In this chapter, you will have an opportunity to meet four women whose life stories illustrate this valuable character strength. They demonstrate endurance, persistence, and grit, and have survived in the face of many challenges to achieve their goals. They demonstrate a wonderful blend of courage, ingenuity, and stamina.

as possible, maintaining the ceremonies and celebrations as well as they could. But, life had changed dramatically.

When Dr. Shakur disappeared, Set's mother tried to maintain her job and financial security; but within a short time, she, too, was in danger of being arrested and was losing ground financially. By the time Set was eight, her family could no longer hang on in New York, and they moved to Baltimore, where they had family connections. They had been plunged into poverty. While they had lived a life full of culture, pride, and community in New York, what awaited them in Baltimore was quite different. "It was barren in Baltimore," Set says. "The people were ignorant, mean, and small minded. I had dark skin, short hair, and dressed in African-style clothes. They said things to me like, 'You're black as the street!' It was horrible. Then my brother moved out of the house and my mother fell into deep despair. Eventually my mother's younger boyfriend moved in with us and I didn't like him. When I began to enter puberty my personality changed. I wasn't that sweet little girl anymore."

At twelve, Set was sent to Marin City, CA, for the summer, to live with the wife of a family friend. The summer came and went, and Set remained in Marin City. Baltimore was not a good place for the family and eventually her mother and brother joined her in California and they lived with one of her aunts. This particular aunt was stressed with the arrival of more relatives in her home, and Set says she thought this woman was mean. In retrospect, she thinks it must have been hard to care for a displaced young teenager, but at the time, the woman just seemed nasty. By the time Set's mother arrived, Set was no longer speaking to the woman and her mother asked her why she was silent. "Speak up!" her mother encouraged. "I hate her," Set answered sullenly. Set's mother was adamant in saying that if that was how she felt; they should pack up and leave immediately. "If that is how you feel, she shouldn't have to have someone in her home that feels that way about her," her mother said. "We had no where to go and no place to stay," Set explains. "It was the beginning of our being homeless. My mother taught me the hard lesson of standing behind my words. She did not blame me and she never spoke of it again. I know that my mouth can be sharp and I am sometimes willing to cut off my nose to spite my face. But, if it comes out of my mouth, then I'll stand behind it."

Set is quick to say that she does not blame the woman she said she hated. "She was actually sweet in many ways. She was just tired and I was twelve and thirteen. Marin City is a tough place and it took away the sweet baby girl in me. Whatever Baltimore didn't drain from us, Marin City did. There was such ignorance there."

"Tupac had arrived that first October and by May he had left to pursue his career. I was there essentially by myself. Everyone in the community was depressed. My mother was mostly absent, and I was left to raise and fend for myself. I became the girl who didn't fit in and got beat up on a regular basis. I no longer had my big brother to protect me. There was just no protection for me."

Set had found some solace in her church's Christian Youth group, but by the time she was thirteen she had stopped going and had begun hanging out with the "bad girls." "I was drinking alcohol at thirteen and had a twenty-three year-old boyfriend when I was fourteen. I had gone from being this good, good girl, to being horrible. I was drinking, fighting, and skipping school. My friends were smoking marijuana and some of their parents were "crack heads." One day I was handed marijuana and for some reason I just saw my life fast-forward to what it would become. I had been kicked out of a store for some sort of misbehavior and Tupac and his girlfriend wouldn't help me. In school I was getting all "F's." So, I made arrangements to go back to New York to be with my Aunt Gloria. Aunt Glo's husband, Tom, drove the subway, and there was stability in their home. I got a job at Love's Rite Aid Beauty Supply and finished high school in two years with straight "A's." I also worked in the school office. My mother eventually moved back to New York and began getting her life back together."

Prior to this, in 1986, when Set was ten years old, her father was apprehended and arrested in California. She says she was really happy when he was found because she thought he was dead. But, then she was disappointed, because he was not safely in Africa, as she had hoped.

Dr. Shakur stood trial in 1987 and according to Set he was convicted on the basis of the sole testimony of a confidential informant. He was sentenced to forty years in prison and remains incarcerated at the time of this writing.

Set was fifteen when Tupac Shakur made his first movie. He was nineteen, and though they were fairly distant, she was proud of him. He sent their aunt a check for $100 every month to help support his sister.

Set says that nobody realized that Tupac was her brother until he came to New York on tour. She heard a song he had performed on the radio that he dedicated to her. It was titled, "Pretty Brown Eyes," and she hadn't known about it. She says that when he was in New York, she would go to his hotel room to visit him. "I never asked him for money," she says. "I would make myself busy by straightening up his hotel room. Of course, since hotels have maid service and housekeeping, there wasn't much straightening to do. He would try to pay me and I would take the money and then hide it where he would eventually find it, like in the refrigerator. It bothered him that I wouldn't take his money. Some people in the family may have taken money from him, but those of us who were closest to him from the old 'little rascals' gang didn't. His fame really had no part in our relationship," she says.

When Set's uncle retired, he and his family moved to Atlanta. She did not want to move. Her mother said that if she could find a place to live, she could remain in New York. She stayed awhile in New York and eventually joined her family in Atlanta.

When Set was eighteen she had her first child, a daughter she named N'Zhinga. Though she was a single mother, she says that she never felt like a single mother, because when she left N'Zhinga's father, she always had a boyfriend. Within a short time, she had met the man who would become the father of her son, Malik, who was born when she was nineteen.

At this point, Set says that her brother had become a bigger part of her life inasmuch as his financial success allowed him to be more like a father and a protector. "He took care of me and my children and many of the children of our former 'little rascals' gang," she says. But, when Set's son, Malik, was nine months old, Tupac was killed in Las Vegas in a crime that was never solved. Shortly after Tupac's death, Set's God brother, Yaki, was murdered. He was one of the 'little rascals.' He looked up to me," Set says. "He taught me that I could be admired. Because I am so sensitive and emotional, his admiration bonded us."

Insightfully, Set explains: "The absence of my father stamped everything in my life. It influenced my relationships with every boyfriend I ever had. I felt dingy and insecure, and that I had no firm ground to stand on. I was clingy and terrified of abandonment." She also points out that she is proud of her father's pride in himself. "He's a Leo, and such a lion. He taught me how to have that pride, but his absence really affected me."

Set was able to see her father infrequently after his arrest. When he was moved to the penitentiary in Atlanta, she was able to see him weekly. He is moved from time to time, which makes it difficult for Set to see him with any regularity. Though held in a maximum-security prison, Dr. Shakur continues to correspond with and talk to his children frequently; attempting to be the best father and grandfather he can be under the circumstances.

Set speaks in a straightforward way of the rage in her that would break through her more typical sweetness from time to time. "I'd have a huge rage at least once a month. It would happen when I would interpret something as abandonment. Maybe it would come out when Tupac would go out with friends, or when he'd have friends over and I might get teased. I didn't know it, but I probably also had post-partum depression." At any rate, shortly after Tupac and Yaki were killed, Set broke up with Malik's father. She says that she felt fat and ugly. "I just felt that I could not go on without my brothers. I was beginning to have suicidal feelings, just wanting to be with my brothers. I called my mother and let her know this was it. There were other friends around me who were dying, and some by suicide; one of them cut her own throat. I just couldn't understand it and I asked my mom, 'Why? Why? Why?' My mother said that some people were just sad beings, that they had a sad spirit. I asked her if there were any sad beings who 'made it'. She was very quiet and then she thought of the name of one who had 'made it' and gave me her phone number. I had bought my first house and my mother hadn't been there yet, but she came there and stayed up all night to keep me safe. During that time, I believe that I saw God and both my brothers. I was thinking to myself that God would not be mad at me if I just wanted to come home and be with my brothers. But, what I saw was that all three turned their backs on me, and so I decided not to kill myself. My mother asked me if I wanted to go to a hospital or a spa. I said, 'a hospital,' and someone recommended Sierra Tucson in Tucson, Arizona."

Sierra Tucson is a unique treatment center dedicated to the prevention, education and treatment of addictions, and behavioral and psychiatric disorders and Set does not remember how her mother found out about it.

This month-long hospitalization was to be the beginning of Set's new life. But, it was not an easy experience. "I was one of a handful of urban black people they had treated, and they didn't really understand me or my experience. I had to teach them, get help for myself, and be with all these white people and try to understand them, too. But, I was able to step away from the urban environment I had been in and find some peace. My friends and family coined a phrase about my volatile emotions. They would say of me, 'Set trippin.' I found out that that wasn't the real me that was so crazy, it was a chemical imbalance in my brain. I learned I have a condition I can control, but I had to attack it the way I attacked my schoolwork. I have wished that my whole nuclear family could learn what I learned in that month. Sierra Tucson saved my life!"

After her discharge from Sierra Tucson, Set settled in Sausalito with her children. She attended intensive psychotherapy for two years, combining individual and group therapy with 12-Step meetings of Codependents Anonymous and Sex and Love Addicts Anonymous. She was determined to continue to heal herself and create a foundation of mental health. She says that her rages all but disappeared and she became more aware of herself. Set makes the point that some aspects of mental health can be hereditary as well as environmental. "If you are continuing to have emotional problems or are continuing to use drugs, or going to jail, look into it," she says. "There is help available."

Once Set's emotional health stabilized, she felt ready to return to school. "I'm dyslexic," she explains. "I was six before I could spell my own name and I couldn't read well. I hated to read out loud the way you have to do in grade school. And for the longest time I didn't believe I could have a career. I thought maybe I could do something simple. I tried going to cosmetology school after Tupac died. But, there was too much gossip and everyone always asking, 'Who killed Tupac?' I just couldn't stay. But, I am ambitious and I decided I needed to get the basic skills I had missed in high school. I enrolled in The College of Marin, a local community college near where I was living in California, and I learned so much! In high school I had learned that I could *be* somebody, but now I learned academic skills I really needed."

When Set returned to Atlanta, she gained entrance to Clark University. She remained a student for one year, and though she says that she doesn't remember much of what she learned there, what she did get was the confidence to pursue a career. There were several fitful starts and stops, with Set gaining experience along the way. She opened a beauty salon, but had trusted the wrong person as a partner, and had to leave that behind. She loved fashion and wanted to design clothes, but didn't find a lot of support. Even so, she persevered and created her clothing line, Madame Velli, based on her own designs. She was determined to bring her ideas to market. "Before I went to Sierra Tucson I was overweight, had no confidence, and didn't think of myself as pretty," she says. "My idea of myself was what I saw reflected from the men and what they said about me. I just thought I couldn't compete. When I received money from my brother's endowment, I began to wear high fashion clothes, and I saw how I was judged differently as a result. I could see that the clothes were a distraction from me. They held me in a particular way. I wanted to design clothes that empowered women to be themselves."

Set says that she decided to continue recreating herself. She had some cosmetic surgery despite disapproval from others. "Its what I wanted, and I just didn't care what others said about it." She married Gregory Jackson, in a magnificent and meaningful ceremony in her mother's backyard. "Greg is totally supportive of me," she says. "He adds stability to my life and I enjoy being a stepmother to his children."

Nowadays, Set is one of the proud owners of a boutique clothing store in Decatur, GA, called The Wild Seed, in honor of her favorite author, Octavia Butler, who wrote a book by the same name.

"I'm a girl who most people wouldn't think I'd read Octavia Butler. But I began reading her stories and books when I was eighteen or nineteen years old. I wept when she died recently and I wanted to acknowledge her in this way."

In addition to her work at The Wild Seed, Set serves on the Board of Directors of The Tupac Amaru Shakur Center for the Arts in Stone Mountain, GA. She is the liaison for "Pac's Kids," who are students at the Center, and teaches healthy empowerment classes to them in the summer program, employing some of the ideas and techniques she learned during her own recovery process.

Set is an advocate for mental health whenever the opportunity arises. She is emotional and adamant when she says, "I truly believe that improving people's mental health and addressing depression and post-traumatic stress disorder would lessen poverty, domestic violence, child abuse, drug addiction, and gang activity." She alludes to a recent trip she made to South Africa where she visited in Soweto. "There was so much despair and depression and it reminded me of what I felt like when I was depressed. When a person is depressed, there is just a feeling of nowhere to go. This is an issue that needs addressing worldwide. So, my best advice is to attend to your mental health. Doing that changed my life."

Denise Stokes

*"I can't be who I am,
if I don't know
who I am."*

I heard about Denise Stokes through another woman I interviewed for this book. "You should really be talking to Denise Stokes," Sonya Lockett said to me. "She is amazing in her work educating people about HIV and AID's."

I went to Atlanta, Georgia to meet with Denise, who came to my hotel wearing a beautiful dress with a flowing cape over it. She looked absolutely elegant, and though she has been HIV positive for many years now, she is the picture of health.

Denise has also been in recovery from drugs and alcohol for many years. And so, we had a brief discussion about my career treating substance abusers before moving on to talk about her very remarkable life.

Denise Stokes says that she grew up in a family that was secretive and confusing. She never really knew her father, and her mother had a fury in her that kept her children from asking any questions or approaching her much at all. Denise found out that she had older siblings when she had a crush on a neighborhood boy and her cousin explained that he was actually Denise's brother. She found out about a sister by noticing a photo in an album at her grandmother's house and asking whom it was.

Trying to figure out such basic information as family ties made Denise quite a detective. Her mother told the children very little, and though she could be fun and outgoing, she didn't know how to express love for them. There was little in the way of conversation and no affection whatsoever. It was a barren environment.

Denise found comfort in all types of music. She found that certain song lyrics seemed to validate her feelings. When she heard Prince sing "Let's Go Crazy," it let her know that someone else understood the way she questioned the world and its meaning.

She also loved words and the dictionary. Denise would write poetry as a way to express her feelings and then hide it so that no one would see it.

Early on, Denise was labeled as a bad child. Since there was no one to explain things to her, she explored and tried to figure things out on her own. This frequently got her in trouble. For example, there was a black cat at her grandmother's house that everyone chased away. Denise was only seven at the time and she thought that if this cat weren't black, he would have a better life. So, she got a can of white paint and a brush and painted the cat white. The poor cat died and the word went out that Denise hated the cat and intentionally killed it. Nothing could have been further from the truth, but the "bad" label stuck.

Denise says that she comes from several generations of abused and abusive women, so it is not surprising that she began running away from home when she was eleven to escape the cruelty there. She was always returned to her mother, where she endured the instability of many moves and a string of stepfathers.

When she was in the ninth grade, a construction worker raped Denise near her home. Her mother's rule was that Denise had to be home when the streetlights came on; and, because she was late, her mother began hitting her with a belt as she came in the door. She was in shock and never said anything about the sexual assault. But, she wrote poems about her experience and through this poetry she expressed herself without concern about judgment.

Denise was fifteen when she began dating a twenty-one year old man. She was convinced that she was in love. He gave her things that she wanted and said nice things to her and about her. He saw how attractive she was in every way and encouraged her. He also read the poetry she wrote, and really understood it.

When her mother forbade her from seeing this man, Denise became defiant. She wasn't about to give up the positive attention she was getting. So she ran away again, this time for four months.

Denise was eventually caught and placed in a Youth Detention Center as a runaway. Though she tried to explain herself and her situation to the staff, it was no use. Finally, Denise figured out that if she just said what the staff wanted to hear, such as, "I've been bad, but I promise to appreciate my mother," she would be sent home.

When Denise went home, she had had that four-month taste of freedom. And when she was sixteen, her mother turned her over to this same young man.

Denise says that there was really no one to talk to about any of this. She had been emotionally abused, and had had no help with the trauma of the assault. She wondered if her mother had ever even wanted her.

Denise tried to make a life with the young man she now lived with. There was a lot of drinking, but no drugs. She had been a brilliant student, but living on her own, staying up late and being wild ended her academic success during twelfth grade. It wasn't until many years later that she finished high school.

With the inevitable end of Denise's relationship, she decided to enter the military. She was intrigued by the idea of the GI bill for education and signed on with a recruiter. Denise was not quite eighteen years old when she passed the entrance exams with high marks. The military doctor who had performed her physical called her back. With absolutely no emotion in his voice, he informed her that her tests indicated that she was HIV positive and was unacceptable for military service. "You'll be dead in a year," the doctor announced impassively. The rape she survived at thirteen had come back to haunt her in the form of HIV.

Denise went back to her apartment in shock. When her landlord got home, she asked him to go to the liquor store for her. Teetering between numbness and terror, her drunken state became the norm and soon she began to associate with the neighborhood cocaine dealer. This began a year of unimaginable degradation.

"Cocaine eventually led to crack," Denise says. "I was running all over and could not land. I was becoming more and more degraded, and I crossed every moral line you can imagine. I would have occasional moments of consciousness, and then lapse back into that dark, dark world of crack addiction and alcoholism."

Denise awoke from her fog one morning to realize that she was twenty-one years old. The doctor had said she'd be dead and she wasn't. "What happens if I live?" she wondered. She had never considered this possibility and had hidden her pitiful state from her family.

"I really wanted to live. I thought it might be great to live, to write again, to listen to music, and enjoy the sun."

Denise went through several treatment programs trying to get clean and sober. She kept relapsing. At one point, someone had broken her jaw and she was found wandering the streets of Atlanta.

Finally, her stay at The Fulton County Drug and Alcohol Treatment Program, followed by living at Saint Jude's Halfway House allowed Denise to obtain and maintain her sobriety.

"I loved the 12-Step work," Denise says. I talked and talked and talked, and everyone listened. It felt so good to share. I had been waiting a long time to have people to relate to and talk to. There was real dialogue, and it was a power base for me."

One day, a woman named Dottie came to visit Denise at the treatment center. Denise told her about being HIV positive. Dottie told her that there were many women who needed to hear her story and arranged for Denise to meet and encourage other women facing the same challenge. Because her health was compromised, she was able to receive disability payments to survive during this period of time.

Denise began doing outreach work as a peer counselor at a local AIDS clinic, where she eventually served on the board. She delivered culturally sensitive HIV/AIDS education, incorporating messages about addiction and recovery. She says that she constantly rode the bus here and there for speaking engagements related to AIDS education. She tried to convey to infected people that they had a right to live productive lives despite their HIV status.

When Denise had been sober for three years, she received what she thought was a crank call. The person on the telephone said he was a White House aide and asked if she would be interested in working in Washington, D.C. for the Clinton administration, advising the President and other government officials on AIDS policy. He went on to say that her name was on a very short list of possible appointees. "I thought it was just some weirdo," she says. But, very soon a packet of papers appeared in the mail that made the offer official. Her appointment to The National HIV/AIDS Advisory Council began to be noticed by the press and she received numerous notes of congratulations from various government officials. People approached her and asked, "Now that you have the ear of the President, what are you going to do with it?"

Denise thought about her constituency of disenfranchised people with HIV and AIDS. Some had addiction problems. Many had been hurt by homophobia and/or racism. She knew that what she wanted to do with "the President's ear" was to represent these people. She wanted the President to know about the problems they faced. She says that she focused on writing sound policy and making sure the focus was on practical help and getting things done.

Denise says that from 1995 until 2000, when her term ended, she put her whole heart into this work. "My integrity spoke for itself and my voice was heard," she says. She goes on to say that President Clinton was attentive to the issues she presented and appreciated her.

"This is how I finished growing up," Denise says. "I went from the crack house to the White House and I found my womanhood. To this day, I can go to the White House website and pull up speeches I gave. I am proud of what I was able to do there."

Denise has continued her public speaking engagements. She has spoken at two Democratic National Conventions, including one for nominee John Kerry. She is a regular speaker at NFL Rookie Symposiums and on Black-Entertainment Television's, *Rap It Up*, HIV/AIDS education programs.

"I tell my story," she says. "I don't like telling people what to do or not to do, or how to behave. I just tell them where I've been and what I've done. People melt into the feelings and they relate to the feelings. I want them to be introspective and realize how their decisions affect themselves and others. I let people come to their own resolution."

In addition, Denise is an emerging writer, with work contributed to James Adler's *Memento More —An AIDS Requiem*. She has released a spoken word project called *Elevation*.

In reflecting on her life, Denise says that she sees the connection between having no father and being attracted as a teenager to an older man. "It took me a long time to let go of my father. I had no consistent father figure and it left a hole in my identity. I had no idea about how to do a relationship. But, I now know what I want and where my lines are. I won't move my lines for anyone."

She goes on to say, "My life had begun to unravel even before I knew I had HIV. With the diagnosis, I became immobilized. When I realized that I would live, I had no idea *how* to live. I just knew I didn't want to hurt inside anymore and that there were things I needed to learn. I had spent so much of my life trying to get my mother to love me. I tried to *earn* her love and this spilled over into my other relationships. It just didn't work."

"So, I realized that I can't *be* who I am if I don't *know* who I am and I set about to find out. I found my passion in life and that's when I found myself. When the noise in my head stopped, and I got other people's voices out, I could just really be me."

Victoria Rowell

"Wow is me!
Not woe is me."

I received an invitation to a "High Tea at the Beverly Hills Hotel" benefit for Victoria Rowell's nonprofit foundation, which provides money to children in foster care for lessons of various sorts in the performing arts. It was a beautiful invitation, but I couldn't afford to go. I'm not a television watcher, so I had not heard of Victoria. But when it was suggested that I interview her for this book, I decided to find out more about her. I read her book, *The Women Who Raised Me*, and was amazed by her story.

I made arrangements to attend her fundraiser the next year with my daughter-in-law, and it was great fun, as well as a delicious and elegant tea.

When Victoria modeled her cute outfit for the audience, I loved it when she made mention that she was experiencing menopause and that it was definitely changing her body. "It's a natural thing!" she said so publicly and easily as she walked down the stage runway.

Victoria Rowell is an accomplished and successful dancer and actress. She is living proof of her advice to others, which is: "Do not let your circumstances define you, but use them as a cornerstone of your strength."

Victoria was born as a ward of the state of Maine. Her mother had received no prenatal care and was kept in quarantine because she was mentally ill and filthy. Victoria's first five days were spent with the nuns at Mercy Hospital before she was transferred to The Holy Innocents Home for orphans. Her Caucasian mother immediately lost custody of three other children, due to her continuing mental illness and instability. Her father was an unknown black man.

Ultimately, her mother gave birth to six children—three boys and three girls. The boys remained virtually unknown to Victoria until she searched for and found them when she was an adult. She and her sisters all had fathers from various minority groups. Her brothers all had white fathers, which made them acceptable to her mother's white family. Victoria and her sisters were rejected and referred to as her mother's "nigger children."

At three weeks of age, Victoria was placed in foster care with a white family. The mother of this family, Bertha Taylor, had to argue with the social worker to take this baby home. Social Services did not believe that a minority child should reside with a white family. In fact, there were antiquated laws on the books in Maine at that time disallowing adoptions of black children by white families. However, adoption was never an option for Victoria anyway, as her birth mother refused to relinquish her children, hoping to be reunited with them at some later time—an event that never happened.

Though Victoria has no memory of her two years in the loving care of the Taylor family, she says that she knows that the time spent there, surrounded by love and kindness, gave her a foundation of resilience so essential to healthy emotional development.

Though the Taylors had every expectation of raising Victoria to adulthood, this dream ended when the Child Welfare department determined that the "racial difference" between her and the Taylors would present a problem in the future. No amount of pleading on the part of the Taylors or their close friends could persuade the social worker otherwise.

And so, Victoria was removed from the only family she had known and placed with a new foster family on a rural farm. Interestingly, this family was already providing foster care for Victoria's two sisters. So, she was reunited with them, though she had never previously met them. The social worker had hoped to find adoptive parents for Victoria, but again, her biological mother objected.

Mrs. Armstead, Victoria's new foster mother, moved her foster children to Dorchester, Maine where she could enroll them in a local Head Start program. She believed this city could provide the girls with a better education. But, they would return to the Maine countryside, which they loved, each spring.

Victoria says that like many children who struggle with instabilities in their home and family lives, she learned to depend on her early observational skills for stability. She says that she became a close personal friend of the ultimate mother, Mother Earth, herself. She speaks of her deep gratitude for the grounding effects of growing up off and on at "Forest Edge," the Armstead's farm. "When you care for a garden, reap a harvest, can identify flowers, birds, animals and trees before you can read and write; this is to understand basic survival. It is so important. Mother Earth has been my most influential mother," she says.

Mother Earth and Mrs. Armstead taught Victoria that there are no shortcuts in life to completing a full cycle. It was not how life or nature worked. Indeed, she learned that follow-through and completion were the one and only means to a desired result.

When Victoria was six, Mrs. Armstead noticed that she wore holes in the toes of her Keds shoes faster than the other children. When asked about this, Victoria demonstrated how she emulated dancers she saw on television by standing on her toes and dancing in the barn. Thus, holes in the toes of her Keds launched Victoria's dancing career, as her foster mother recognized a creative potential in her and arranged for her to have lessons. Victoria says, "At age eight, I began to understand that physical struggle was part of learning to dance. I also realized something else that became clearer later on – that my love affair with ballet was a double-edged sword, a dance/fight to channel pain, to stave off exhaustion, to defy gravity, and to make something extraordinarily difficult appear effortless."

When Victoria was nine, her foster mother looked in earnest for formal ballet training for her and Victoria received a scholarship to The Cambridge School of Ballet. She had arrived for her audition in Boston on a Trailways bus with homemade sherbet-colored interfacing strips, instead of ribbons, sewn onto her black, mail-order pointe shoes. Up until then, her ballet lessons had taken place in her living room, with a doorknob substituting for a ballet bar and her foster mother coaching her from lessons read from a book on ballet. She had neither leotard, nor tights.

Victoria expresses the utmost gratitude for the tutelage of her first formal ballet teacher, Esther Brooks. She learned the simplest, most universal truth from Miss Brooks; that one person could make a world of difference in someone else's life. Victoria attended The Cambridge School of Ballet for the next eight years, funded by a scholarship from The Ford Foundation.

During this time, Victoria developed a socially debilitating malady called hyperhidrosis. The physical symptoms of this genetic anomaly are extreme, excessive, and uncontrollable perspiration of the hands and feet.

For Victoria, this meant that she was reticent to touch others, even just to shake hands, as perspiration literally dripped from the ends of her fingers and palms. At school, she kept an extra piece of paper under her writing hand so that she didn't leave a puddle on the desk or on the paper she wrote on. She tried numerous difficult, expensive and painful procedures to little or no avail. For seventeen years she wore gloves to hide her symptoms. She was secretive and ashamed of her condition. It was not until she was thirty-one years old that this could be corrected through a dangerous, but ultimately successful surgery. She had lived her life until then, being afraid to touch or be touched by anyone.

Throughout Victoria's junior high and high school years, ballet and her ballet teachers were the constant in her life, along with her social worker, Linda Webb, to whom she expresses deep gratitude.

She traveled among various other foster placements, formal and informal, during her years in Boston. She learned that her fate often rode on the kindness or whims, positive and negative, of others.

But, as for all foster children, at the age of eighteen, emancipation loomed for Victoria. There would be no more support checks from the Child Welfare Department of Maine. She was expected to be completely self-supporting by May 10, 1977.

Fortunately, Victoria had become a professional member of The American Ballet Theater's second company. She was thrilled to be able to survive, but just barely. In addition, she had landed work with *Seventeen* magazine as a model. She kept herself on a strict diet. She had learned without quite knowing how, that she could deny herself food in order to not feel. Likewise, she could do the opposite and overeat and stuff herself in order not to feel. Eating had been problematic off and on since childhood. Victoria was well into adulthood before she could feed herself easily and adequately, and understand the connection between her eating problems and her losses in early infancy and childhood.

Victoria's years as a dancer were marked by very hard work and gradual success. She was paying her dues, touring with the Ballet Repertory Company and then on circuits performing with other ballet companies. This allowed her to earn money, as well as have travel and adventure. But, a real crossroads came when she was asked to work with choreographer Twyla Tharp on the feature film of *Hair*. She had to make a choice between this opportunity and furthering her dance career with The Julliard School of Dance as a ballerina. She chose to do *Hair*. When it was completed, she returned to her dance career. Victoria danced with numerous companies; but, she also took other jobs to stay afloat financially. She discovered that she wasn't much good at clerical work and was a poor typist, although she did both at times.

Victoria began to try to make contact with her biological mother and her three brothers. Her mother's sister always blocked her access to her mother until she took it upon herself to show up uninvited at her mother's funeral in 1983. She was able to learn the details of her mother's long struggle with paranoid schizophrenia, and in addition, she was able to locate and meet her brothers.

Victoria says that during this time, she had to remove herself from a relationship with a man who had provided for her, but had become controlling and threatening. This is an all too common experience for young women who are emancipated from foster care. Because they are needy of love, attention, food, and a place to live, they are vulnerable. The intricacies of intimate, mutually supportive relationships are unknown to most foster children as they navigate the field of broken attachments or no attachments. Fortunately, for Victoria, she was able to recognize her situation and move on from it.

She secretly continued her battle with hyperhidrosis, soaking her hands and feet in pure aluminum chloride and wrapping them in plastic bags secured with rubber bands. An additional regimen of immersion in positively and negatively charged water allowed four perspiration free hours per day.

Her career continued to grow by fits and starts. She was dancing, modeling, and acting. When she was finally able to be represented by a pair of agents, her professional life began to blossom.

Ultimately, she has become an award-winning actor, veteran of many acclaimed feature films and several television series, including eight seasons on *Diagnosis Murder*, and thirteen years as Drucilla Winters on CBS's number one daytime drama, *The Young and the Restless*.

Today, Victoria is using her creativity in yet another venue – writing. She has been writing since she was a child; writing to the various women who raised her and saving their letters to her. She speaks of the spiritual component of writing when one puts pen to paper in a personal communication so absent from email. The paper is sacred space for her.

Victoria has written her first book, *The Women Who Raised Me: A Memoir*, which stands as a collage of women so central to her life, and to her own tenacity and resilience. She has written a children's book that is ready for publication. She makes the important point that to do this writing has meant letting go of a lucrative income in show business, to return to the basics. It has been a leap of faith.

The mother of two children, Victoria has married and divorced. She says that the defense of detachment that exemplifies many adults, who were foster children, makes issues of intimacy and lasting relationship challenging. She wholeheartedly endorses psychological help as a means for bridging that gap to healthy relating. She says that her journey in therapy was "relieving—as though a weight had been lifted. It allowed me to be honest about my circumstances, lifted my shame, and acknowledged how strong I was."

Victoria is adamant in her advice for all women. "The only way to sustain our strength is to honor ourselves with rest. There are so many demands on women today as mothers, wives, workers, and volunteers. We must listen to our minds and bodies. Otherwise, we leave ourselves open to peril and depression. We women are susceptible to compassion fatigue, because we feel the sorrows of the world. So, honor yourself with rest, time, and sisterhood. Understand that the world's work will never be completed; it will always be there. So, replenish yourself."

Victoria is the founder of The Rowell Foster Children's Positive Plan, which provides scholarships in the arts and education to foster youth. She speaks on behalf of foster children and the issues they face while in the foster care system and upon their emancipation. She is a tireless traveler and speaker on behalf of disadvantaged and at-risk youth.

Lastly, Victoria advises women to pray. Though baptized Catholic, she practices no particular religion today. She says that she prays as a spiritual exercise and her vision of God is in the biggest sense and includes all ancestral mothers. "The landscape of Mother Earth is my church," she says, "So, lean into the bigger message."

Vickie Stringer

"There are so many doors that we don't go through. Always be ready, because preparation makes opportunity."

My friend, Martin Shore, heard about my book-writing project and called me to say that he knew of someone I should interview. He said that this woman was the owner of a publishing house; the largest African American female-owned publishing house in the United States. He made an e-mail introduction for me, but Vickie said she didn't know Martin. As it turned out, Martin knew someone who worked with Vickie, and so the connection was made.

Vickie was friendly and generous from the beginning. She sent me copies of books she had written and a book about the publishing business that has been helpful.

When I sent her the draft of her interview, it came back to me by return mail with her corrections. She is efficient! And when I arrived at my office the next day, there was a box that had arrived with gifts for me. I received a

T-shirt with her logo that says "I Read Triple Crown Books," which I have done and that I wear to the gym. There was a coffee mug with her logo, which I use daily, and it was filled with candy.

Vickie Stringer is the second to the youngest of seven children born to her parents, who divorced when she was seven. She says that apparently her parents had conflicts, but she wasn't aware of them and didn't feel tension at home. "I wouldn't trade my childhood family life for anything. Everyone looked out for me and so I was spoiled."

Vickie's father was an engineer at General Motors in Detroit, and her mother was a schoolteacher. They lived a middle to upper middle-class life. At Cass Tech, the best high school in Detroit, she was quiet and studious and "nothing to write home about." She had four sisters who were her friends and being home with them was definitely more fun than being at school. As she reflects on this now, Vickie says that though she loved being with her sisters, at the same time she believes that it was limiting, inasmuch as having girlfriends outside her family would have broadened her perspective at that time.

Vickie graduated from high school at sixteen. She wanted to go away to college and chose Western Michigan University, where she pledged a sorority and majored in business administration. She was smart and has been described as charismatic. After her freshman year in college, she transferred to Ohio State University.

Vickie was at a fraternity party when party crashers arrived and one of them caught her attention. She noticed his nice car and his good looks. She claims that it was "love at first sight." "He seemed like a nice guy," she says, "but not a good influence." As she spent more time with him and his friends, "The Triple Crown Posse," her values began to change. Eventually, she dropped out of school and followed this man into a life of crime, which culminated in her becoming pregnant. At that point, her boyfriend abandoned her and married someone else.

Indulged as a child in her family, Vickie's life with the father of her son had been one of indulgence, as well. She didn't really know how to manage money and she was struggling. Since crime was what she had come to know, she continued on this path, starting her own escort service as well as drug trafficking. Vickie says that she developed an addiction to money, which she believes was her downfall. She was arrested for drug trafficking when she was twenty-six years old, and a year later she pleaded guilty to money laundering and conspiring to traffic drugs. Prosecutors had agreed to a lighter sentence in exchange for her cooperation against others involved in the case, though she actually never had to testify against anyone. Eventually, Vickie served seven years in federal prison, which she describes as "the most trying time of my life". She was absent from her son's life. He was only two when she was arrested. Thankfully, her mother and stepfather raised her son while she was away. During those long years, she only saw him once.

Incarcerated in Texas, far from family and friends, Vickie had a lot of time to reflect and to think about what she really wanted for herself and her life. "I decided to use that time to heal myself," she says. "I had learned that association brings assimilation, and so I read extensively and wrote in my journal." Reading works by Donald Goines, who was also an ex-convict, inspired her.

Vickie began writing her own stories. She would go to the prison's law library and hang a sign saying, "Research in Progress," on the window to discourage others. There, she would move into the life of her fictional character, Pamela Xavier. She says that she often cried as she wrote, and eventually completed the first drafts of *Let That Be the Reason* and *Imagine This* while still imprisoned. She tried out these stories on her fellow inmates and received high marks for them.

In addition, Vickie wrote a powerful letter to God with a list of her goals and desires. In a way, it was a challenge to God. She was essentially saying, "Since you're God, you can do this!"

"It's been a blessed experience," Vickie says emphatically. "God showed me that He is a restorer. He restored me. We often don't have much faith in restoration and we need to have more."

Vickie's list of goals and desires has been met. She has a lovely home, the car she hoped for, clothes, a computer, financial stability and an emotionally fulfilling job. She has blessed her mother; and, she has done good things for her friends and family, just as she desired.

These more tangible goals were fulfilled by persevering through twenty-six rejection letters she received from mainstream publishers whom she approached to publish her manuscripts. She redirected her entrepreneurial abilities and charismatic people skills that had made her a good criminal, and self-published her first novel, *Let That Be the Reason*. She proved herself a creative marketer, traveling on her own to many cities and selling copies of her novel out of beauty shops and through friends. Vickie's first printing of 1600 copies sold out in three weeks, thereby negating the concern that her hip-hop audience simply weren't readers, and wouldn't buy books. They were and they did!

A small New York City publishing house bought her book in 2002 and gave Vickie a $50,000 advance. She was on her way as an author, but really wanted to be a publisher for other authors with the hip-hop audience in mind. By December of that year, Vickie founded Triple Crown Publishing, revolutionizing the literary industry as a pioneer of the Hip-Hop Literature genre. She has signed thirty other authors to her publishing house, and has published over thirty-six titles, distributing over one million books to bookstores and libraries worldwide.

The intangibles she longed for from her letter to God were to be at peace and be happy, to hear the voice of God, and to have a clear vision for her life. She paraphrases a Bible verse in which God promises, "I can restore unto you that which the locusts have eaten." And she gratefully acknowledges that God gave her her life back and then some.

"I'm not afraid of challenges that I am faced with today," Vickie says, "Because things can and do change with what God is able to do."

Upon being paroled from prison and returning to Columbus, Ohio, Vickie lived in a halfway house, worked twelve hours a day and performed community service to prove her reliability and to pay restitution for her crimes. She was working tirelessly to demonstrate to the authorities that she was able to parent her son. She wanted to regain custody of him. In addition, she wanted a good father for him.

Vickie has been out of prison for over nine years now. She says her family was willing to support her in *not* breaking the law. She has a new man in her life, and a new baby. She has custody of her older son, Valen, and in 2004 she founded The Valen Foundation, a nonprofit organization named for her son and dedicated to reuniting and restoring bonds between children and their incarcerated parents.

Vickie Stringer and Triple Crown Publications have been featured in such prominent news media as *The New York Times*, *Newsweek*, *MTV News*, *Publisher's Weekly*, *The Boston Globe*, *Vibe*, *Essence*, *Inc Magazine*, *The Washington Post* and many others. As an inspiration and motivation to aspiring authors and self-publishers, Vickie has published her advice in *How to Succeed in the Publishing Game*.

Vickie has much to say to other women. "Divine intervention changes lives," she says. "Have faith that miracles overcome obstacles."

She goes on to say, "Trust your gut. The Holy Spirit is your intuition. It never will fail you. I am God fearing and happy to be so. I would also tell every woman to Be Ready! There are so many doors that we don't go through. Always be ready, because preparation makes opportunity. I have a sense of expectancy and I make sure I'm ready. My credit is good; I've taken classes in time management, among other things. I got a speech coach to help me to improve my speaking ability. Look good! Fortify who you are!" And finally, "Be Blessed."

CHAPTER 3

The Inspirers

*For every one of us who succeeds, it's because
there's somebody there to show you the way out.
The light doesn't necessarily have to be in your family;
for me, it was teachers and school.*

— Oprah Winfrey

African American women have traditionally been inspirational and encouraging to others in their communities. They have been the bedrock of their churches, for example, and have provided spiritual nourishment to their children, grandchildren, and extended families.

Often, in the course of resolving problems or issues within themselves or their own families, they provide inspiration to others to do the same, without even knowing that they are having that kind of influence or that anyone else is observing their process. Helping one another and modeling success is critical to improving the self-esteem and self-confidence of those who are less aware or confident of their own possibilities.

Inspiring women are essential to their communities because they provide hope. They model the attributes of courage, commitment, confidence, and spiritual vitality so essential to successful and meaningful lives.

Inspirers encourage just by their presence. They come from all walks of life, and social and economic strata. They are not necessarily famous, though some are, but they serve as competent coaches and role models, encouraging others to take stock of their own possibilities and to make the most of them.

Inspirers are generous in their praise and acknowledgement of other's attributes. They encourage lavishly and criticize when they believe the criticism will be helpful in a particular situation. Every woman interviewed for this book spoke of people along the way who had inspired her, with either a personal touch or as a model to emulate.

In the course of writing about inspiring African American women, one of them explained to me the truism that, "Sometimes when I want to be inspirational, I put my backside to the business at hand and push from behind. A tugboat doesn't always pull, it mostly pushes." Her statement made me laugh at first, and then I realized that it was a good illustration of the diverse ways in which Inspirers affect others and sometimes effect change.

As I interviewed each of the following women, I was not only personally inspired by their stories, but I could see that they had had broad influence on the people around them because of their ability to be flexible and purposeful, and have courage and integrity. They made others better just by association.

Sonya Lockett

"If you don't give back, your blessings have been wasted."

I introduced myself to Sonya Lockett when I was on retreat at Miraval, a wellness resort in Tucson, Arizona. I had watched her and her friend, wearing bathrobes fresh from the spa, visiting over lunch, and asked if she would like to join me for dessert. It took some nerve for me to approach her and I worried that she would think I was rude or too pushy. But, she was really friendly and we exchanged enough personal information for me to learn that she was Director of Public Affairs at Black Entertainment Television (BET) in New York City. She had won an in-house weight-loss contest at BET, as part of their educational initiative targeting obesity in African American girls and women. In twelve weeks, she had shed twenty-five pounds and won a weekend at Miraval as her reward. As I was to learn during the course of the interview I requested of her, this was a great example of her determination in plotting her own life course, as well as inspiring others to improve themselves through making educated choices.

Sonya also exemplified how sometimes when we have to give up a dream we have held onto, in her case, the dream of being an actor, the new dream emerges and turns out to be highly fulfilling.

She was quite modest, telling me that the person I really should be interviewing for my book was not her, but Denise Stokes, who she claimed was a REAL hero in the fight against AID's. And so, Sonya helped me contact Denise, who is represented in the chapter on Survivors. This is an example of the way in which much of this book evolved. I would contact a particular woman and she would tell me that she was not "the one"; that "the one" was someone much more accomplished than her. It is refreshing to hear women pointing to other women as examples of accomplishment, rather than criticizing them, as so often happens. At the same time, it is critical to understand that most women are inspiring to someone, and that leadership involves claiming one's own accomplishments, as well as highlighting others.

Sonya's home life while growing up in Baton Rouge, Louisiana, was like *Ozzie and Harriet*, she says. Her parents, both professional educators, were strict, Catholic, and provided a good foundation for their two daughters. Sonya's parents taught her that, "no one is better than you, but as a black girl, you will probably have to work harder than others." She felt mostly protected from racism in her Catholic school environment, even though she was one of only six black students in her class of 120. She says that she loved the structure, the nuns, and the whole experience. "Being black didn't stop me," she says. "I was class president my sophomore, junior and senior years in high school and I just didn't view myself differently. Nothing made me think I should have."

Sonya is emphatic when she says, "You have to be comfortable with yourself to be comfortable with people different from you. If I'm the only black person in a situation, I'm fine with it. I always see myself as just another person." When speaking of racism, Sonya says that she entered school after integration was underway. "I just handled it. At that time, any racism I experienced from white people came more from stupidity, rather than viciousness."

However, Sonya experienced more hurt from the inter-racism, based on skin color and hair type, that she says is common in Louisiana. She heard comments like, "You are too dark," or, "You have nice hair for a dark-skinned girl." She acknowledged the painful affect this attitude had on her and saw how it affected other girls. The message was that to be attractive, you had to look more white than black. Internalized racism among African Americans is a challenge.

After high school, Sonya attended and graduated from Howard University. She had wanted to go away to school and her father believed strongly that she should attend a traditionally Black college for the support. Feeling stifled by the cliquishness of Baton Rouge and believing that her father's notoriety as a professor at Southern University would have been further restricting, Washington, D.C. promised a bigger worldview. Being at a historically Black college, she also felt the relief of having "no burden of my race. I didn't have to be a token."

Though she had planned to major in drama, Sonya eventually chose public relations. She was politically active in the undergraduate student association and the D.C. Young Democrats.

Sonya loved being in Delta Sigma Theta, a women's sorority that emphasized public service. She loved learning the lineage, the songs and traditions that had been passed down to them as a legacy from the founders.

She embraced the largely unspoken, but clearly understood commitment that if you were a Howard University graduate, you would go out and change the world.

While Sonya says that her sister was extremely focused on becoming a physician, she, herself, wanted to do everything and lacked clear focus. As a result, she says she had some trouble growing up, which she wasn't even sure she wanted to do.

After a stint as a bank teller, she got a job with The D.C. Department of Human Rights as a public affairs specialist, writing press releases and speeches and developing brochures. She credits Janice Smith with being a great first boss, and attorney, Maudine Cooper, head of The Urban League, with being an excellent mentor.

Sonya was certainly getting great experience, writing speeches for the mayor and learning the intricacies of special event planning. But, her original dream of being an actor was always in the background. And so she auditioned for The American Academy of Dramatic Arts in New York and was accepted. Though her family was nervous and she was terrified to leave a promising career and start over at age twenty-five that is what she did. "I was either brave or stupid," she says now. Although Sonya was successful at The Academy, being told that she was talented and had a strong presence, she was not thin and she didn't sing or dance. The older she got, the more discouraged she was because there was so little work available for black actors – female or male.

In 1999, she was auditioning and working as a restaurant manager/

bartender, while quietly believing that she had more to give. A man whom she had met previously, while doing freelance public relations work, came into the bar. Tim Rosta was the Executive Director of LIFEbeat: The Music Industry Fights AIDS, and as the evening progressed, "and the drinks flowed," he asked Sonya to contact him at his office. She did, and he offered her a job serving as the LIFEbeat representative on The Lilith Fair Tour, which was a traveling music festival and concert tour featuring exclusively solo female artists. Sonya's job was to coordinate the AIDS outreach activities on the tour, but with her public relations background, she began to create press opportunities for the organization, too. After speaking at one of the tour's press conferences praising the tour's efforts to have organizations that combat AIDS, breast cancer and domestic abuse be a part of the festival, she was asked by tour founder, Sarah McLachlan, to speak at every press conference. This insured that LIFEbeat was mentioned in tour articles. She says that, "Tim Rosta is still one of my biggest supporters."

After Lilith Fair, Sonya was asked to be project manager of the Levi's sponsored "World AIDS Day Concert," which was another LIFEbeat event. She arranged for numerous artists such as In Sync and Destiny's Child to give public service announcements. As a result of the success of this event, Sonya was asked to join the staff full-time and eventually became Director of Communications and Marketing for LIFEbeat. After three years with the organization, and though she loved non-profit work and had learned so much, she needed more income.

Around that time, a sorority sister from her Howard University days, who was now at BET (Black Entertainment Television) reached out to her and in 2002 she went to work for them as Director of Public Affairs; her job at the time of this interview. She has since been promoted to Vice-President. In this role, she creates pro-social initiatives, such as Rap It Up, an HIV-AIDS prevention campaign that is presented to a variety of audiences and tailored to the needs of the particular population being addressed. "I am so proud of what I've been able to accomplish," she says. "We've expanded our partnerships with educational campaigns. We've been recognized internationally for our work. The United Nations put our 'Global AIDS Initiative' up as a model. I expanded grassroots HIV testing events and teen forums. We want our programs to serve communities. We partner with local radio stations, look for a local physician to be on our panel and bring in youth living with AIDS, a celebrity and a representative from BET. The program is called Choices, and it focuses on the implications of choices we make in our lives. We try to clear up misconceptions regarding HIV and AIDS. We do prevention and education, and try to reduce the stigma usually associated with this disease. I'm so happy with what I'm doing. I see the young people being changed by what they have experienced with our program." Her enthusiasm and pride are readily apparent.

But, Sonya's enthusiasm wanes when we touch on the subject of significant men in her life. "What's the deal?" she asks. "There is this phenomenon of so many great women who are alone. Most of us would like to meet a nice guy. We date, but rarely find ones who are ready or willing to commit. I am stumped and disappointed about this."

Nevertheless, Sonya is resolute in her advice to other women. "Stay true to yourself, no matter what the situation," she emphasizes. "Integrity is my favorite word. Never let others dictate who you are and what you think.

Don't 'dumb' down for someone." She acknowledges that she sees some of her friends do this and it saddens her.

"The thing I like best about myself is that I am non-judgmental," she says. "I may not approve of or like something you do, but I respect your choice. And more than anything, I know, for sure, that I have been so blessed. If I don't give back, then my blessings have been wasted. Be yourself. Don't hide your light."

Sonya has shed the light of health education to countless people, male and female, adults and youth. She is indeed blessed, and a blessing.

Karolyn Ali

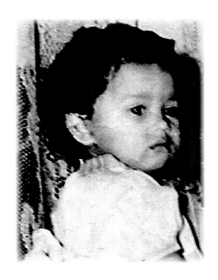

"Ground yourself in some form of spirituality. Love yourself and go forward."

I met Academy Award-Nominee Karolyn Ali when my son, Simon, was hired as an intern at Amaru Entertainment in Santa Monica, CA. Amaru represented the estate of the late rap star, Tupac Shakur, and it was a college student's dream to work in such a setting. Karolyn was kind as well as strict with her new intern. And I, as Simon's mother, was grateful for her guidance and direction for this teenager who was so excited to be working in the music industry.

I got to know Karolyn during the time Simon worked for her and found her to be as beautiful in her spirit as she is in her physical appearance, with her long, flowing hair, and her regal presence. She remained a mentor to Simon throughout his college career, having written a recommendation for him when he applied to The Berklee College of Music, and taking his phone calls from Boston when he was at Berklee College studying music business. She was also inspiring to me in the process of writing this book, offering her encouragement when I was challenged or feeling like Sisyphus, of Greek mythology, endlessly rolling the great stone up the mountain, only to have it roll down again. Karolyn was helpful from beginning to end. Early on she agreed to chant, in her tradition, for the best outcome for all concerned with the project.

Karolyn Ali was born Carolyn Jeannette Brown in Washington, D.C to parents who soon divorced. Her mother, Jennie, moved with her two daughters to Cambridge, Massachusetts, where they lived for a time with their great-aunt. She describes this period as hard for them, but they made it work; and eventually settled into what she describes as a comfortable life in Springfield, Massachusetts revolving around school and the Baptist Church.

Karolyn and her younger sister really had little relationship with their own father, but came to deeply appreciate their stepfather, Hammie Golden, who came into their lives when Karolyn was thirteen. Together, they regularly experienced family outings to a different New England city or landmark every Sunday and Karolyn speaks of her mother, Jennie, and stepfather with great fondness and respect. Hammie, or "Pop" as they called him, "was an uneducated Southern gentleman with a heap of common sense and a big heart...a beautiful man," Karolyn says. He was a decorated Army soldier, who loved animals and loved to fish. He loved bringing his catch home for his family and the neighbors, too. Although both her parents worked full time, their jobs were menial with low income. But, Karolyn explains, "We didn't know we were poor. For Blacks at that time to have a home and two parents together and with jobs, well, that was rich." Eventually, her stepfather owned his own dry-cleaning business where Karolyn worked part time.

Unlike her younger sister, Daa'iyah—a linguist with a Master's degree in Education, French and Spanish—Karolyn, regrets that she did not identify herself as an academic. She says that as a youngster, she knew she was endowed with the work ethic and just couldn't wait to join the workforce, starting with a job at the public library when she was fifteen. She worked through junior college and held a dream of having her own business. Within six months of receiving her Associate of Science degree, United Airlines hired her as their thirteenth black flight attendant. "My mother was an emotional wreck over me flying for a living. What did we know about airplanes? Black people didn't fly."

It was 1965 and because of issues of segregation and prejudice, Blacks were not welcome in the South. United Airlines did not require their African American crewmembers to fly south of the Mason-Dixon line, but Karolyn says she thought, "I'm not going to let that fear keep me from doing my job." And so she accepted flight schedules from her Chicago domicile to all destinations. She served many dignitaries and well-known people, including Duke Ellington, Senator Everett Dirksen, Richard Nixon's presidential campaign press plane and Muhammad Ali. Of the latter, she says they became friends after a turbulent flight between New York City and Chicago, where The Champ became so fearful that he accidentally pulled the shade off the window. His first comment to fair-skinned Karolyn was, "Are you passin?" in reference to her position as a black flight attendant. After the flight, he and Howard Bingham gave her a ride home. They have remained friends for forty years.

During her stint as a "stewardess," Karolyn maximized her days off by modeling. Shortly thereafter, she was discovered by *Ebony* magazine for their '67 national Fashion Fair. United granted her a leave of absence to join the fashion tour where she held the distinct privilege of closing the show each night as the show's "bride." Her groom was Richard Roundtree. On her return to the airline Karolyn was selected into United's management training program and groomed for various management positions. Her first assignment was as an appearance counselor for flight attendants who were all women at the time; teaching trainees about grooming guidelines, which included wearing girdles, and strict weight control. From that position, she moved on to be an in-flight supervisor, anonymously evaluating crewmembers on random flights and writing reports regarding issues of safety and quality control.

It was around this time that Karolyn married John Ali who was introduced to her by The Champ and Howard. While she enjoyed being treated like a princess by John, the confines of a traditional marriage did not suit her ambitious professional goals. Karolyn got a divorce and continued her climb up United's corporate ladder and beyond.

Ultimately, Karolyn was appointed Director of In-flight Services Training. She designed and wrote training manuals for In-flight safety and dining services, including galley and serving procedures, menus, service-ware —all the most minute details of In-flight service. She was one of the few black women in management, and says it was a fabulous experience that prepared her for corporate life and allowed her to travel the world.

Karolyn began mingling with popular recording artists and took another brief leave of absence from United to explore the entertainment industry. She was invited to join Bob Marley's management and music publishing company taking up residencies in London, Jamaica, New York and Los Angeles.

But, in contrast to her "charmed life" with her family and at United, Karolyn's personal life was marred by a devastating relationship with an abusive man—a "Jekyll and Hyde." She had to literally run for her life, slipping away from their digs in the middle of the night and begging the doorman not to reveal seeing her. She took a bus home to her parents, who sheltered her and nurtured her back to health. This experience, though a dark chapter, planted a seed of a dream, which she still holds, of one day creating a documentary for and about abused women. Its purpose will be educational and, hopefully, preventive, as it will encourage women to keep their power and not give it up to any man. She laments that "in the name of love," so many good women are filled with drugs and then emotionally and physically beaten by men who claim to care about them. This is a theme that many of the women I interviewed echoed, and I look forward to Karolyn's dream coming to fruition. "I became empowered through determination," Karolyn says today. "My naiveté was gone after the experience of physical abuse, and I simply took an attitude of *no fear*."

Strengthened and reinvigorated, Karolyn bounced back in New York as the Executive Assistant to Bennie Ashburn, manager of The Commodores, which included Lionel Richie. She traveled the world promoting their image and reputation, and helping keep their corporate profile intact. This gave her an opportunity to interface with agents, concert promoters and sponsors.

In the early eighties, Karolyn was tapped by Dick Griffey of Solar Records and moved to Los Angeles to manage the artists they represented, including The Whispers, Babyface & L.A. Reed, and Shalamar, to name a few. During this decade, that saw the birth of the music video, there was concern that their recording artists' themes and concepts portrayed on film (the combinations of imagery with songs) were not impactful enough to compete successfully with well-known white acts. Karolyn convinced Mr. Griffey that she could better present their acts. She went on to produce music videos for all of the Solar Records artists. Her work with Solar resulted in one of their groups, Lakeside, receiving a CEBA award for best video and Shalamar's, *Dead Giveway*, which was filmed in London, became an early MTV hit.

With the rise in her success as a music video producer, Karolyn joined forces with several filmmakers she had employed to direct videos. The team's independent production company became a powerhouse for music videos, concert films, and commercials. Her clients ranged from Stevie Wonder to Sinbad, from Steele Pulse and Ziggy Marley, to Dionne Warwick and Burt Bacharach. She produced numerous television commercials, including spots for Cherry Coke, featuring Cameo, and Jesse Jackson's 1984 presidential campaign (both CEBA award winners), as well as for the twenty-first anniversary of McDonald's Big Mac. She produced Stevie Wonder's concert film, *Live at Madison Square Garden*, celebrating his twenty-fifth year in show business, and corporate films for Nissan and Peter Ueberroth's, Rebuild LA.

Like most successful people, not all of Karolyn's projects have had the hoped for level of success. For example, the industry considered her debut feature film, *Kla$h*, a "Jamaican film" and did not recognize it for theatrical distribution in the U.S. It went to DVD distribution and the cable. But, she counts it as a success anyway, in that it brought a great new friend into her life, Jasmine Guy, whom she refers to as "a dear." Ms. Guy appreciated

Karolyn's person and her skills as a producer. When Tupac Shakur passed away, Jasmine Guy asked her to produce his memorial service in Atlanta. Tupac's mother, Afeni Shakur, was pleased with the service for her son. Some years later, Jasmine recommended Karolyn to head up Amaru Entertainment, which continued to produce Tupac Shakur's legacy of artistry.

The position at Amaru led to Karolyn producing the documentary feature film, *Tupac: Resurrection*, released by Paramount Pictures for which she received the prestigious Academy Award Nomination. It was a stunning achievement that she says was the culmination of a lot of hard work by a lot of dedicated people.

Karolyn says that she feels a spiritual connection to Tupac Shakur, though she never met him personally. "I feel hand-picked by him," she says. Karolyn was also editor of the companion book, *Tupac Resurrection 1971–1996* for MTV Books/Atria Books, distributed by Simon & Schuster. In addition she shepherded the production of *Afeni Shakur: Evolution of a Revolutionary*, written by Jasmine Guy for Atria Books/Simon & Schuster.

The recipient of numerous honors, Ali has earned the prestigious Lillian Gish Award from Women in Film. She was also selected as the NAACP/Legal Defense Fund's, AT&T Entrepreneur of the Year.

Back in 1986, Karolyn joined forces with its Founder/Executive Director Sheila Scott-Wilkinson and became a founding member and board member of Theatre Of Hearts/Youth First. The Los Angeles-based nonprofit that empowers underserved youth and their families through mentoring and instruction in quality, multi-disciplinary fine arts educational workshops has served over 75,000 youth countywide.

Karolyn seems amazed, herself, at the serendipitous chain of events that have allowed her to fulfill so many of her aspirations. She is clearly as beautiful on the inside as she in on the outside, and exudes kindness, generosity and competence. She has provided inspiration to countless others, not only through her person, but also through the media she has inspired.

Over the past twenty-five years Karolyn has practiced Buddhism in the Nichren Daishonin tradition. Her chanting practice—"Nam-myo-renge-kyo"—bespeaks a devotion to the universal law of cause and effect through sound. Buddhism aims to prove the true dignity of human life through the individual's life and his or her actions to help others do the same. It is a means to connect with one's highest and best self and to manifest that best self in all one's affairs. This inner journey has fortified her with "preparedness and perseverance," she says. She emphasizes the need for women to embrace some form of spirituality that grounds them and allows them to love themselves and go forward in the world with confidence.

Karolyn continues to work in the music and film business that she loves.

Lovie McGee

*"Excellence is
the highest form
of rebellion."*

I was shopping in Santa Fe, New Mexico, when I saw a magazine with a picture of Lovie McGee on the cover. She had been named, "Woman of the Year" by the governor of New Mexico, and I picked up the magazine to read about her. I was amazed at all of her accomplishments and especially struck by the fact that she said she certainly liked the financial results of selling an expensive home, but that her real joy came from showing people who never thought they would be able to own a home that they could. She helped them make a long-term plan for home ownership and then followed their progress.

Lovie was the first woman I interviewed for this book and she was patient with my anxiety and my inexperience. She had some suggestions, which I followed.

In a meeting with her over a year after that first interview, Lovie instructed me to return to my hotel room and look for the Gideon Bible in the desk drawer. "Look at the passage in Habakkuk, Chapter 2, Verses 2 and 3, then do what it says," she instructed. Well, I did as I was told. And here is what it said:

"Write the vision; make it plain upon tablets, so he may run who reads it. For still the vision awaits its time; it hastens to the end— it will not lie. If it seems slow, wait for it; it will surely come, it will not delay."

When I got home, I followed the instructions I had been given and re-wrote my intention for this book; that it would be inspirational to many women of all ethnicities, and especially honoring of African American women, who have endured so much to take their rightful place in American society. That piece of paper, placed inside a gold-colored, metal fortune cookie, has remained on my windowsill for all the months since that coffee date with Lovie.

Lovie McGee, owner of Love Realty in Albuquerque, New Mexico, is a true Inspirer. She is a passionate woman – passionate about her family, finding homes for people, teaching, music, helping children, and life, in general. Lovie says that she is in her sixties, which is surprising. She looks many years younger sitting at her desk, surrounded by pictures of her family and her many awards for public service.

The First State Bank honored her with the "Smart, Savvy, Successful Women in Business" award, but she says emphatically that it was not always so. "I was really dumb!" she says of her early adulthood. "I lived in a fairy-tale fantasy world and I didn't know anything else." She is talking about the first half of her life.

Lovie was born the fifth of six children, and there was a big space of years between her and her younger brother. "I was the baby for a long time and I guess you could say I was spoiled." She described growing up in a closely-knit family, where her maternal grandfather, a Church of God in Christ pastor, was the acknowledged patriarch. "What he said went!" Lovie recalls emphatically. She was not allowed to wear lipstick, shorts, pants of any kind, tennis shoes or sandals. Showing one's feet was not permitted. Her family produced and prepared all their own food, including curing their own meat. Very few items came from a grocery store. However, since Lovie was the last of the girls, she was mostly shooed out of the kitchen when food preparation was going on. She never really learned to cook.

Having been born in Oklahoma, Lovie's family soon moved to Missouri, where she grew up. Two months after her 18th birthday, she married. Even so, her mother prepared all the food for her and her husband and delivered it to them. Since she didn't work and she didn't cook, she had lots of time for fun. Nine years later, when her twin sons, John and JoRon, were born, the fairy tale began to unravel. Not only was Lovie unprepared for motherhood, but also both her sons were chronically ill with severe asthma from infancy. She says that her oldest sister, "the mother hen of the family," helped her enormously. "She helped raise my children and saved my life," Lovie says. The boys were so ill that they spent about three months of every year in the hospital. Many treatments and medications were tried, none with much long-term success.

Lovie was very candid in emphasizing again and again that moving from her parents' very protective care to her husband's home in marriage, had left her extremely naïve about life outside this very insular environment. She says that she truly did not understand the deeper and long-term implications of her children's illnesses, and so when their doctors advised that they be moved to an arid climate, like Arizona, she discounted it, largely because she could not imagine life away from her family.

When the twins were four, JoRon was hospitalized with asthma for the umpteenth time. The doctor said, "He's not going to make it." "My sister was crying, but I didn't understand what that meant. I heard JoRon calling faintly for his brother and I felt God wanted me to bring John to him." So, even though the hospital had strict rules against children visiting, and even though she was advised not to leave her dying child, Lovie went home to get John. "I told John, 'Hold onto my hand as tightly as you can and don't let anyone separate us.'" Though many hospital personnel tried to stop them, Lovie brought John to JoRon and put John in bed with his brother. JoRon's vital signs began to respond immediately and he ultimately recovered. Several years later, another severe medical crisis occurred with her sons and when they, once again, pulled through, she said that if God had saved her children so many times, she had to make good on her vow to God to leave her family and follow the doctor's orders to move to Arizona.

She packed her clothes, a TV set, and an alarm clock and headed out alone, leaving her husband and boys behind until she could find a place to move them. She stopped off in Oklahoma City and stayed with a cousin, who said, "Lovie, you are so naïve, the world is going to kick your ass and kick it good." Lovie tells this part of the story with a rye laugh. "And you know," she says, "the world did kick it good!"

Lovie stopped in Albuquerque, New Mexico, to stay with a friend from high school. Her friend's husband was in the military and insisted that the climate was right for her boys and that if she stayed, he would help her get a job at Kirtland Air Force Base. She had never really worked at a steady job and had no job skills, but she took a part-time job at the commissary on the base and sent for her husband and children. "My drive was always about having witnessed my son suffocating and there wasn't a damn thing I could do about it. I was willing to do anything to save his life," she explains. Lovie is tearful, we are tearful together, as she explains that there are things in a person's life that they can never forget and that motivate them to action. Seeing her son's nearly lifeless body was such a thing. She is quick to emphasize again that other than the challenge of her children's illnesses, she had lived a fun, fantasy-filled life and had no clue about what she would be facing outside the confines of her known world.

Lovie's husband, a ground traffic controller, was never able to find work earning more than $3.50 an hour in their new location. He made the decision to return to Missouri to work where he could better help to support his family. It was 1980 and Lovie was left alone in an apartment with two boys and two big dogs. Though he came to visit on weekends and holidays when he could, the couple gradually drifted apart and eventually separated. "I really panicked then," she said.

In addition to her job at Kirtland Air Force Base, Lovie started her own janitorial service. She worked days at Kirtland, was with the boys when they arrived home from school, and cleaned until 2:00 or 3:00 a.m. "But, I never missed a basketball or football game," she says proudly.

Employment at Kirtland proved daunting. Lovie says she experienced the most extreme forms of bigotry and prejudice that she had ever known. "I could not leave a cup of coffee or food on my desk because people would spit on my desk, in my cup or food, or worse. Very nasty things were put on my desk." She survived the inhumanity of this treatment and it strength-ened her resolve. She arrived early, stayed late and worked through lunches. When she complained about the bigotry to a supervisor, she was told she was lucky to have a job. She tangled with superiors on numerous occasions over issues of fairness and never backed down. "My grandfather taught us to speak up and I did," she says.

As time went on, two significant events occurred. First, having grown tired of apartment living, Lovie began contacting local realtors about buy-ing a house. But she didn't know the term, "down-payment," and had little money. When the realtors discovered this, they dropped her. However, eventually one stuck with her until a home was found. Her gratitude to this person is evident.

Secondly, Lovie was passed over for a promotion she had worked for and believed she deserved. A white woman who had been an art teacher was hired instead. When Lovie protested, she was told that this woman had a college degree and was, therefore, more qualified. "What a degree in art had to do with missiles, bombs, and hazardous waste, I didn't know, but I decided that if they wanted a degree, I'd get them a degree." And so, she did. When she got her Associate's degree, they said the other woman had a Bachelor's degree. And so Lovie got a Bachelor's degree in Computer Sci-ence with a minor in Business Administration. She graduated in four years while working full-time at Kirtland and running her janitorial business after family life and class at night school. "I would clean toilets until 2:00 or 3:00 a.m., sleep until 7:00 a.m., and then get the boys off to school and go to work." As her cousin had predicted, life was kicking her ass and kicking it good. "My anger at the treatment I received gave me an incentive," she says.

While getting her degree, Lovie met a fellow student who was a realtor. He encouraged her to get her real estate license. And so Lovie added a real estate license and finally a broker's license to her list of academic accomplishments. At Kirtland Air Force Base, she had eventually become the Black Employment Program Manager, which was a collateral duty. Her tenure at Kirtland ended in 1999. When outsourcing threatened her job of seventeen years, she was able to take early retirement. The timing was perfect, as she could devote her time to selling real estate. One month after passing the test for a broker's license, Love Realty was up and running. It was another agreement she had made with God. A sign in Lovie's office quotes the prophet Isaiah, Chapter 94, Verse 17, "No weapon formed against me shall prosper." She is certainly living proof of this affirmation.

Lovie has never forgotten the help she received to buy her own home. Her grandfather was a vocal advocate of property ownership and had owned over 200 acres of land. In an article written about her in *New Mexico Woman*, she states that her greatest job satisfaction comes from helping people who otherwise would not be homeowners; people who never thought they could own a home. Two of those clients stick in her mind. One was a homeless Gulf War veteran whom she helped to find a home of his own. He cried at the closing because he thought he'd never be a homeowner. Another client was a woman in an abusive relationship. Her sister brought her to Lovie, who assured her that "of course she could own a home." It changed the woman's whole outlook on life and her self-worth when she moved into her new home.

Lovie admits to having little free time. What she does have she spends with her family, including fifteen grandchildren. She loves music, dancing, and exercise. She practices T'ai Chi and says that yoga changed her life.

She has been a strong activist in the community as a member of the National Council of Negro Women, the African American Cultural Association, the Albuquerque Public Schools Superintendent's Council on Equity, and the African American Task Force. She is past chair of the Housing Committee of the N.A.A.C.P., and Vice-Chair of the Chelwood Vista Neighborhood Association. She served on the Albuquerque Human Rights Board for eight years, is a member of the National Association of Women Business Owners, and, as a member of the Democratic National Committee, she serves as ward chair of seven voting precincts.

Lovie has found herself involved in some areas usually associated with parents, not grandparents. Even with her own children successfully launched in life, she finds the time to be active in her grandchildren's school, serving as past president of the Hoover Middle School P.T.O.

Finally, and possibly most important, she has launched the Community Academic Initiative Resource Center (C.A.I.R.) to help close the achievement gaps in New Mexico schools. Lovie still finds time to be active in her church, New Hope Full Gospel, where she has been a Sunday School teacher and is active in a program to feed the homeless.

Her awards are equally impressive. She has received the Governor's New Mexico Distinguished Public Service Award, The Public Service Award from the Albuquerque Realtors' Association, the People's Choice Award for Favorite Real Estate Agent, and PNM's Entrepreneurial Leadership Award. In 2002, she was ranked 42 in the list of the Top 50 Women-Owned Businesses in New Mexico, and climbed to 32 in 2003.

"I love serving better than anything," she says. "Making a difference, teaching kids that there's a better life, a better way, being an inspiration if I can be. I work with the elderly as well because I look at my mother, my grandmother, myself and see that we're all in this world together. If we don't help each other, it's all for naught."

Lovie stated emphatically, "Many women are put down and alone. If you want to be a rebel, then be successful. Action speaks louder than words. Stop wallowing in self-pity and see that your life is all about your choice."

Lovie advises young women seeking success in life, "It's all in your mind. If you think you can, you can. If you believe you can achieve, you will. Don't let anyone tell you that you can't become something, because you can."

Listening to Lovie McGee's life story was awe-inspiring. She exemplifies the energy of the Inspirer, showing people the way to home ownership, as well as in so many other endeavors. Lovie tells me that she occasionally sells a very expensive home, and that that is fun and financially rewarding. "But, the real joy is finding a home for someone who thought they couldn't own a home," she says. "That's where my real joy is."

Lovie goes on to say words that I have used since hearing them from her, to inspire teenagers and others in my psychology practice, "Excellence is the highest form of rebellion!"

Ysaye Maria Barnwell, Ph.D.

"Don't be afraid to be multi-dimensional. Claim your contradictions. If we don't claim them, we can't resolve and integrate them. Then, strive to find the truth."

Twenty years ago, a woman in one of my therapy groups spoke of her devotion to a singing group called, Sweet Honey in the Rock. I had never heard of it, but the name was interesting and I stored it away in my memory. Fourteen years later, I saw a small advertisement for one of this group's concerts and talked my husband into attending. It was fabulous! We loved it! I invited all my friends and my sons to their concerts for the next few years and everyone loved them. And though the concert halls were always full, the people I invited had never heard of this group.

When my husband and I took our sons on a trip to Washington, D.C., we arrived fairly late at night. We asked the concierge at the hotel where we might catch a quick late-night bite to eat and he suggested a restaurant a taxi ride away. When we arrived, the host walked us to the back of the dining room, and as we passed the other diners, I noticed a member of this singing group I had become so enamored of. I told my husband that I knew it was "that woman." He said it wasn't. I said it was. I took one of my business cards and wrote her a note telling her that I was a great admirer of her work and thanking her for her contribution to my life and the lives of so many. I asked the waiter to deliver my note, which he did. Well, she came right over and we introduced ourselves and hugs went all around. She gave me her card.

When she was in Santa Cruz, CA on a retreat, I went to interview her. Again, it was one of my first interviews, and I was nervous. She was as regal in her "civvies" as she is gorgeous in her stage costumes. Her silver jewelry is her trademark, as is her black lipstick and nail polish. She is stunning in her unique style!

Some months later, when I was invited to present a program for the Tupac Amaru Shakur Center for the Arts, I asked Dr. Barnwell to help me. She suggested that we have a community singing day in which the children who come to the center and their parents would come for a day of "Singing in the African American Tradition." What a day it was! We sang from morning until early evening, beginning with sounds of the rainforests of Africa, and extending through the Middle Passage, field hollers, spirituals, gospels, songs of the modern-day Civil Rights movement, and so on. It was the most amazing history lesson I have ever had. In fact, I can easily say that it was one of the most meaningful days of my life. It was fun, too!

Ysaye Barnwell is the only child of parents who she describes as strictly disciplined, themselves, and strict with her. Ysaye says her father, a self-educated man, studied the violin his entire life and played professionally, as well as teaching, for over sixty years. He had hoped that Ysaye would be "the best violinist the race had ever known." To this end, Ysaye was his student for fifteen years, at which time she left home for college. He was also an inventor and held several patents on such things as home and auto alarm systems and air conditioning filters, to name just a few.

Her mother was a registered nurse. In 1927, because there were only two schools of nursing for "colored" women in the United States, she traveled alone, from Los Angeles to New York City to attend school. She had bought a train ticket for this journey, and then had to sue the train company to be able to use the ticket, as they were not going to allow a "colored" woman on board as a passenger. It was after nursing school that she met the man she would eventually marry. In time, they had Ysaye, who completed the new family.

Ysaye was named after Eugene Ysaye, a violinist and composer. She began violin lessons when she was two and a half years old, with her father as her teacher. "Every day was a lesson," she says.

Her mother had a nursing colleague who believed that teaching children about Black history was very important. Her mother agreed and Ysaye attended a Black history class for a small group of children on Saturdays. These lessons were foundational in her ability to pass on what she had learned to others when she was in college, because they provided a historical perspective for her and cultural pride at a time when this part of history was absent in the mainstream school curriculum.

Ysaye majored in music at Newton High School in Elmhurst, New York. She was a violinist in the New York City All City Orchestra all four years of high school and it was there that she experienced her first major racial insult. She had been assigned a place in the last row of the first violin section of the orchestra. From time to time, guest conductors visited. The famous conductor, Leopold Stokowski was one of the guests, and when he heard Ysaye play, he moved her forward to a more advanced position. Once he left though, the regular conductor moved her to the last row again. The message was clear!

Ysaye describes herself as a very average academic student. She had to have a math tutor, and her academic prowess was yet to be discovered.

When Ysaye was fifteen, she had an experience that was to influence the rest of her life—she saw *The Miracle Worker* on Broadway. She became fascinated with the idea of deafness. As the child of a musician, she had been raised and immersed in a world of sound. "I wanted to be a miracle worker and teach deaf kids to talk," she says. Soon thereafter, she met a deaf girl from Haiti. Of course, they had no common spoken language, but Ysaye was intrigued by this beautiful girl, and really wanted to communicate with her. Although they played together at times, they could not have a conversation. This encounter further encouraged her in pursuing the study of speech and language.

Ysaye began applying to colleges and looked for schools with strong speech pathology programs. The State University College at Geneseo, which was part of the SUNY system, accepted her. It had a well-known speech pathology and audiology department and she was accepted into the department. She went without ever having seen the campus and knowing nothing about the surrounding area.

When Ysaye arrived at Geneseo, she discovered that there were very few African American students. In fact, she was one of just seven Blacks on campus, including faculty, staff and students. All the negative racial stereotypes were intact in this Snow Belt, thirty miles from Buffalo. "I never saw so much white in my life," she says. "White snow that never melted, white sheep all over the countryside, and nothing but white people." When she received the names of her future roommates, she wrote to both and told them she was a Negro. Upon arriving at her dormitory room, she heard the father of one roommate arguing with his daughter and saying, "I've always sent you to private schools to keep you away from *them*." The other roommate never showed up. This was her welcome to college life.

Upon her arrival in the speech and audiology department, she discovered that they specialized in the treatment of stuttering. There was no training in speech acquisition for the deaf. As it turned out, Ysaye's dream of teaching deaf people to speak really ended there. Throughout the rest of her academic training, which includes a master's degree and a doctorate, she never did work with a deaf child.

Other opportunities presented themselves in Ysaye's undergraduate days. She discovered that only three miles from the college campus were migrant worker encampments filled with illiterate black farm workers. She began walking the three miles to the encampment, to teach the migrant workers to read and write. Today, the Board of Cooperative Educational Services (BOCES) hosts the Geneseo Migrant Center; something that grew out of the seed she planted.

Ysaye's father had been part of the Harlem Renaissance, and her family had books in their home written by and about black people. Some of them were written in French, as well as English. She went home and retrieved some of these books to set up a library of Black history books in her dormitory room. She was aware of the influences of Martin Luther King, Jr., Malcolm X, and the Black Panthers. She wanted to go to the South to do civil rights work, but her mother forbade it because of the very real danger. So, instead, she was a founding member of The Northern Students Movement at Geneseo, teaching fellow students about issues of civil rights, and preparing them to go to the South, if that was their choice. Ysaye says that the confluence of these various experiences led to her politicization in 1967 and 1968.

Throughout her college career at Geneseo, Ysaye sang with the Geneseo Chamber Singers. She listened to singers such as Nina Simone, known for her emotion-laden blues and jazz singing, Miriam Makeba who helped her understand what was going on in Africa and particularly apartheid in South Africa, and Odetta, whose folk songs, blues, and spirituals reflected issues of social justice. All were politicizing forces. She sang folk songs and studied the guitar due to the inspiration of those three women. Ysaye had sung Negro Spirituals in a community choir while in junior high school, and remains in contact with the man who directed that group. The fusion of music, issues of social justice, and activism were coming together in Ysaye's personal life in ways that would inform much of the rest of her life.

Ysaye was deeply immersed in her speech and language studies: so immersed, in fact, that she didn't realize until years later that she had not learned much about deafness, which was her original intent. But, she says now that in hindsight she was actually being prepared in a much broader way for her career in the field of speech and language. Geneseo was an immensely challenging place to be for a black woman in 1963. It is important to remember that Ysaye was one of only seven black people on the whole campus! Other challenges manifested in a number of ways, including receiving lower grades than she deserved; a fact that was noticed by several of the faculty. One of these professors, who observed this, provided Ysaye with encouragement and support. They had had numerous discussions over the years, and this mentor taught her to be observant and to think critically. She was also instrumental in encouraging Ysaye to continue on to graduate school. Thirty years later, when Ysaye received an honorary doctorate from Geneseo and gave the commencement address, her mentor was there to share her observations of her former student. She indicated that she had understood the pressures and prejudice that Ysaye faced.

Ysaye sums up her years at Geneseo by saying, "You can have a center that is different from everybody else, and it can make a difference." She emphasizes her point by saying that if she could live and thrive in Geneseo, which was so unwelcoming, she could do the same anywhere.

In March 1968, Ysaye finished her Master's degree in speech pathology at Geneseo and had no idea what she wanted to do. Did she want to work in a hospital or school as a speech pathologist? Could she have a career as a folksinger? She didn't know. But, on April 4, 1968, Martin Luther King, Jr. was assassinated. That very night, Ysaye made a personal decision and commitment regarding the importance of teaching black students at a historically Black college. She wrote letters to every historically Black college she had ever heard of requesting a teaching position. Howard University in Washington, DC invited her to interview and she was hired immediately.

Ysaye arrived at Howard University with a deep commitment to teaching black students. This commitment had heightened her radicalized perspective. She was twenty-two years old, wore her hair in an "Afro," and wore African clothes. And she was very well qualified for her position. Because she had had to work so hard to make her way successfully at

Geneseo, she had not had the experience of the more insulated culture she found at Howard, where students had not had to struggle in the same ways that she had experienced because they were mostly children of the middle class. They had more time for things like sororities and fraternities and Bid Whist, a very popular card game, which were completely foreign to Ysaye. The students at Howard at that time were just at the beginning of the ferment and foment of the times and had not figured out yet how it all applied to them. It was hard for Ysaye to understand and accept, given her own experience. It was a challenge to her values.

Ysaye was initially hired in the College of Liberal Arts department. Across the hall from her office was a man named John Lovell, who was writing a book about Negro spirituals called, *Black Song: The Forge and the Flame*. He was an anchor for her and inspired her musical interests, from the standpoint of the historical and cultural aspects of African American culture and music in this landmark work.

In 1969, Ysaye joined the faculty of Howard University's College of Dentistry. Like college departments in most professional schools of that time, men dominated and ran the department. "Because African American professionals who trained in traditionally Black colleges could not find positions in white institutions and had to return to Black institutions for professional employment, all the disappointment, hostility, and anger they felt was often seething just under the surface skin, and influenced the attitudes with which these people taught. There was an attitude of, 'I got mine! You got yours to get!' It was not friendly or collaborative. So, what was there was generation after generation of angry folks damaged by racism. I was definitely an outsider—a Ph.D. non-dentist, a woman, and someone from the outside who had very dark skin. They didn't really want me." After three or four years, I was up for promotion and the secretary to the dean said, 'You won't get it because you are too dark.' In most any black institution, it is those with light skin who rise to the top." The challenge of color stratification was another of the lessons of this time. "It took eleven years to rise through the ranks to become a full professor, but without tenure."

In 1973, Ysaye decided to continue her education and get a Ph.D. She was granted a two-year leave from her job at Howard to go to The University of Pittsburg. At her preliminary exams, she told the faculty that she had only two years to complete her studies, including her dissertation. They laughed and said it was impossible. She finished in two years and one month.

When Ysaye returned to Howard University to continue teaching, there had been a transformation in her interests as they related to her career in speech and language. She had never satisfied her dream of understanding deafness. But now, she was more interested in the cultural aspects of the deaf community, rather than in "fixing" deaf people.

Ysaye went to Gallaudet University; the only liberal arts university in the world established for deaf students, and began studying Sign Language. Gallaudet provides educational opportunities for students beginning in pre-school and continuing through the Ph.D. in several areas of study. In 1978, she completed a ten-week intensive program in Sign Language interpreting. She began teaching dentists how to take a medical history with deaf persons. "You have to ask about symptoms, rather than use the name of the disease, because of a lack of exposure to medical terminology," she explains. "If a patient reports 75% or more of the symptoms, then they have probably had the disease."

In the same year, Ysaye had joined a Unitarian Church and began singing in their choir. She noticed that there were few black people in the choir, though there were many blacks and others in the congregation who wanted to be included. These people couldn't be in the choir because they didn't read music. So, Ysaye set up a choir for people who did not have to read music. She arranged and taught them spirituals she had learned in the junior high school choir she belonged to so long ago. Shortly after, her pastor asked her to interpret a worship service. Her choir members encouraged her to sign and sing a solo. She agreed.

On that same Sunday, Bernice Johnson Reagon, founder of Sweet Honey in the Rock, an African American women's a capella singing group, happened to attend the Unitarian Service and observed Ysaye singing and signing. She was impressed with what she saw and was intrigued by the fact that Sign Language had the capacity to interpret subtle aspects of African American culture. In the mid 1970's, Sweet Honey had been invited to tour with pioneers in the Women's music movement. The leaders of the Women's movement were advocating for inclusivity of all sorts, including accessibility for all people, and had asked Sweet Honey to provide Sign Language interpretation for their music six years prior to this.

Dr. Reagon got a glimpse of what was possible as she observed Ysaye interpreting music using Sign Language in such a way that it expressed the musical, rhythmic, and emotional aspects of what was being sung, rather than just a literal interpretation of the words. She invited Ysaye to come the next day to audition for Sweet Honey. The auditions were three hours a day, every day for thirty days. This was in addition to her full time job. Ysaye learned all the vocal parts to about forty songs, and at the end of the month, she was chosen to be part of the group. Her choice was to join the group as a singer, and a decision was made to add a Sign Language interpreter to accompany Sweet Honey. And so, these disparate aspects of Ysaye's training were brought together in an amazingly creative way.

Ysaye continued her career teaching at Howard University. In September 1979, another major, historically Black university began courting her, and though she told them she intended to stay at Howard, in January 1980, they sent her employment paperwork anyway. She sent it back with a firm "no." When she told her department chairman what she had done, he said she should have taken the job. He knew what she did not yet know, that although she was up for a full professorship with tenure, she would only receive the professorship without tenure. He let her know that come fall, she would be out of a job. She realized with dismay that she had not learned to play the game. She was a woman and an outsider. She was a Ph.D. in a world of D.D.S.'s and tenure was reserved for the dentists.

"I was devastated," says Ysaye. "I had really believed that if you worked hard, you would succeed. Many people supported me. My students signed letters that had been written on my behalf, as did numerous faculty members. It made no difference."

Ysaye says that 1980 was the most difficult year of her life. "I had a crisis of values. I couldn't understand what all my hard work had meant. I was in deep despair. A close friend had died of asthma. I had an affair that ended with an abortion. I had to figure out if I could apply to another university and start over. I seriously contemplated suicide. I entered psychotherapy and received help with the depression and despair that had taken over my life."

Ysaye applied and was accepted into Howard University's School of

Public Health for a Master of Science degree in Public Health, a ten-month intensive program, open only to M.D.'s and Ph.D.'s. At the same time, Sweet Honey was invited to do a month long tour in Japan, which meant that she would miss a whole month of the ten-month public health program. She had to convince the faculty that she could manage both. She went on tour with Sweet Honey for the month, and it proved to be an opportunity for her interest in research and science combined with music to come together.

In her public health curriculum, Ysaye had studied the disaster in Minimata, Japan, in which mercury had leached into the water, killing fish and causing birth defects and brain damage to humans. The results of this toxic exposure had come to be called Minimata Disease. When Sweet Honey traveled to Minimata, she asked local people if they had songs about this tragedy, because in many cultures, as in the United States, there are songs to describe all types of hardship or tragedy. The answer was "no." It occurred to her that the industrial and occupational songs of industry laborers could be used in epidemiological research. All her different "pieces" were coming together: music and speech and language, public health, research, epidemiology, and education.

Ysaye began collecting the songs of ordinary laboring people. She analyzed them to determine how they might describe diseases and the symptoms intrinsic to their particular occupation. She collected and analyzed over 1500 songs of coal miners and textile workers, and the people in the Public Health School were stunned to see how ordinary people had documented their lives and their work, and their illnesses in songs. Ysaye collected songs that had been recorded, were in stores, and were easily available. At the oral defense of her research, she asked the faculty to identify the disease described in each of the songs. There was 100% accuracy!

Obviously, there is much more that can be said about Dr. Ysaye Maria Barnwell's professional life. But, it can certainly be summed up in "the whole journey of people who don't hear," giving voice to people and empowering them. Her ability to integrate her formal training in speech and hearing with her lifelong love and study of music and the oral tradition, have created her unique contribution. She is a commissioned composer. She has taught deaf African Americans to do AIDS education in their community. She has worked in the area of child protection. She says that her work in public health is meant to energize and heal people's spirits, as well as their physical and mental health. "When I added Sign Language and a knowledge of Deaf culture, I was able to be an advocate for the Deaf in medical situations and make Sweet Honey concerts more accessible. I have combined community health with community singing, and song gathering events. You just don't know how you will use your pieces. But, our lives are composed of these disparate threads that come together."

In conclusion, she offers this advice, "Everything, and I mean everything, matters. If you think it doesn't, look at people not in public office because of what they did in their youth. Don't be afraid to be multi-dimensional. Claim your contradictions. If we don't claim them, then we can't resolve and integrate them. Then, strive to find the truth. And finally, "Where do you find and how do you use your voice? That is the real question."

Chiquita Stephenson

*"I don't allow
anyone or anything
to define me.
God comes first."*

met my friend, Gloria Bouknight in New York City to go to the theatre
before attending the "Women, Peace, and Power" conference at The
Omega Center in Rhinebeck, New York. During our dinner after the
theatre she said that she had arranged for a young woman to come to her
house the next morning for me to interview for this book. I reminded her
that it was now midnight and we would be leaving fairly early the next
morning, and there might not be time. Besides, I had no idea who this
woman was. Gloria didn't even know her last name. "Don't worry," she said.
"I told her to come over at 7 a.m. I don't really know who she is or much
about her, but I just have this feeling about her. She is something special."
And, so it was that Chiquita Stephenson rang the doorbell the next morning at 7 a.m. sharp. I was still asleep, and so I conducted this impromptu
interview in my pajamas. Chiquita didn't seem to be the least concerned

about any of this. She was quite clear that she had a story to tell and she was ready to tell it. I was impressed with her clarity of purpose and her unwillingness to be defeated anywhere along her very remarkable path.

By the time I had returned home and completed writing up this interview, Chiquita had had yet more heart surgery. She affirmed to me on the telephone that so long as God had saved her again from an early death, she had an obligation to devote her life to service. That is what she has done and what she is doing.

Chiquita Stephenson grew up in the wealthy town of Stamford, CT, but she is not from a wealthy family. She is the only child of her parents, though she has half-siblings from her mother's second marriage. Her mother is a survivor of incest and abuse, and had, herself, been born to a thirteen-year-old mother.

Her father was a chemist at ACME. He had been born prematurely with a heart condition and died when Chiquita was ten.

When Chiquita's parents married, they were just teenagers. His family was opposed to the marriage because they were middle class people and her mother was from a poor background. Her paternal grandmother actually had tried to ruin her parent's romance but failed. They were 17 and 19 when they were married.

Chiquita says that it was her maternal great-grandmother, "Big Ma," as she was called, who was "the glue that kept us together." She had assisted in raising Chiquita's mother while working cleaning houses and scrubbing toilets, and she was fiercely loyal to her family. When Chiquita complained to Big Ma that someone had "looked at her funny," she said, "Kita, never let anyone define you!"

Her father had a twin brother, who was a veteran of the Vietnam War, and had come home a very disturbed man. Because of his brother's war experience and family loyalty, Chiquita's father felt an obligation to help him, even though he drank heavily, made sexual passes at her mother, and created all sorts of drama in the family. "There were violent fights every weekend because of my uncle," Chiquita says now. "I didn't understand it and I would ask God to take my life, because I thought I was the problem."

"My father called me 'rabbit,' and he and my mother were beautiful together. But, my uncle created fights and he and my father drank together, and then my father would come after my mother. He was six foot five inches tall and very frightening in that state. One time when he was beating my mother badly, I called the police and then I crashed a huge jar of coins over his head to try to make him stop. I was only eight! I somehow got into my mother's arms with him still hitting her. The police arrived and it took eight Stamford policemen to pull him off of us and get him under control.

"Of course, my mother went to the hospital. While she was there, she asked me if I wanted her to go back to him. I said, 'no.' After that, my father stopped taking care of himself. He wanted his family back.

"The last time I saw my parents together was at my baptism at Faith Tabernacle Church when I was eight. My father died two years later from his heart condition and many times, I wondered if he would still be alive today if I had told my mother that night at the hospital to take him back but, in the back of my head, I can't help but wonder if my mother would have been dead!

"There were lots of secrets in my family. I never knew what was what. My mother had so much anger that I didn't understand. She always tried to define me (because of her past choices), telling me who I was and what I was. A lot of it was harsh words because that's all she knew. It was difficult for her to express love because she never experienced a mother's love. She married my stepfather and had my sister Shondell and my brother Glendell. It wasn't long after that that I decided no one was going to define me anymore."

In junior high and high school Chiquita was a good athlete, playing basketball and running track. She met a young man who showered her with praise, telling her how smart and beautiful she was. By the time she was fifteen she was pregnant. The baby's father wanted her to have an abortion, and so her uncle took her to New York for the procedure. When her mother found out that Chiquita was on her way to New York, she came to get her before the abortion took place.

As a result of all of this, Chiquita says that her relationship with her mother deteriorated. Her mother became resigned to the idea that her daughter would turn out badly. She did not want Chiquita to follow in her footsteps. Chiquita says that it was education that made all the difference.

Chiquita went on to have her baby. The local high school tried to block her from continuing as a student. They said they had no provisions for unwed mothers. But, Chiquita wanted her education. She knew it would be her chance at a productive life. So, she researched the laws in the area and found that they could not deny her school entrance unless she brought a weapon to school, something that had never entered her mind. When she won her case, and returned to high school, she and her son were living in a $20 a day hotel. She was working at Macy's and for the attorneys who had helped her press her case. Her son's father did not contribute financially and she made too much money to apply for welfare. Her main goal was to secure stable housing for herself and her son.

Of her return to high school, Chiquita says that some of her teachers had discarded her; but, Mr. Sylvester, her math teacher, babysat for her while she took her tests. He helped her get what she needed so that she could graduate. "Several other teachers came out of nowhere to help me. They gave me something positive every day so that I couldn't give up. Thank God for Mr. Nast, Mr. Tucci, Mrs. S and the Stamford High student body who all gave me support."

During high school, a childhood friend re-entered her life and wanted to be involved with her and her son. Donavan soon became an integral part of their lives. They bought their first home in July of 1991, and they were married in August of 1991 when Chiquita was twenty-one years old.

The father of Chiquita's son became jealous when he found out that Chiquita was engaged. He laid in wait for her, hit her over the head with a gun, kidnapped her to a hotel in Norwalk, where he beat and raped her. He put a gun to her temple and pulled the trigger, but the gun jammed. He put her in his car and took her to an icy river to throw her in. Thankfully, a woman saw what was happening and intervened. Chiquita was able to get away. He fled to North Carolina and ended up doing time in prison. By the time he got out of prison, Chiquita and Donavan were planning their wedding. She and Donavan invited him to dinner when he was released. "I wanted to show him that I had no fear of him," Chiquita says. "There was no point in him getting out of prison and me feeling imprisoned."

Chiquita continued in school and received an Associates degree in political science. In Stamford, CT, she ran for and won a seat on the Board of Education. "Donavan and I were focused on building our family and serving in our community," she says of that time. "When I was elected to the Board of Education, the first thing I was asked was, 'What do you want to say to all those teachers and administrators who wanted you out of the system?' I had run against a white male, and I think that people saw that I was transparent with a GREAT education from the Stamford Public Schools, and I wanted to be a part of building the community in which we all lived. So, with that question, I could see that I could either blame them or look at them as stepping-stones to my later successes. I decided not to blame anyone."

Chiquita says that although Stamford, CT is a beautiful place, it also has lots of "demons." She saw that some people seemed to prosper over the pain of others. She saw quite a few young, black men in gangs. There were turf wars between Latino, black, and Albanian groups who were selling drugs to kids. She was disturbed that the local police were prospering from the gang activity by making overtime wages. "I just wanted people to be empowered by knowing these various truths. I also knew that it is easy to say that you want change. But, if you really want change, you have to know that it will cost you, because it will."

Chiquita's outspokenness did not make her popular with everyone. She said that she received threats that became so virulent that she became fearful of eating at events for fear of being poisoned. But she stood by her statements and what she believed in.

Chiquita has had heartache with her son. In his attempt to have a relationship with his biological father, he began to walk in his footsteps, which included battling with police and community politicians who opposed her political views. "He was a victim of chance and took some wrong turns and is serving six years in CT State prison. He is my first-born – a fighter and a young man of God who will not be moved or stopped because he is destined for greatness," she says. He has had his own son as a teenager, whom Chiquita raises. However, Chiquita says he has sorted his life out and sees the results of the choices he's made. He is now able to be inspirational to other men and help with community organizing, getting out voters, and providing voting literature. "When my son fathered a baby as a teenager, I was upset. 'Why is he repeating the cycle?' I asked. I had to repent and thank God that I have a grandson. God has a purpose for everything. My son came to change my life and I believe that his son came to change his."

Chiquita's energy and determination to help others better themselves is incredible! She helped to establish SStoneage, Inc., which is a teen center in Stamford, providing tutoring, mentorship, apprenticeships, and leadership training for clients, ages eleven to twenty-five. They house a food bank, provide job training, give seminars in financial literacy, parenting, and a homebuyers training. She was instrumental in arranging for the building to be provided at a cost of $1 per year.

It is no wonder that in 2002, the African American Affairs Commission and Governor named her Woman of the Year for the State of Connecticut.

Chiquita was Executive Director at Malta House, an organization under the auspices of the Catholic Church, meant to break the cycle of single women with children. They have a house with ten beds available and do outreach to 350 women, providing information on housing, budgeting, and communication skills. The stated goal of the organization is to build women, one at a time, to be able to re-enter the community as mothers, women, and competent individuals within their community. Chiquita says that an important aspect of the program is to help these women know that an integral part of their success is their ability to know who they are and what they were created to do. "The board members are all white, except for me, and they are not impoverished. They were not used to someone like me telling them what would work and what wouldn't."

Chiquita also went to city council meetings and spoke up on such things as issues of zoning. "I'm determined to fulfill my destiny," she says. "I cannot tolerate negativity or injustice."

Chiquita and her husband Donavan were instrumental in creating a transitional home for women and children. It is called Victory Gardens. "We give them tools to have a better life," she says. "We also literally, give them gardening tools to work in the garden." "Virtuous Women in Victory" is a program within Victory Gardens, presenting women with a life map of their past, present, and what they hope for their future. The map allows the women to see the pains and challenges that are hurdles to the future, and to make plans to address these issues positively. Chiquita says, "I have the ability to see all these women as survivors. They have reached out for help to raise children who will become better citizens. I have to see to it that they are helped."

Chiquita and Donavan, work as a team. Among other things, he does carpentry for their women's shelter and gives the women honest feedback about all kinds of things, including their appearance, attitude and outlook on life. Her children act as babysitters for the women and help with distributing supplies to the families coming in."

"I remind the women on a regular basis that if you want something, it's going to cost you," Chiquita says. "God has put me here to be a voice for those who have no voice. I am here to make change, and change costs!"

In 2003, Chiquita was ordained as a pastor in a non-denominational international church, called God's Kingdom of Restoration. She makes time to interact with the younger women, trying to be a life example for them, and helping them to do better. "I continually try to do better, too," she says.

In 2005, Chiquita found that she had heart disease and underwent three heart surgeries. The first doctor she consulted about her problem said that there was no problem and that it was "all in her head." When she consulted a second doctor, Keith Landsman, M.D., he sent her straight to the hospital. By a series of little miracles, it was discovered that Dr. Landsman's father had operated on Chiquita's father twenty-five years earlier and could look up his records to determine the genetic links between his heart problems and Chiquita's. Chiquita went to her spiritual father, Derek L. Calhoun, founder and Pastor of New Vision International Ministries, and began to have the members at God's Kingdom of Restoration fellowship worship with the family of New Vision International Ministries. A month prior to Chiquita's heart surgery she spoke to Pastor Calhoun and shared with him that she believed God had told her to bring the members of God's Kingdom of Restoration to New Vision. Eight weeks after it was agreed, she was told that she needed immediate heart surgery.

"Surviving those surgeries is how I really know I have a purpose," she exclaims. "I am an ambassador for the American Heart Association. I wake up knowing that in all we women have faced, there is purpose. My deepest loss is the angel who fought to save my life. He told me that I would be at my children's graduation. Dr. Landsman lost his battle with cancer in 2008. He was only thirty-seven and gave me his all. I was present for my children's graduation, but, on a daily basis, I am praying for his wife and two children. I am grateful for all that they've done and continue to do to help women like me!"

"My mother and I now work together at the Victory Gardens (shelter). We have power as a team. We help women re-unite with their mothers and families. It makes it more powerful for the men we are raising."

"I didn't understand why I was a teen mother, or abused. I didn't understand why landlords or employers cheated me. I didn't understand why I would have heart disease. But, I see now that it was all important in my understanding of what challenges others face and how to be compassionate."

Chiquita also has worked for the Jackie Starks Foundation, working with individuals and organizations that are interested in community building through health, education, and wealth assessment and training. She is the Director of Development for Norwalk Economic Opportunity Now, Inc. (NEON) serving families 200% below the poverty level.

"Life is what you choose to make it!" Chiquita emphasizes. "You were born with a purpose. Never let anyone or anything separate you from your heart's desires. So, spread your wings, focus on your target and you will find success and happiness. If something is not working right, rethink it, and ask God if it is His will for you at this time."

Chiquita ends by saying, "I don't allow anyone or anything to define me. God defines me. God comes first."

CHAPTER 4

The Nurturers

*When we had finished our Thanksgiving dinner, I saw people
in the back of the parking lot going through the dumpster
for food. I said to my husband, we're not ever doing this again.
From now on we will serve Thanksgiving dinner in the
parking lot and we will feed anyone who comes.*

— Carolyn Hall

The strength and energy of the Nurturer is historically evident in the lives of African American women. Throughout the history of the United States, these women not only nurtured their own children, families, and extended families, but the children and families of the white community, as well. Some may see this role as a pattern that is "less than" or insignificant. I don't see it that way. Early in the course of this project, Karen Holmes-Ward, who is included in this chapter, asked me what "thread" I had noticed that ran through all the interviews. I didn't know what it was at the time. It was too early in the process. But, I came to see that something that seems to be inherent in the characters of the women I interviewed was their commitment to service. And service usually means nurturing in one form or another.

Clearly, the overall health of a community is dependent on those who know how to nurture and support children, partners, bosses, the elderly, to name a few. It is through empathy, sacrificial love, and compassion, combined with practicality, that Nurturers consider the needs of others, particularly youth, those who are dependent, or those who are in need of support and guidance.

Every woman who takes time from her own busy life, which may include academic or career goals, or hobbies and interests, to nurture others, is heroic. In addition, sometimes her very occupation has to do with full time care giving.

To be a Nurturer may mean accepting a role outside the spotlight and with few, if any, material rewards. Nurturers, who actually receive money for their role, often are among the lowest paid service providers. They do not choose their roles or jobs to become rich or famous. For many Nurturers, there is little or no training; they simply use their own kindness and compassion, combined with practicality to get the job done.

All of American society owes deep gratitude to the African American women who have nurtured generations of this country's families and children, as cooks, care providers, housekeepers, mothers, nurses, and more, as you will see as you read the following stories, which richly illustrate the myriad ways in which Nurturers contribute to all of our well-being.

Carolyn Hall

"Invest in something other than yourself."

found a brief article about Carolyn Hall in People magazine. Apparently, she helped homeless women and children get off the street and stabilized their living environments long enough for them to stabilize their lives. How did she do it, I wondered? Homelessness is an intractable problem and Mrs. Hall was succeeding in her endeavor. When I called her in the winter of 2006, her sister said that Mrs. Hall was too ill with the effects of chemotherapy to come to the telephone. She suggested I call back in the spring. Sadly, I never had a chance to meet Carolyn. I had actually planned to go to visit her, if she allowed it, when she was well. I had attended the University of Southern California, not too far away from where Carolyn was now doing her work. I had been a student teacher and a substitute teacher in the Watts area of South Central Los Angeles in the late '60's, so her neighborhood was well known to me. As it turned out, Carolyn called me before I had a chance to call back and told me her story. It wasn't long afterward that her daughter called to tell me that Carolyn had died. She sent me the funeral notice and the program from her memorial service. I tell you the truth: though I never actually met Carolyn, I cried and cried over her loss. She and I had cried on the telephone over the death of her foster child and the way in which her hard work with that child's siblings had been spoiled. I guess when women share tears together, they have a bond even if they never meet.

Carolyn Hall was sixty years old at the time of our interview. She was born the eleventh of twelve children and her parents were married to each other until their deaths. Neither of her parents had more than an elementary school education, which was not uncommon in Alabama at that time. Her father was a coal miner for over fifty years, having gone into the mines when he was fourteen. Her mother was a homemaker. This was a source of pride for her mother, as most black women in the small town of Docena, Alabama traveled eleven miles into Birmingham each day to work as domestics for white families. Their small home had two bedrooms and no running water. Clothes were washed by hand, outdoors in a wash pot. They had few material possessions. Her father grew crops on the empty lots adjacent to their home and fed his family and many neighbors from what he harvested. "That's how I learned to give to others," she says. "I watched him give sacks of potatoes and vegetables that he had grown to our neighbors, sometimes just leaving them on their porches without saying a word."

Carolyn says that her mother was meek, quiet, and non-confrontational. She had a very dark complexion and had been raised in an area of Alabama so rural that her parents arranged her marriage because she knew no men.

Her father was of mixed parentage and had been raised on a plantation in Georgia. Though he could have passed for white, she says, he chose not to.

Carolyn recalls that when she was eleven, her family was home on a Saturday night when they heard a big commotion. There came a stream of about twenty cars with horns blaring. She recognized the local sheriff's car among them. When the procession came around the corner, she could see that it was the Ku Klux Klan and they had lit a burning cross. They would stop at one house or another and go into it to terrorize the occupants. Carolyn reports that there were frequent acts of racism and violence in her small town. It was a puzzle to her because the men, white and black, mostly worked in the mines together, and the black women worked for the white women, taking care of their homes and children. But, she says, the local white people purposely put fear in their black neighbors and the tension was palpable.

Carolyn's parents could not vote because they were too poor to pay the poll tax, a common deterrent for poor, black people.

She recalled a day in the tenth grade when a caravan of buses rolled up on to the grass of her segregated school. They were white people – "freedom riders." They began speaking with bullhorns, telling the students that they were not second-class citizens, but that they were being denied regular citizen's rights. "They gave us such hope," Carolyn says. The "freedom riders" invited the students to a rally downtown at the Sixteenth Street Baptist Church. Her mother, fearing violence, said that she could not go. Carolyn was not happy about it, but was obedient. Many of the men and boys went to the rally and were set upon by attack dogs and the police. The Southern Christian Leadership Conference continued meeting in various churches every Monday night. Her parents and their children were among the six to seven hundred people in attendance. One Sunday morning, while in church, Carolyn heard and felt the bomb blast in Birmingham, eleven miles away, which killed three little girls attending Sunday school. She says the bomb was so powerful that their church shook, though they were nowhere near the blast.

This event, plus the lack of jobs in her hometown, led Carolyn to join her oldest sister in Los Angeles, California in 1965. She arrived just as the Watt's riots ignited and she wondered if she had made a mistake and should go home. "I thought I had arrived in some kind of hell," she says. She stayed. She worked in a factory a few days a week for $1.25 an hour. The money was insufficient. She found a mentor in an Italian man, Mr. Fabiano, at the unemployment office. "He changed my life!" she says with great emotion. Before sending her out to an interview at Crocker Bank, he demanded to see her. "Go home, take off that mini-skirt, put on nylons, and wipe off all that make-up," he ordered. Fortunately, she took no offense because she sensed his concern. "He really tried to help me and he did. It was a life-changing moment," she says. She got the job and stayed for twenty-five years, moving up from being a page in the mailroom to working in customer service.

During those twenty-five years, Carolyn married Larry James Hall, and had a son, Larry, and a daughter, Erika. Her husband worked at Lockheed until they both decided to retire and enter Christian ministry work full time, establishing a small Apostolic Church in their neighborhood. It was at about this time that crack cocaine invaded their neighborhood and it became infested with drugs, drug dealers and their children. "The dope dealers became the gate keepers of our community," she said. Carolyn and her husband made the decision to continue living on the church property, rather than be an absentee pastorate. This is different from pastors of many churches in dangerous or less desirable areas who come to the church once or twice a week, but live elsewhere. They wanted to be a presence in the community.

In 1987, a neighbor's house burned down. Carolyn found clean clothes for the family. This began her ministry of collecting and giving away nice, clean clothes to people in need, from a card table in front of the church. That same year, the Halls had a big Thanksgiving dinner after a church service and Carolyn said that afterwards she observed people eating out of the trashcans and she told her husband, "We're not doing this again. We will have Thanksgiving in the parking lot of the church for anyone who wants to come."

Soon after that, a woman with six children, one of whom was a six-week old baby came to a clothing giveaway and asked if she could leave the baby with Carolyn for a few hours. She showed up to retrieve the baby four days later. Carolyn asked for the family's address and began going there several times a week to deliver food and clothes and take them to church. She had no idea that she was going to a crack house. Through a long series of events, Carolyn was asked to foster four of these children, all less than four years old. Her husband agreed. The Hall children participated in caring for their new charges and Carolyn says it taught them to be more loving and giving.

The Halls parented these four children, in addition to their own, for four and a half years, at which time their grandmother petitioned the court for custody. There was nothing anyone could do to stop this action and Carolyn told me that handing the children over to their grandmother and aunt was one of the worst days of her life. Within six months, the baby girl was dead. The children were disciplined by having their heads held under water and the baby had drowned. Her little body had been dumped by the side of the road in a rural area. Carolyn said she had rarely spoken of this incident, as the pain is so great. We were silent awhile, digesting it all. I didn't know what to say.

In 2002, the Halls moved their home and church to a permanent location on Vernon Avenue in Los Angeles. They continued their food and clothing give-away. They began to notice homeless mothers with children and made a decision to open a part of their Victorian house to these people, in hopes of helping them stabilize their lives to get into permanent housing. They could accommodate four women at a time, or six, if there were no children. Carolyn said that she tried to select women between the ages of eighteen and thirty, who were willing to take direction. She had a written protocol or program for each woman. Most of them had been on skid row. She gave them a week to rest and then set them on the road to recovery by connecting them to social service programs she had selected. "Homelessness is like an addiction," she said. "Some women are able to escape it. Some are not." Carolyn received no government funding. She had her own set of restrictions and guidelines, which the women agreed to while living with her. The first restriction was that they must be willing to drop any relationship they had to a boyfriend or the children's father. She believed that this began the process of each woman taking full responsibility for herself and her children. Each woman was evaluated for skills at the African American Unity Center in Los Angeles, and then connected to suitable welfare to work programs in the area. The entire process of empowerment took six months to a year, and Carolyn succeeded in moving many women and their children off the streets and into productive, satisfying lives.

One of Carolyn's first charges was a woman who had given birth to her daughter when she was twelve years old. By the time Carolyn took them in, the mother was twenty-three and had spent years on the street. They are now stable and living on their own!

The Halls were in the process of building a new shelter to serve ten to twelve women at the time of this interview. "Larry and I don't have much to give, except wisdom and structure," she said in her modest way. She said that they were working to break the cycle of homelessness and had had a fair amount of success doing it. Campus Crusade for Christ sends college students to volunteer from time to time, doing outreach in the inner city. The Halls have housed them in the church and taught them about homelessness. They served them Barbeque on their last day to thank them.

Somehow, *People* magazine learned about Carolyn Hall's work and sent a reporter to spend a day with her to verify the story. They ran an article about her and sent a make-up artist and hair stylist to do "make-overs" for all the women in the shelter. Carolyn said that the magazine people could see that there was no ulterior motive in their work and the article and attention boosted everyone's morale.

"I learned from my father's example that it truly is more blessed to give than to receive. I learned on my own that many social service agencies have money, but lack wisdom. I have wisdom, but not much money. The return from what you do for others will be about wisdom, not money," she says. She continued, "We must step up and do what we know is right. I invested in something other than myself. People gave to me and helped me. And I know I am not going to live forever. I want the women I help to pass it along." With a chuckle, she added, "My husband says I'd give away the roof on the house if he wasn't here to hold it on."

It was with great sadness that I received the news of Carolyn's death from her daughter, Erika. Her cancer had returned, but her legacy of compassion and her nurturing spirit lives on in the lives of the many women and children she helped into safe and productive lives. Carolyn's husband and daughter have continued her work in her memory.

Diane Hambick, M.D.

*"Find a good mother.
You <u>need</u> a mother—
a soft place that
is not critical.
It will be like honey
on the end of
your tongue."*

O ne of my male colleagues said that I *had* to interview Dr. Diane Hambrick. He said that he had met her years earlier when he was hospitalized and treated for his drug addiction. He went on to praise her for her kind but firm stance with him while he was in treatment and trying to tell her how to do her job. She did not shame him, but helped him to relinquish control and accept her recommendations.

I visited with Diane in her beautiful home in Northern California, where she continues her work as an addictionist at St. Helena Hospital. When we completed the interview, she showed me a collage of family pictures, including those of four generations of college graduates and three generations (including herself) of physicians. If you can appreciate what a rare thing it is to have four generations of college educated people among the general population, then you can understand how amazing it is to be that fourth generation person in an African American family, where access to a college education is, even now, not something to be taken for granted.

When Sweet Honey in the Rock came to Davies Hall in San Francisco, Diane wrote to me and asked if I would like to come to the Links, Inc. benefit reception to meet her friends. Links, Inc. is an organization of accomplished African American women dedicated to service and philanthropy in their communities. Of course, I agreed, and she was so gracious, introducing me to beautiful women, in some of the most gorgeous clothes I've ever seen. She reminded me that her mother had been a founding member of this Links chapter in San Francisco, and said that her mother would have thought she was too casually dressed for the event. I guess we never do escape our mothers' opinions about us, even when they have passed on to the world of Spirit!

Diane Hambrick, M.D., says that she is the classic oldest child—calm and compliant. The brother and sister born after her were rascals, by comparison.

Diane comes from a long line of scholars, being a fourth generation college graduate and a third generation physician. She says that when she was only three years old, she was able to demonstrate her family's racial pride by reciting in a strong voice, "I stand on my Constitutional rights! I will not be segregated."

She was born in Memphis, Tennessee, but moved to San Francisco as a toddler. Her father had a general medical practice in San Francisco, where initially he was not allowed to admit his patients to the hospital, except under the direction of a white physician. Since African Americans could not belong to the American Medical Association, he belonged to the National Medical Association for Black Physicians.

Diane's mother had worked with the Signal Corps during the war, and then taught high school English and history. The Hambricks were definitely an upper class family, with a social life and educational expectations that matched their place in the community. Nevertheless, Diane was raised with a social conscience that is reflected in the Bible verse often recited in her home, "To whom much is given, much is required." We laughed about the fact that my mother quoted the same verse, and we commiserated about how much we had disliked hearing it all the time.

As previously mentioned, Diane's mother was a charter member of the San Francisco Links, Inc., which is an invitation only, African American women's philanthropic organization. Her mother's charity work informed much of Diane's approach to life. Diane graduated from Lowell High School, where she was one of only twenty African Americans in this school for honor students only.

She decided to attend Fisk University in Nashville, Tennessee because it was where her mother had gone to school and she had extended family there. But, before she left for college, her mother sat down with her on the front steps of the house and said, "Anything you could ever even think about doing, I've already done. So, don't be afraid to tell me anything."

"I've had what so many women want in a mother," Diane says today. "I've learned so much from her."

Diane entered Fisk University in 1963. She says it was strange to be at an all-black school, because she had lived such an integrated life. But, she thought it was wonderful. She loved seeing the paintings in the library done by a famous black artist, and noticing the university buildings named for black historical figures. Fisk participated in the nationwide observances of Negro History Day and Black History Week. Nashville was also her first experience with institutionalized segregation.

Diane remembered to stand on her Constitutional rights, and was jailed for participating in the boycott of a restaurant that would not serve blacks. When she arrived at the jail, she stood before a man who sat behind a card table. "You have been charged with conspiracy to obstruct trade and commerce," he said. "How do you plead?" Even though Diane was guilty, she said, "Not guilty."

The jail was segregated and she and her co-conspirators were placed in a huge cell furnished only with cots, and filled, she says, with scary-looking black women. The dean of women visited them in their cell and said she would notify the girls' parents. White church parishioners came on Sunday to read Bible verses and sing hymns. But, they wouldn't come to the black women's cell and so the jailed women drowned them out with their own hymn singing. Local black citizens, including Diane's uncle, came and offered their personal property for bail, and they were back in class by Monday morning.

Back in San Francisco, Diane's little sister told her all white classmates at "Show and Tell" that her sister was in jail.

When the case went to trial, their lawyer was repeatedly silenced and the co-conspirators were jailed for another three days. They were bailed out again and the case was continued. When President Lyndon Johnson passed the Civil Rights Law of 1964, their case was dropped.

Diane says that her college years were the best years of her life. Since her parents financed her schooling, she was free to just be a student, and though she majored in biology, she also took lots of humanities and social science classes just for the love of learning.

These particular years were also tumultuous for the entire United States. President Kennedy was assassinated and the Birmingham bombings occurred in Diane's freshman year. By the fall of 1967, the federal law calling for desegregation had passed.

In the summer after Diane graduated from college, and as she was waiting to enter medical school, she traveled to West Point, Mississippi, to Mary Holmes Junior College, where black children were being tutored in anticipation of entering previously all white schools. Since many of the children had received an inferior education up until then, despite "separate but equal" opportunity, a tutorial program was necessary. There was no set curriculum and so Diane taught biology, German and drama. The Ku Klux Klan rode by the junior college periodically and scared everyone.

The staff decided to take the children on a field trip to New Orleans, Louisiana. Diane and two white, male staff members followed the school bus in a private car, with Diane lying down on the back seat so as not to be seen by white passers by.

When fall came, Diane entered Meharry Medical College, where her father, grandfather and two great uncles had graduated to become physicians. There were eighty students in Diane's medical school class. Ten of these were women. At the time, this was the largest number of women in a medical school class in the United States. The student section of the National Medical Association, of which Diane was a member, held a convention with Howard University medical students, and any other black medical students they could find. They organized a letter writing campaign with rows of students typing at typewriters, and informing deans of medical schools across the United States of the need for more minority students to be admitted to medical schools to at least serve the needs of their own communities.

Diane got married the day after her graduation from medical school.

She and her husband served internships in Nashville, with Diane eventually training in family practice during a residency at Howard University. Her husband proceeded to Johns Hopkins University for graduate studies in public health.

When Diane and her husband discovered they could not have children, it was what she describes as, "The hardest thing I faced in my life." It was painful to watch as all her friends began having babies.

Soon, they adopted a son, who came to them when he was just five weeks old. Sadly, the marriage had begun to dissolve. When the baby was only two, Diane took him with her as she returned to her family in San Francisco. She says now that the subsequent divorce, though civil, was horrible. Her attorney tried to seduce her and she believed that she had to keep quiet about it. But, more importantly, Diane says that she felt her strength and power as a woman had over-powered her husband. "I felt like I was the mythical Amazon woman…. eating men. It wasn't a good feeling."

As for her son, Diane says that if she could re-do something in her life, it would be her child rearing. "If I could do it over, I would stay home with him full time. My son had many problems, as many adoptees do. I was conscientious in many ways," she says sadly. "I was a Cub Scout den mother and room-mother, and a Disneyland kind of mom. But, there is a difference between child-rearing and parenting, and for child-rearing, you have to be there on a daily basis."

Diane says that in her family practice, she kept running into people with alcoholism and addiction problems. There was no formal training in addiction medicine at that time and few, if any, experts in the field.

Diane found an externship program in San Francisco, called The Center for Special Problems. There were two sections to the program. One was a methadone clinic for heroin and other opiate addicts. Methadone was new and no one had any idea of what an appropriate dosage was. To qualify for the Methadone program, a person had to prove five years of addiction and have a job.

The second section was for what was then considered sexual deviancy: homosexuals, bisexuals, transvestites, etc. Diane was in her early twenties and she says she looked like she was twelve. "I was doing group therapy with so-called deviants. It follows you. Every time I turned around, there was someone saying, "Oh, you're the one who knows about alcohol, drugs, and deviants. Could you talk to this person?'"

Diane was called to minister to a forty-five year old alcoholic woman, who had been set on fire by her boyfriend. She was completely burned from the neck down and her skin was so contracted that she could only lie on a couch. "When people are grotesque, no one touches them," she says. "I touched her and told her if drinking whiskey was the only way she could get through, then she should be allowed to do it. It seemed merciful."

"I could see that I needed more training," she says. And, she learned more as Medical Director of the Alcohol and Drug Program at The House of Uhuru in the Watts section of South Central Los Angeles, California.

Diane worked at 80th Street and Figueroa Boulevard in Los Angeles. It was a dangerous assignment. There was an armed guard at the front door, and about 200 people came through the clinic each day. PCP was the new street drug, and people under its influence were severely psychotic and very dangerous. The hospital emergency rooms were afraid of these people, as were the police. The only treatment available was Haldol, a strong tranquilizer. "The drug dealers didn't like us," Diane states. "Our work meant they lost customers. But, they never touched my car, or me because my addicts protected me. I loved my addicts." Diane says that although there were many tension-filled moments, she was never really afraid.

Diane was struggling emotionally. She was a single parent and was depressed. She hadn't dated anyone in a long time. She had gone to a party where football star, Lynn Swann, was the bartender and many celebrities were in attendance. When Diane asked Lynn Swann what he did for a living, he answered that he entertained the people of Pittsburg. Another man gave her his business card, as did many other men that evening. The man's name was Whitney LeBlanc, and he asked her to dance. She gave him her business card. When Whitney called two weeks later, he said that if he had known she was a doctor, he wouldn't have talked to her. He, too, was from an upper middle-class family and he assumed she was practicing in an "uptown" location. He invited her out to lunch and was surprised to pick her up in the ghetto, and to be met at the door by an armed guard.

Whitney was a successful Hollywood producer and director, with numerous television shows and movies to his credit, and worked with such great talents as Norman Lear, Dinah Shore and Redd Fox.

Diane and Whitney married a year later. She says she inherited two ex-wives and three kids.

When Whitney was offered a job at KQED in San Francisco, Diane jumped at the chance to return home and work with her dad. She had to work hard to prove herself; because everyone knew her father and she needed to establish herself as competent in her own right.

She says that the five years she practiced medicine with her father were wonderful. She had a general practice in San Francisco, and continued her work with alcoholics and addicts, as a true pioneer in addiction medicine.

While at a medical conference in Scottsdale, Arizona, Diane was offered the assistant medical directorship at a cutting edge facility for addicts and alcoholics in Orange County, California. The program was for adults and adolescents, and catered to athletes and celebrities. Diane took the job and says it was fun and she was paid handsomely. But, she began to doubt the ethics and integrity of the program. She believed it was compromised by the administration, and decided to take "an indefinite leave of absence." Now, twenty some years later, she's still on leave.

While Whitney continued directing *The Young and the Restless* and *Generations*, Diane became Director of Addiction Medicine for FHP Corporation, with a large territory to cover, flying to her assignments in the corporate jet. She and Whitney were living in Southern California again and she had developed severe rheumatoid arthritis. Diane says that she was seeing patients far less sick than she was, who were on total disability.

Her doctor recommended thirty minutes in the Jacuzzi every single day. He added that her husband must participate in this treatment. She could not drive and she was medicated for the chronic pain.

By now, Diane and Whitney were "empty nesters." Diane says that Whitney is a romantic and he wanted to leave Hollywood and open a Bed and Breakfast Inn in the Napa Valley. They began looking for a place to buy. The Inn never materialized, but they found a wonderful house in the small, predominantly Seventh-Day Adventist community of Angwin, California. There, Whitney is able to indulge his artistic talent as a commissioned stained glass maker. Diane came out of retirement to specialize in Addiction Medicine and Pain Management at the Alcohol and Chemical Recovery Program at Saint Helena Hospital, working with the addicts she loves.

"I owe everything to my mother," Diane declares now. My mother was raised by her grandmother, because her own mother had died in childbirth. Her grandparents had moved from Charleston, South Carolina to Boston, Massachusetts with nine children. Traveling north by train, her grandfather passed for white, and her grandmother pretended to be his servant. Her mother was the oldest and had had polio. "My mother felt that she had to apologize for living, as her grandmother had lost her own mother and her daughter on the very same day. We always knew that my mother was the strong one. She was everyone's rock," Diane says emphatically.

Diane has welcome advice for other women. "I talk about my mother all the time. Other people wish they had her for their mother. Women need mothering. So, if your own mother is unavailable, find another good mother and go to her for advice. You need a mother who provides a soft place for you to land and who is not critical. It's like honey on the end of your tongue." She says this while touching the end of her tongue dramatically.

Diane is aware that for most of her life, people, and especially women, have looked up to her. "They see something in me that they want to emulate and I am honored by that. The thread that runs through my life is that there has not been a moment when I haven't been loved. I am so grateful for that."

Diane ends our conversation by offering the Hambrick family's prayer, said at all family gatherings. It comes from The Bible, Revelation, Chapter 7, Verse 12.

Saying Amen! Blessing and Glory and Wisdom and Thanksgiving and Honor and Power and Might belong to our God forever and ever. So be it. Amen.

Valata Jenkins-Monroe, Ph.D.

"If not us, then who?"

I was teaching a weeklong class on group psychotherapy in Puerto Vallarta, Mexico for mental health professionals and Dr. Valata Jenkins-Monroe called to register for my class. We were together every day for a week, and after class one day, we went into town to do some shopping. As we were browsing at my favorite store, Querubines (Cherubs), a voice came across the rows of interesting goods, "Is that you, Ladybug?" It was Valata's cousin from North Carolina and they had no idea that they would run into each other, as neither knew the other was in Mexico. Ladybug, indeed!

During the week, several of the nurses and therapists shared their experiences conducting group therapy with various types of groups. But, when Valata began talking about having half of her therapy group die from one week to the next, we were all stunned. One or two of us had lost a group member to death over the course of our careers, but to lose half of a group from one week to the next? And then, to have the same thing happen again, and then again, due to the AID's virus? We couldn't imagine it. But, that had been her experience when she went to East Africa on a Fulbright scholarship. Her brilliance and her compassion were amazing.

Valata invited me to her home in the Oakland Hills in California at Christmas time to see all her Christmas trees. She said that she put a decorated tree in every room in her house. Valata lives in a spacious home with lots of rooms. And she does, definitely, have a Christmas tree in every single room, even the bathrooms. They all have themes and are surrounded by African American Santa's, angels and Nativity scenes.

In addition, Valata is a "fashionista"! When we met in San Francisco for her interview, she was wearing a gorgeous, chartreuse green leather skirt and jacket, with matching accessories. She had just come from teaching a psychology class at Alliant University, and I imagined that her students were just as enthralled with her appearance as I was.

Valata Jenkins-Monroe was part of a blended family before the term was invented. Her parents separated when she was very young. Her mother, who was half Cherokee, remained in the public housing projects with her children in Newport News, Virginia. She struggled to support her family working as a housekeeper. Her father moved to Buffalo, New York after the separation, where he had lots of extended family. He had been a cook in the Army, and then worked at a Westinghouse factory and as a nurse's aide. Valata says that he was a handsome man, who would play Santa Claus for his children so convincingly that they never guessed his true identity.

Valata's father remarried and her new stepmother, Evelyn, became a significant person in her young life. She was about ten when her mother sent her to her father. Valata just thought it was to be a visit. She did not realize that her mother was having such difficulty financially that she had made a decision to send her, along with her older sister and brother, who were also her father's children, to Buffalo permanently. "I went from the projects to a middle class home," she says now. "It was a very hard transition for me and I was really scared." Valata realizes now what a huge sacrifice her mother made so that her children could have a more secure life.

Her stepmother was loving and patient and treated the children as though they were her own. She taught the girls about making their environment beautiful, as she was creative about the use of color in decorating and fashion. She was an educated woman who exposed her stepchildren to plays, museums, and the arts, as well as being very socially active, and a devout Christian.

Though it was difficult taking up an entirely new way of life and meeting a new set of relatives, Valata made the transition. Her brother and sister had more difficulty adjusting and continued to struggle. Valata says that she became active in the "Y" and her church group. She made friends in Buffalo. Eleven of the group remain friends to this day.

During high school, Valata's family had friends whose families traveled to various places on vacations. She accompanied these families as a nanny and thus was able to become more traveled herself. She says that these experiences brought her new awareness and the families became various and valuable models for her.

But, during the summers, when she went to stay with her mother, she was challenged in a different way. Before her mother had sent the older three children to Buffalo New York to be with their father, she had had three more children. Valata could see how different these younger children's lives were from her own and she says that she felt terribly guilty that they did not have the same opportunities as she had. While her mother and stepmother had a collaborative relationship regarding the children, being generally protective and warm, the younger sisters regarded her as "rich" and "other." Her maternal grandmother and aunts were highly suspicious of her stepmother, Evelyn, and her motives, but as time went on, they became accepting and trusting of her.

"I had great respect for Evelyn, and how she managed this complicated situation," Valata says. "But, I also felt very protective of my mother. She was not as educated or aware as my stepmother, and there was considerable disparity in their circumstances."

Valata's maternal grandmother taught her by example to integrate her Cherokee spiritual traditions and ceremonies into her everyday life. She taught her about elements of Earth Spirituality, and focused on such things as acknowledging the origins of the various foods eaten at their mealtime.

So, there was a unique richness to Valata's early spiritual life that combined the beauty of Cherokee ceremony and tradition with the devotions of her membership at the First Church of God in Christ.

Valata attended an integrated, middle class high school. She was an honor student, an athlete, and Vice President of her class. She was voted "most likely to succeed." Though she had been a quiet, "Southern girl," she began to come out and shine.

After high school in Buffalo, Valata came to California to attend the University of San Francisco on a full academic scholarship. She knew that she wanted to study psychology. Her extended family had experienced the challenges of mental illness, autism, and developmental disabilities, and she wanted to understand it. She now sees that there is significant post-traumatic stress disorder in her family, as well, but, at the time, she didn't know what that was.

While Valata was at USF, a family member suffered a crisis of mental illness and was taken to a distant state hospital. Valata was in a panic to try to get to him to see how she could help. A fellow student, whom she knew only in passing, saw her distress and offered to take her to the hospital, which was at quite a distance. This act of kindness on the part of a casual acquaintance would eventually lead to a marriage that has lasted over three decades and produced two wonderful children, Marlon and Mignon.

Valata was the second member of her family to finish a higher education. Her older brother is also a college graduate. She is the first in her family to finish a graduate degree. During college in San Francisco, she met Price Cobb, the author of *Black Rage*. She worked for him as a research assistant and a receptionist. When Mr. Cobb's wife was dying of cancer, Valata moved in with his family to help out with their young children. He became her mentor and friend, and she credits him with having had a great influence on her life. In addition, when she and Leon married, it was Price Cobb who gave their wedding reception in San Francisco.

Valata was admitted to the University of Cincinnati's first multicultural Ph.D. program in psychology. She was one of twelve African Americans admitted to the program that year. They were called, "The Famous Twelve."

But, while in Cincinnati, Leon Monroe proposed marriage, and so Valata decided to return to San Francisco to complete her doctoral studies there, so that she and Leon could be together.

Valata is acutely aware of her minority status as a psychologist and professor at Alliant University. She welcomes the opportunity to influence her students by way of multicultural awareness and diverse perspectives as it relates to mental health and emotional well-being.

In 1991, the famous and devastating Oakland Hills fire occurred and took the home Valata and Leon had so lovingly created. Their home burned to the ground in this fire that devastated an entire community. She says that the hardest part was losing items of great sentimental value from her mother and grandmother. When one realizes that her grandfather, a preacher, literally bought her Cherokee grandmother from an Indian reservation, and that some of the items lost in the fire had been passed down from this grandmother, the enormity of the loss can be understood. Her grandmother had been only thirteen years old when she began having her six children, Valata's mother being the oldest daughter.

Valata and her husband rebuilt their home again. They literally rose from the ashes.

In 1995, Valata applied for and won a Fulbright Scholarship to create mental health programs for children suffering from the effects of the AIDS epidemic in Uganda. She received the first Fulbright scholarship ever given to an African American woman. And so, she went to Uganda, not quite knowing what to expect, but filled with anticipation. She took her daughter, Mignon, with her and they stayed a year and a half. Leon and her son, Marlon, stayed behind, but visited from time to time. Valata's family had just barely moved back into their rebuilt home when it was time for her to leave for Uganda. She was responsible for developing a children's mental health clinic. The building provided to house the clinic had been built in the eighteenth century. The children with AIDS were tied down in their beds. They were all orphans, as their parents had died of AIDS and they were wild with fear. In addition, Valetta taught psychology to medical students. She was considered "a miracle worker." Her students would line up around the building and wait for days just to get a chance to talk to her. There were ten textbooks for one hundred students, so each dormitory had one text to share, and Valata taught introductory psychology and child development. When she was asked why she had decided to undertake such a difficult task, she simply said, "If not us, then who?"

Valata says that going to Uganda gave her a feeling of "going home." Though it was terribly hard because of all the death and dying around her, she also saw the incredible resiliency of the women. She eventually wrote an article about the resilience of Ugandan women, who provided all the nursing care for the hospitalized children, while often in the process of dying themselves.

In addition to her work in Uganda, Valata provided psychological services at the American Embassy in Zimbabwe.

Valata's advice to women is to pursue their dreams. She encourages reading, as she explains that books helped shape some of what she thought was possible. She says that she consciously chose a mate who supported her dreams and remains her best cheerleader.

In closing, Valata says that being the kind of caretaker she has been – not only in her family, but in her role as psychologist, professor and in her work in the world – takes a toll on her: "People don't always realize that I get needy, too. I do get torn because I have been so blessed." Learning to keep her nurturing spirit in balance is her challenge.

Karen Holmes-Ward

"Don't listen to 'no'!"

As I lay in bed on a Sunday morning reading the newspaper, I noticed an article and pictures in the "Wine" section (well, I live near the wine country) on the Divas unCorked. They are a group of African American professional women who are wine buffs and they had been visiting the world famous Napa Valley wine country. The article spoke about the fact that these women met regularly for wine tasting and educational events having to do with the appreciation of fine wine. They were mostly residents of East Coast and New England cities and they would travel all over, even internationally, to enjoy and learn about the world's wine growing regions. I thought it would be fascinating to meet one of these women. Since one of them was from Boston and I was going to visit my son, who was in college in Boston, I chose her to try to contact. Locating her and arranging an interview wasn't as hard as I had anticipated. I was full of anxiety as I drove into the guarded parking lot at her TV station. I was going to interview a professional interviewer and my cousin, Jay Stallman, with whom I was staying, had told me she was a local celebrity. "Everyone knows who she is," he said. So, I was nervous as I waited for her. But, my fears were needless. Karen was warm and gracious. Her office was absolutely amazing, inasmuch as it was covered, and I mean covered with plaques, certificates, and awards of one sort or another, having to do with her service to the community and her career accomplishments.

Since I was in town for my son's birthday, she gave restaurant recommendations (Hammersly's in the South end). It was wonderful! When my whole family gathered for my son's college graduation (finally!), I called Karen again for her dinner recommendation. "Definitely go to Sibling Rivalry," she advised. This was especially fitting, as my older son had graduated from law school two years earlier and it was fun to have the sibling rivalry theme out in the open. Again, she was right on. If you want a great restaurant recommendation, call a Diva unCorked!

Karen Holmes-Ward was about five years old when her family became the first African Americans on her street. During the early sixties, she began attending Freedom School, an extra-curricular activity for African American children provided by the NAACP. This was an opportunity for children to learn about Black History and related topics. As she was drawing a picture at Freedom School, her teacher said, with awe, "Oh, your father is Clarence Holmes!" It was the first time she realized that her father was someone important. She describes him today with awe in her own voice, as an endlessly interesting and learned man, for whom she has the utmost respect and admiration. Her parent's history is important to her own story, as they built a firm and conscious foundation for their three children's remarkable success.

Clarence Holmes was one of nine children born to a poor family. Though he was very bright, he had to stay home from school for months because he had no shoes. He graduated at the top of his high school class, took a competitive scholarship exam and was awarded a college scholarship by Pepsi Cola. Since he could not use it to attend the University of Alabama in his home state due to segregation, he went north to Case Western Reserve in Ohio, where he met and married a fellow student. His wife, Etta, attended Columbia University graduate school and was a teacher until her children were born. Clarence went on to law school at Case Western Reserve School of Law. Since most law firms would not hire an African American, he joined with other black lawyers to form their own firm. They took many cases involving civil rights, helping to gain jobs for African Americans and to work for integration. Mr. Holmes also served during this time as president of the local NAACP.

During this time, Karen says that she was rather unaware of the ever-present danger resulting from her father's civil rights work or of the roles her parents played in the larger community. However, she is surprised by her own tears, and I am surprised by mine, as she tells of answering the telephone as a young child to hear a threatening voice say, "Your father won't be coming home tonight." Though he did come home that night, it was a poignant moment, and representative of only a fraction of the dangers he faced for his activism.

Equally significant events were happening on the home front. Karen was attending Ludlow Elementary School; one of six schools that fed into

Shaker Heights High School. The Ludlow Experiment, as it was called, was a successful plan in how to balance and integrate a neighborhood to prevent "white flight" from the local area and maintain property values. Although the original deeds to homes and property in Shaker Heights specifically excluded blacks and Jews from ownership, by the 1960's these restrictions had been legally challenged. The families who participated in The Ludlow Experiment did so thoughtfully and consciously. Each family who remained made a conscious choice to experience integration. The neighborhood was still predominantly white, with some Jewish and African American families, and a smattering of Asians. They were all there on purpose. Karen describes the experience as "unusual and wonderful." Everything was integrated: church, birthday parties, scouts, etc. Her mother was a typical 1960's mom, leading a Brownie troop, joining the PTA and involving herself in her children's schooling. Karen says that at the beginning of each school year, her mother would invite each of her children's teachers to lunch. As the children looked on with some embarrassment, Mrs. Holmes told each teacher, in no uncertain terms, what she expected of them and of her children.

When the "Ludlow Kids," as they refer to themselves, entered high school, things changed. The usual cliques formed, often along racial lines. However, the Ludlow bond remains. "It is a testament to all our parents," Karen says proudly. Many of the "Ludlow Kids" went on to Ivy League schools and prominent positions. They still maintain a loose bond and Karen is in contact with many of them.

Karen was always encouraged by her parents to speak her mind. Teachers often called on her to recite at the front of the class and as her father was a lawyer, oration came easily. In high school, she made the loudspeaker announcements, such as, "Bake sale in the cafeteria after school." She became the first girl to do play-by-play announcing for the Shaker Heights High School basketball games.

Though she was a National Merit Scholar, her high school counselor advised her not to seek entrance to an Eastern or Ivy League school. She was told that her grades were probably not high enough. Thankfully, Karen recognized the inherent racism in this advice and ignored it. Ultimately, she entered Boston University, having convinced her father that since Martin Luther King, Jr. had gone there, it must be all right. When she entered Boston University in 1973, many schools were actively recruiting African American students. Lots of her African American friends had gone on to Ivy League or upper tier schools, as opposed to historically Black colleges, just because they had finally won the opportunity to do so.

While at Boston University, she pursued her interest in broadcasting, and upon graduation, she went to work for an African American radio station WILD, in Boston, as the afternoon drive announcer. After two years, she was hired by WCVB-TV Channel 5, where she has been since 1981.

Karen is adamant when she says, "For any woman to be successful, she must have a foundation of self-esteem. It's like a positive brainwashing and mine came from my parents. I believe I have combined the best of my parents." She explains that she has combined her mother's ability to teach and be creative with her father's legal mindedness, to be able to make a case and present it for whatever goal she may have in mind.

As Director of Public Affairs and Community Services, as well as host and executive producer of *City Line*, WCVB-TV's weekly magazine program, Karen addresses the problems, concerns, and accomplishments of people of color living in Boston and its suburbs. She has interviewed many notables, including Minister Louis Farrakhan, Attorney Lani Guinier, Oprah Winfrey and Denzel Washington, among others, for *City Line*.

Karen also oversees WCVB's public service and community outreach efforts, which illustrates her Nurturer's spirit. This work includes the station's work with Habitat for Humanity, raising awareness about the need for affordable housing in the Greater Boston area, and WCVB's first-of-its-kind web-based initiative, Commonwealth 5, which was nominated for a national Emmy award. This on-line project promotes philanthropy by matching viewer-donors with non-profits via the Internet. She is proud of one of her creative projects in Boston, called Extreme Makeover-Boston Edition, which identifies local non-profit organizations, whose facilities need extreme makeovers. She solicits local businesses and advertisers to donate time and materials to achieve the desired result. The Boys and Girls Club, a block in East Boston, a residence for homeless women, and The Home for Little Wanderers are among the recipients of this beautification and nurturing.

In 1999, Karen served as Executive Producer for *Return to Glory*, a one-hour prime-time documentary hosted by Emmy Award-winning actor, Andre Braugher, about the famed Massachusetts 54th Regiment. *Return to Glory* was syndicated nationally and seen in over eighty percent of the country. She produced the Emmy-nominated WCVB prime time special, *Through Children's Eyes: Remembering Dr. Martin Luther King, Jr.* hosted by Julian Bond and *Sesame Street*'s, Oscar the Grouch. Her creative credits are amazing and all these projects reflect her ability to nurture them from start to finish.

Karen's awards and achievements are simply too numerous to chronicle here. However, it is obvious from sitting in her office, where every inch of wall space is covered with awards and plaques commemorating her service, and achievement plaques and certificates are stacked two, three and four deep, that she is a woman committed to service. Her leadership is remarkable.

When asked about her advice to other women, she is clear and forceful, "Just because someone says no to you doesn't mean you have to believe them. For me, often when someone says no, I set out to prove him or her wrong. This is not from my arrogance or ego. I've just had to realize that they may have reasons for not wanting me to succeed. Don't listen to 'no'!"

CHAPTER 5

The Crusaders

"Don't feel entitled to anything you didn't struggle and sweat for."

— Marian Wright Edelman

African American woman have been crusading for issues that are important to them or their communities since early in this country's history. The Crusaders whose stories are told in this chapter have deep passion for their particular issue or cause, and have been willing to take very public, and often, dangerous stands to make their voices heard and accomplish their goals.

When a woman is operating from the energy of this strength, she must be inherently a risk-taker, whether she sees herself in that light or not. The Crusader is not one to hide out. Because she believes strongly in her cause, she cannot afford pretense, political correctness, or some of the other methods of remaining below the radar. At the same time, she must exercise good leadership skills, with a persuasive presentation, or she will fail in her crusade.

Crusaders know what they believe to be right and they have the courage of their convictions. They speak the truth as they see it, and are often in the position of speaking truth to power. The risks a Crusader takes are very real, because when she speaks her mind on a particular topic or issue, she knows that many may find her views unacceptable. If she has good leadership abilities and others are following her, she must be mindful of the risks that her followers may face at her behest. In addition, there is always the possibility that she could be proved wrong headed in her crusade and face public humiliation that occurs in these circumstances. So, the successful Crusading woman has courage, moral conviction, and passion.

Crusaders need to have clarity of purpose, but they also need to be flexible in order to change course, if need be, to accomplish their goals.

In the book of Luke in the New Testament of The Bible, Chapter 17, Verses 20–21, it says we only need to have faith as large as a mustard seed to succeed. Here are some "mustard seed" stories of women who have successfully crusaded and prevailed.

Linda Pondexter-Chesterfield

*"Don't just sit at the table,
set the table."*

"Meet me at the state capitol in Little Rock, 9:00 a.m. Monday," she says on the phone. I was headed to Little Rock to visit my dear friends, Dr. Rick and Rev. Susan Smith, and so I agreed to meet her. She was dressed in a cool, smart, pale blue, seersucker pants suit and her smile was easy and reassuring.

"I don't think I'm the right person to interview," she said. "There are so many African American women more important than me, who blazed the trail for me." She mentions Irma Hunter Brown, Libby Kontz, and Mary Hatwood Futrell, among others, as her 'she-roes,' as she refers to them, and role models. It is quite clear that Linda has been observing women and emulating the ones she found admirable, starting with her mother, grandmother, and great-grandmother, for a long time.

How did this woman in her late fifties from Hope, Arkansas, become the

Chairperson of the Democratic Black Caucus and a Representative in the Arkansas State legislature, I wondered?

Linda tells me she grew up "poor as Job's turkey." But she didn't realize it until college. Her father was not a significant figure in her life, though he was a decent man. She received three things from him: a blender, a suit, and a flag at his burial. Her mother, Ernestine, grandmother, Ophelia, and great-grandmother, Millie, made up for his absence. These women were amazing cooks, who knew how to create beautiful meals and gorgeous deserts, even when money for food was scarce. They used the fruit from their trees to make preserves, as well as pies and cobblers, and each of the four children always had their favorites. Linda's was chocolate meringue pie and her eyes sparkle at the memory of it.

Linda's mother walked several miles to work as a domestic, raising the children of white families. And though her grandmother worked, too, Linda spent a great deal of time walking and talking with her. "If I'd be sad or upset about something, my grandmother would say, 'It's a long train, don't have no end. It's a bad wind that don't change.' I'd have no idea what she was talking about, but those wisdom sayings stick with you and now I know she meant that no matter how bad it gets, things change, and often for the better."

But mostly, Linda recalls with fondness the fun she had using her imagination to make up games and pass-times with her three brothers. "Ricky and I would play *Gunsmoke*. We'd make our pretend whiskey out of vinegar and salt and toss it down and grimace, just like on TV. And, we'd play *Hopalong Cassidy*. I still have scars on my knees from running and jumping onto my bicycle, just like Hoppy jumped on and off his horse. (I loved telling Linda that I had waited on "Hoppy" and his wife at a local dinner house in my hometown, when I was working my way through college as a waitress.) We'd swing on old tires and climb trees. My family says I still drive a car the way I rode my bike."

Linda's grandmother was an avid reader and although she had only finished the 7th grade, she insisted that Linda and her brothers read. She also made sure that they knew the "moral of the story," or they'd have to read the story again. Her grandmother and mother demanded that she and her brothers graduate from high school.

Her grandmother took a job as the manager of the school cafeteria, in part to keep an eye on her grandchildren, and also to move out of having to work in the cotton fields. Her grandmother would attend the annual teachers' meeting to find out more about what was going on in education.

Linda is passionate about education! She emphasized, with tears in her eyes, that every school employee, and not just teachers, plays a part in a child's education. She illustrates her point by recalling how her grandmother would send her and her cousins to pick blackberries and make cobbler from them. She would feed what she had made to children so poor that they did not have the ten or fifteen cents for lunch. Service and caring for others was expected.

She emphasizes that at Hopewell Elementary School, it was simply assumed that no one was unable to learn. The school was excellent. There was great emphasis on discipline and hard work; recitation and language skills were an important part of the curriculum, and the children knew the difference between a gerund and a participle when they left. There was a spirit of competition and a drive to do well. When Linda's fourth grade teacher whipped her and left a welt on her leg, she ran to her grandmother, in hopes of defense. But, her grandmother said, "I guess you won't do that again!" *In loco parentis* meant just that and parents deferred to and supported teachers.

Linda's first experience of overt racism came from her fifth grade teacher, a light-skinned African American woman. She didn't like Linda's dark skin and would not call on her. She called on the lighter children instead and Linda remarks that this type of internalized racism within the black community has been very damaging. She says that she and her dark-skinned brother were advised to use Nadinola to lighten up. "I was deep chocolate with short hair, and I was not cute. But, my grandmother said, 'You've got it!' meaning I was capable and I understood."

But in sixth grade, a wonderful thing happened. Linda had Electa Mae Yerger as her teacher and principal. "She believed in me," says Linda. "She invited me to put up a bulletin board and let me know that she really cared about me. In fact, she still comes to see me when I speak." Linda graduated from Hopewell Elementary School as Valedictorian and she went on to Yerger High School. She emphasizes that Yerger was one of the few accredited Black high schools in Arkansas at that time. Many of the teachers had Master's degrees and the teaching was exemplary. Linda credits the many opportunities for public recitation that were provided in her segregated school, as well as her church, for her ease in public speaking today. All the students were required to give speeches and oratories, and grew more confident in the process. "My verbal agility has been invaluable to me," she emphasizes. This verbal agility also translated into a 'smart mouth.' "I've always cussed and I couldn't have survived without being like that," she says with a twinkle in her eye. "I was near-sighted and wore green, cat-eye type glasses with white edges. I was a size two and I was teased constantly and called 'bird legs.' In the Black community, if you didn't have 'tits and ass' you were undesirable. So, I argued and questioned, and stuck up for my brothers, my cousins, and myself and it got me in trouble on a regular basis. But, I was also in charge in my family a lot. I changed a lot of diapers, disciplined a lot of kids, and learned how to buy groceries, clean house, iron, and pay the gas, water and light bills. I learned about keeping good credit and that your word is your bond, no matter what."

In high school, Linda competed to be first or second in her graduating class to win the coveted college scholarship. And she would have, too, except that in the end, social studies grades were eliminated from the final figuring of grade point averages. She was third and sobbed openly at school when she heard about it.

What Linda didn't know was that the National Achievement Program that had been founded by the National Merit Foundation had established a program for outstanding black students in 1965. Linda received scholarships from seventy-five colleges and universities all over the United States! Her principal failed to inform her about her scholarships. She happened to go into the office and saw the mail with her name on it. She says that once again she learned, "If you're yellow, it's mellow. If you're brown, stick around. If you're black, get back," referring to the internalized racism amongst African Americans of that era and the fact that her principal didn't like her. But, she received her scholarship as she walked across the stage wearing the black patent leather high heels her brother, Don, bought her.

Hendrix College in Arkansas sent Reverend James Major to recruit

Linda and she accepted their offer of a full scholarship. It was the Fall of 1965 and Linda got on the bus to travel to the school wearing a green print dress she had made herself, white socks and white tennis shoes. She got rid of the green cat-eye glasses. Dr. Ella Meryl Shanks, Dr. Helen Hughes, and Ms. Lily Major met her bus. She was one of two black students and she says that Hendrix not only made a decision to integrate, they also made a commitment to their minority students. "They must have taken our pictures (Emily's and mine) to all the surrounding stores, theaters, and so forth, because while the average black person could not try on shoes in a store or sit in the main part of the theater, Emily and I were allowed those courtesies. There were those at Hendrix who would not speak to us and we got nasty looks. It was the height of the Civil Rights Movement and the class had been discussing the death of Viola Liuzzo (sic) when a boy in the class said, 'She got what she deserved.' But, the school took pains to make it go smoothly. I had great professors overall and Professor Bobby Merriweather taught me to argue both sides of an issue effectively, which has come in handy in my political career. I had the opportunity to attend school with true geniuses and compete with academicians."

In 2000, Linda was named Distinguished Alumna of Hendrix College. She had graduated from Hendrix with a degree in History and Political Science. Although her career as a high school teacher spanned thirty-three years, she was fired from her first teaching job for insubordination, because she brought noted Civil Rights activists to campus to speak to her classes. She thought it was important for her predominantly white, wealthy students to understand that blacks did not just work as maids and butlers. She instituted the first Black History program. The administration was unimpressed, and let her go.

Pulaski County Schools hired her as a teacher, and she settled in as a strict disciplinarian and rigorous taskmaster. Her students nominated her for, and she was elected to, *Who's Who Among America's Teachers.*

Linda's political career began with her involvement in the Pulaski Association of Classroom Teachers. She attended her first National Education Association Convention in 1976. She was then chosen to attend the Arkansas Education Association's Summer Leadership conference where she made her debut wearing a tee shirt that said, "Jesus is coming and He's really pissed." She noticed that people avoided her and she really didn't care. But, several women heard her speak and were impressed. That evening she was invited to a dorm room where about thirty women gathered around her to tell her how to act, what to wear, etc., in order to make a good impression and to be identified as a credible leader. "I knew that they cared and so I was obedient."

Her service in the teaching profession has included the following:

- The first African American to represent the state of Arkansas on the National Education Association (NEA) Resolutions Committee and Board of Directors after the merger between the black and white associations.

- The first Arkansan elected to the nine-member NEA Executive Committee.

- The second Arkansan to serve as chairperson of the NEA Black Caucus.

- Co-Chairperson of the NEA Minority Affairs Committee.

- The first African American woman elected as president of the Pulaski Association of Classroom Teachers.

- The first African American woman elected president of the Arkansas Education Association.

- The first teacher-member of the Little Rock School Board, where she served two terms as president.
- Recipient of the Mary HatwoodFutrell Award from the NEA. This award is presented to a nominee whose activities in women's rights have made a significant impact on education and on the achievement of equal opportunities for women and girls.

Linda is tearful when she speaks of her pride in her students. She is passionate about the role education has played in her own life and the lives of her former students, many of whom are now her constituents.

She says she is outspoken and often rubs people the wrong way. "People either really like me or dislike me. I don't lose sleep over it. When I lose a contest, I say to myself, 'No matter what happens, the sun will rise the next day.'"

When she was elected to the Little Rock, Arkansas school board, she won by thirty-five votes. Then she had the unhappy task of fighting openly with the first black superintendent of Little Rock. "There is an unwritten rule that blacks can't argue with other blacks in public. But he had privatized the bus service and as a result poor folks, black and white, lost their jobs, their health insurance, and so forth. I was the only one who had read the contract and I spoke up. We got rid of him. Some people were upset and I got hate mail. But, I will not suffer angst over other people's anger," she says forcefully.

Linda was elected to the Arkansas House of Representatives in 2002. She became the Chairperson of the House Subcommittee on Desegregation and Litigation and the only female member of the House Committee on Agriculture, Forestry, and Economic Development.

Ms. Pondexter-Chesterfield has much to say about political involvement. "Don't just sit at the table. Set the table. Otherwise you will always be in reactive mode. Remember that beauty shines more brightly than ugliness. Blazing the trail for others makes me proud. I may be the poorest financially, but I am the richest over all. I never have to be impoverished in spirit."

She continues, "Where I grew up, people made a sacrifice to vote. There was a poll tax and many people had to decide between choosing to vote and choosing to eat. We voted! White politicians passed out money on street corners for votes. My mother and grandmother wouldn't take that money." She encourages people to vote and worries that many do not.

"Now I am in the legislature and I am the voice of the African American and the poor who have no voice. I am the voice of women and men who have no voice. I give service because so many others have given service before me."

Linda closes the interview with a heart-felt exclamation, "God is omnipresent and omnipotent and has a plan for our lives. It is our duty and obligation to determine how we will serve." Tears are streaming down our cheeks as we conclude our time together.

Majora Carter

"Don't be afraid to live out loud."

I met Majora Carter and heard her speak at the "Women, Power, and Peace" conference at The Omega Center in Rhinebeck, New York. The conference organizers had originally invited Wangari Maathai, the Kenyan Nobel Peace Laureate to give a presentation on her tree-planting projects in Africa, but had invited Majora in her place when Ms. Maathai was not available. She said that she felt so honored to be a replacement for Ms. Maathai, and it was an honor, of course. But, Majora has made her own amazing, and perhaps equally significant contributions to the environmental movement, too. Her presentation on "greening the ghetto" and the social justice implications of waste disposal, and creating greenbelts in inner cities was compelling. "Just call me," she said when I approached her for an interview. Women wanting to have a word with her surrounded her and she quickly passed me her card and her email address. When I called her and arranged the interview, she was surprised at my lack of knowledge about environmental issues in inner cities and elsewhere. "I have to educate you!" she said. And so, she did! She sent me DVD's to watch and steered me to other information and presentations she had made. She is a great example of how a Crusader can sometimes happen onto their issue quite by accident. It changes the course of their lives, and influences and changes the lives of others, too. That's what happened to Majora.

I had to beg for a half hour of Majora's time for the interview, even though all the interviews up until that time had taken two hours or more. Her assistant said she would do what she could to get me any time at all. I was willing to take what I could get. As it turned out, we spent an hour and a half on the telephone before she said she really had to run. She is warm and delightful. She looks far younger than her forty some years. And she seems to be fearless in her crusade to keep the powers that be from dumping New York's garbage in her neighborhood!

Majora Carter is the youngest of seven children born to her parents, Major and Tinnie Carter, in the South Bronx of New York. She says that her father was a rather distant figure, as he was sixty years old when she was born. He worked at a number of jobs from janitor and grocery clerk to long-line truck driver and postal worker. In day-to-day life, it was her mother she wanted to please and who was truly present. She says that her mother was a large woman noted in the community for always wearing fabulous hats and gloves.

Majora says that she was not like her brothers and sisters. She was not cute, not popular, not musical or athletic, in the ways that they were. But, she was smart. Though the others teased her and called her "bookworm," her mother encouraged her studies.

Majora says that when she was a little girl, the South Bronx was a real community. Neighbors knew and watched out for each other, and she had lots of friends.

When she was about seven, she noticed fires in the neighborhood and didn't know why there were so many. What was happening was that landlords had begun to set fire to their buildings to collect insurance money and disinvest in the neighborhood. This set the stage for businesses leaving, and these businesses were often replaced by waste authorities. The South Bronx soon became a place that time and law enforcement forgot.

One of Majora's brothers returned from military service in Viet Nam, only to be murdered in the neighborhood. He was twenty-three years old.

Two apartment buildings on Majora's block burned down. They had been filled with friends of hers; and, the neighborhood began to feel unfriendly, though not scary. She says that even as a child, she felt sad looking at buildings that had once throbbed with life and were now burned out shells.

The neighborhood had also become more dangerous, though she didn't realize it then. But, when a young girlfriend of one of her older brother's was brutally raped and murdered on a nearby rooftop, the danger became apparent.

Majora says that she was miserable as a teenager. She had applied for and been accepted at Bronx Science High School, one of the most prestigious public high schools in New York City. She had been tutored in middle school to take the entrance exam, and she assumed that this was what everyone did to get in. But, upon entering, she almost failed every class. "I discovered that not all things are created equal with education in New York City schools. I had an inferior education coming from South Bronx, and was not prepared to compete with mostly white peers. I began asking how anyone in authority could let this happen." She was one of only a few black students at the school and she didn't feel connected to them or her white classmates. It was a lonely time.

"There was a lot of prejudice within the black community," she says. "I was considered low class and I was really shy, too. So, I was an outsider with the white kids, and an outsider with the black kids. I had no boyfriend. I did have one close girlfriend who remains a friend to this day. But, I knew that school would be my platform to get out of the South Bronx, so I endured."

From a social standpoint, Majora found college to be much the same. She had received financial aid and loans to attend Wesleyan College in Middletown, Connecticut. The school had a good theatre program and she had decided to become an actor. This was an abrupt switch from her high school interest in biology, and her plans to be a doctor or a neuroscientist. But, the theatre intrigued her. She loved directing, and loved the permanent nature of film. She was also good at editing and knew how to tell a good story. In many ways, her experiences growing up in the South Bronx had been the best education of all and she planned that her senior thesis in college would be a film about a young girl growing up in the South Bronx.

It was also true that college was culture shock. She was really on her own, with no family nearby. She says that it took her awhile to see that she had nothing to prove to her fellow students and that she needed to focus on developing and being herself.

Majora was having trouble getting her senior project film made. The burned out buildings of the South Bronx provided great sets, and a local child had her mother's permission to play the starring role. But, Majora did not have the financial resources that other students had to rent or buy the equipment necessary for filming. Because the filming was to take place in a high crime area, no one wanted to rent the equipment to her anyway, not even when the police chief of the local First Precinct wrote a letter guaranteeing its safety and eventual return. The film didn't get finished.

Majora married in her mid-twenties. She sees now that she was too young and too needy to manage a marriage. When it broke up, she moved home to the South Bronx.

She had tried working in film for a time, but it never really worked out. Her time spent working as a receptionist was unfulfilling to her. She would have loved to go to New York University's film school, but could not afford it. She was searching for where to fit in the adult world of work.

During this time, while Majora was living at home and trying to figure out her next move, a brilliant dancer, Bill T. Jones, returned to the South Bronx to live with his partner, Arthur Aviles. This was the beginning of some artists taking up residence and being a presence for the arts in the neighborhood. This was heartening and inspiring to Majora.

She had been teaching creative writing to students enrolled in such programs as the Job Corps, Writer's Corps, and Ameri-Corps. She doesn't think she was a very good teacher, but it made use of her education and her interest in the arts and creativity.

She became involved with other neighborhood creative types and they formed the South Bronx Film and Video Productions, to further implement artistic pursuits in the area. At the same time, New York waste management facilities were coming into the neighborhood. Majora came to the realization that all the art in the world wasn't going to save her community.

At that time, forty percent of New York City's commercial waste was trucked to the South Bronx and added to one hundred percent of their own garbage. The city had plans to add forty percent of the residential waste to what was already coming their way. The health implications were dire, as a higher percentage of the community's children contracted asthma, and everyone was subjected to the toxicity of increased diesel exhaust, as well as whatever toxins were contained in the garbage itself. The South Bronx was already the location of several sewage treatment plants and power plants. She refers to this as environmental racism.

Majora's outrage and concern grew, for herself and her community. She was confronted with the complacency and utterly dejected attitude of the local citizens. Getting this population mobilized would be an uphill struggle.

Majora believes that her time away from the South Bronx had given her a different perspective and frame of reference. She just had to figure out how her voice could help. She worked hard at the grass roots level to defeat New York City's plan to double the amount of waste coming to the South Bronx. It took four long years. She says that this experience helped her understand that these kinds of fights are never-ending; that citizens must be vigilant and active if they are to protect their community interests and receive equitable treatment.

"You can't be that choosy about how to make beautiful things happen," she says. "If an environment is boring, negative and with a feeling of anger, well, bring beauty."

After the waste management battle was waged and won, Majora began thinking about other ideas to revive her community and make it a more positive environment. She came across a research study out of the University of Chicago on urban forestry, showing that where there are clusters of trees in urban neighborhoods, crime and stress decrease, while property values and people's reports of happiness increase. This was the impetus and motivation for her to start a program to reforest the South Bronx. It was called Greening for Breathing, and was devoted to increasing the parkland in the area.

She received a $10,000 seed grant to help revitalize the waterfront. Majora thought it was a naïve and impossible task to try to undertake such an enormous project with so little financial support. But, she loves to tell the story of the day her dog dragged her through a very littered empty lot and showed her that beyond the weeds and litter of illegal dumping, was access to the river that was not visible from the street. Her dog had showed her a possibility for use of the seed money.

Majora and her associates began clearing this lot, which was to become the Hunt's Point Riverside Park, the first new park to be built in the South Bronx in sixty years. That was in 1998. She eventually leveraged that $10,000 into a $3,000,000 park with bicycle paths and water access.

Majora went on to found and head up the Sustainable South Bronx project. She is a visionary voice in city planning, and views urban renewal through an environmental lens. She had truly found a way to combine her scientific and artistic interests in a way that continues to amaze and inspire those who learn of her endeavors.

By 2001, The Sustainable South Bronx had received over $20 million in funding from a variety of sources to continue the environmental revitalization of the area. In 2005, Majora received a MacArthur Fellowship, often called a "genius grant." This is an honor and financial award that one cannot apply for, but is bestowed through a search process, making it especially prestigious.

Majora's advice to other women is not to second-guess themselves. "Don't be afraid to live out loud," she says emphatically. As an example, she explains that in writing the large federal grant that brought $20 million to the South Bronx for "green" projects, she was operating as an outsider. She was not a pillar of the social justice community; she had no standing in established environmental groups. She was not even validated by her peers and she wanted validation. But, she knew that her ideas needed to happen, and she says that she owes a debt of gratitude to the many women, most of whom she never met, who helped guide her through the maze of bureaucracy involved in applying for a federal grant.

"Give yourself credit," she says. "See value in yourself and make others see it, too. Put a value on your time, because if you don't, others won't either. If you give yourself away, you get disrespected."

The Hunt's Point Riverside Park became the beautiful backdrop for Majora's marriage to James Chase. Her dog served as her flower girl. In addition, the park was only the beginning of Majora's plans for other environmental restoration and urban renewal projects, including The BronxEcological-Stewardship Training program (BEST), and The Cool Roofs Project.

Majora points out that economic degradation leads to environmental degradation, which leads to social and personal degradation. Her goal has been to reverse this process, marrying environmental issues to economic and social justice issues for the good of her community. Starting with a grass roots crusade to create beauty out of desolation and degradation is her genius.

Kimberle Williams Crenshaw, Esq.

"Don't allow the expectations of others to squeeze the life out of your dreams."

Kimberle Crenshaw was a presenter at the "Women, Peace, and Power" conference at The Omega Center in Rhinebeck, N.Y. in the year that many female Nobel Peace Prize recipients were the conference leaders. She gave a presentation on "intersectionality," as it relates to civil rights law interpretation. She made a very complex concept relatively easy to understand as she spoke about the ways in which women and minorities face discrimination in the workplace, and the difficulty in proving such discrimination when the issues of gender and race coincide. She was beautiful, brilliant, and clear in her presentation. She also seemed able to laugh easily.

But, make no mistake, this is a woman who knows her subject intimately and travels the world helping to create protections for women and minorities in the workplace and in the larger culture.

When I went to Los Angeles to meet with Kimberle, she had just returned from Japan, where she had been asked to speak to a group of Japanese women on the subject of workplace discrimination and what they could do about it. She has consulted all over the world on these important issues of civil rights.

Kimberle's name is not a household word, but it is important to understand that every working woman, no matter her race or ethnic background, owes a debt of gratitude to her for her work extending legal protection to us from the discrimination that has been our legacy since the founding of our country.

Born the second child and only girl to her parents in Canton, Ohio, in 1962 Kimberle's family moved into the biggest house in a new neighborhood. They were one of two black families in this heavily Italian-Catholic area, where the racism was deeply embedded, and the people knew how to say "nigger."

Kimberle says that she didn't understand what the problem was in her new neighborhood and just wondered why the other children seemed afraid of her and didn't want to play. Or, they would only play with her if no adults were watching so they wouldn't get in trouble.

"My mother had light skin, green eyes and red hair," Kimberle says. "And so, when a white man knocked on our door and my mother answered, he didn't realize that she was African American. The man said that he was sure she knew that the neighborhood was changing quickly, and that he was prepared to make an offer on our home before it was too late!" Mrs. Crenshaw told him she would inform her husband, but that she doubted that they'd be moving anytime soon.

Kimberle's older brother was especially sensitive about the fact that his mother was light and his father dark. She says that if the family went out for a drive, her brother would get angry when he saw people were staring at his family. He'd say, "They're always looking! They think that dad is black and mom is white." Kimberle said, "Well, Mom *is* white." At least that's how it seemed to her. The incident prompted her parents to carefully explain the curious intricacies of racial identity.

As a child Kimberle was quite a worrier. Her worries caused her to be very curious and to ask a lot of questions. For example, she asked her mother what would happen when she went to the grocery store and there would be no more food. She didn't yet know the concept of restocking. Her concerns and curiosity would lead her to think more systemically which would become an asset later on in her life.

Kimberle's father and mother were both public school teachers. Their family was active in a Christian Methodist Episcopal Church, where her mother was the organist and her father was the Minister of Music. They attended church on Sundays and choir practice on Thursday evenings. When the Canton Police Boy's Club wanted to sponsor a choir, Kimberle's mother volunteered her father to direct it. Her brother, Mantel, sang in the choir. And so, the Crenshaw's spent an evening each week rehearsing at The Boy's Club, where Kimberle was the only girl.

Kimberle's family was active in music, and with their various choirs they performed all over the state of Ohio. But, music was only one of their endeavors. Her parents believed in preparing their children to have an opinion and to learn how to express it well. When they sat down to dinner at night, each person reported on something they had learned that day and what they thought of it. They were proud and pleased when this training paid off unexpectedly. News that their third grade daughter had given her first impromptu speech at a hastily assembled memorial service the day Martin Luther King, Jr. was killed, reached their home before she did. When Kimberle came in the door, her dad swept her up in his arms. His tears of sadness were mixed with pride, knowing that his daughter had urged others to walk in Dr. King's footsteps.

Kimberle's father left his teaching career to become an administrator of public housing. He became known for developing scattered site, low-rise, integrated public housing, which was a creative response to the high-rise, segregated, densely populated housing projects of the time. Her dad was very hands-on in the development of these projects and the father-daughter team would make rounds together to inspect the buildings on weekends.

When Kimberle was ten, her father died at the age of thirty-four. It was a great loss. He was so well respected throughout the Canton community, that both a park and junior high school were named after him. Kimberle describes this very sad time as, "like going from perpetual daylight into never-ending darkness. One day I was as happy as I could be, lying in my back yard counting puffy white clouds with my family all in sight. The next day, there was nothing to see but tears." Her mother became very depressed. Her brother was despondent and angry, and ultimately he left home. Her caretaker who had been with the family since Kimberle was three had already left, and Kim and her mom suddenly found themselves alone and isolated in their empty house.

Just a year later, her maternal grandmother, who had been a vibrant member of the family, also died. By this time, Kimberle had just turned eleven. She was attending a white, fundamentalist Christian school and was one of two black children in attendance. She was in the fifth grade and she says the teachers and administrators just didn't know what to do with her. There were numerous competitions with other Christian schools, and Kimberle won the competitions to represent her school. She didn't feel she had the full support of the school administrators and she was sometimes warned by the principal to be mindful of the school's reputation. Simply being herself was sometimes interpreted as being difficult and resistant. For example, when her class made paper mache models of their own heads, she had to ask for brown paint and black construction paper. She had to point out that the paint color called "flesh" didn't match her flesh, and yellow and brown paper for hair wouldn't do for her hair, which made some of her teachers uneasy.

The discrimination she experienced at the school ranged from low-level insensitivity to outright indignities. In seventh grade, these indignities had risen to the level of being called a nigger and being left out of sleepovers and parties. She was wrongfully accused by one of the teachers in the school of stealing a musical instrument from a classmate. "Someone had switched their dirty and broken melodica for one belonging to my teacher's daughter and she just assumed it was me. She called me a thief and took mine." Although Kimberle's mother responded by buying her a professional quality instrument, ("it was almost as big as I was...she wanted to be sure that no one would ever confuse my instrument for anyone else's again") Kimberle had had enough. She got permission to transfer to the majority-black public school where her mother taught.

At this same time, her brother, who had just returned from a tour of duty with the Air Force, was shot to death. He had begun college in Southern Ohio and was attending a party when someone shot into the crowd. This random shooting was the third death in three years for Kimberle and her mother. They had gone from being a happy family to having only each other.

"My brother died just as I was entering a new school where my mom taught," Kimberle says. "I was pretty fragile by then and this new environment didn't help at all." Kimberle remembered, "My mother was very strict, a disciplinarian, and everyone was afraid of her. So, I got a lot of collateral anger directed at me. Here I was thinking that finally I would be with people like me and they would be accepting, but surprise, surprise — I was like a pariah! I'd be crying every night about how these kids didn't like me either, and my mom would say, 'That's garbage! Twenty years from now, these kids will want to say they knew you.' Now what kid thinks like that? Obviously, I didn't care about twenty years from then. I just wanted to fit in and be accepted. But I was small and skinny, wore glasses and had braces. Definitely aesthetically challenged!"

"And then suddenly I was in the spotlight because this incredibly handsome and popular boy said he liked me. I thought it was a joke and I just didn't believe it at first. Then it turned out to be true, and that made things even worse. Although I adored him, some of the mean girls came after me. And honestly, the thought of the two of us seemed kind of crazy to me, too. We didn't match, so I just couldn't be his girlfriend."

At the end of middle school, Kimberle entered a local Catholic High School. Because she was from an "inner city" school, she was tracked out of honors classes, which pleased her to no end since she didn't have to study. "I heard my mom was coming to school and I knew there was going to be a rumble. She came out there and read those nuns the riot act. I was kind of trying to hide behind a book or something, but I remember how she told them that she was in a constant battle to pick me up every time they knocked me down, but that she was going to win. Aquinas was just one stop along my path, and she wasn't going to let them block my success. The next day, they put me in honors classes." In the end, Kimberle didn't even want to graduate from this high school because of the way she was treated there.

The local American Legion post requested that her high school send an African American student to Girl's State, a summer leadership citizenship program that creates mock municipal and state governments. Kimberle's history teacher nominated her. She went, even though the school didn't include her name when they announced the two other attendees. She ran for attorney general at Girl's State - the third highest office - and won. She was the only student from her high school ever to win this high office, and she was subsequently elected as one of three girls to represent the entire state at Boys and Girls Nation in Washington, D.C. though it is customary for schools to celebrate such accomplishments, Kimberle's high school seemed utterly disinterested.

In the Bicentennial year, 1976, the American Legion sponsored Boys and Girls Nation, which is the same as Girls and Boys State, but at the federal government level, in Washington, DC. Representing Ohio, she spent two weeks practicing mock national government with three hundred seventeen year-olds from across the United States. It was a huge honor, but once again, her high school was not supportive. As the other students exchanged memorabilia from their various high schools to commemorate the occasion, Kimberle was empty handed. She decided not to credit her high school and transferred to the local public school, McKinley Senior High School, for her senior year.

Kimberle didn't want to go far from home for her first year of college. She attended Akron University, where she lived on campus during the week and drove the thirty miles home on weekends. She transferred to Cornell University the following year.

Cornell was committed to a diversity program, admitting minority students and providing support for them so that they would be successful. Kimberle majored in Government and Africana Studies. She worked on a radio station that broadcast *Black World News* and *Third World News*, and she rewrote wire stories to be of interest to people of color.

Kimberle began noticing issues of race and gender most acutely in college. In her Africana coursework, for example, gender was rarely discussed in the politics classes. And race rarely came up at all in classes outside the Africana Studies center. Her sense of how these issues were experienced within her own community played out when the Africana Center students organized the annual "State of Black America" conference. The men took over more public leadership roles in the conference while the women worked in the kitchen and stuffed envelopes. The men - all of them friends - would say that no one was being excluded and even most of the women would agree that the arrangements were acceptable. But Kimberle thought: "People would never accept this situation if race was the dividing line, where all the white folks were in leadership and the black folks were stuck in the kitchen. That's when it hit me that issues of race and gender justice were not well integrated."

When Kimberle's father died, he had been in his second year of law school. He left behind his law books and Kimberle had spent many hours as a child pretending to be him with those law books. "I had no idea what forces were at work at the time," she says. But, she continued her father's legacy by entering Harvard Law School. While there, she and a fellow classmate, a black man, were invited to be guests of the first African American member at an exclusive men's club. Very few African Americans had ever been guests of this club since the membership had been historically all white. Her friend was excited by the invitation and said he was going to "walk right on in like I belong there." And he did. But when Kimberle was instructed to enter by the back door because she was a woman neither of her male friends objected. "We had solidarity, except on the issue of gender. I was encountering this sort of thing everywhere, and I realized we women had to start to flex our own muscles."

Kimberle's thinking about this crystallized during the confirmation of Clarence Thomas as Supreme Court Justice. When Anita Hill accused him of sexual harassment, Kimberle realized that the black community saw racism in male terms. "Many African Americans accepted Thomas' claim that this was a high-tech lynching," she says. "I'd hear folks say that Anita Hill was a traitor and ought to be shot. Of course no one said that about Clarence Thomas, who had railed against civil rights leaders and anti-discrimination law. At that point I had a psychological falling out with this simplistic form of black politics." Kimberle supported Anita Hill's legal team during that time.

"I don't pooh pooh the issue of race or the need to stand together against racism. But, we should be as concerned about the women in our community as much as the men. I can have a similar problem with my strictly feminist friends who only see sexism in terms of what happens to white women. What happens to women of color is simply seen as a race issue."

During law school, Kimberle worked in a corporate law firm but the work really didn't appeal to her. "I wanted to think about what I wanted to think about. I didn't like renting out my brain to help the powerful use law to defeat the interests of less powerful people, which is how it seemed to me."

Kimberle began teaching at UCLA, and in her second year there, she wrote an article on the intersectionality of race and gender. She also organized race scholars into a network that she called 'Critical Race Theory' – a marker for people who want to write about race in complex ways. She brought her concept of the intersection of race and gender to the international stage at The World Conference on Racism, among other places. She has published extensively in the areas of civil rights, black feminist legal theory and race, and racism and the law.

Kimberle is now a law professor at Columbia University in New York, as well as UCLA. She teaches courses on race and gender equity and intersectionality, and constitutional law. Twice she was voted professor of the year. She takes her students to India and Brazil to see the deep parallels in other countries regarding equity issues and helps to build networks for the next generation.

Kimberle lectures nationally and internationally on matters of race and gender to audiences in Europe, Africa, South America and Japan. Her work on race and gender was influential in drafting the equality clause in the South African constitution. In 2001, she wrote the background paper on Race and Gender Discrimination for The United Nations World Conference on Racism. She also served on the National Science Foundation committee to research violence against women.

Opining that because what most Americans think about race comes from the entertainment industry, Kimberle asks her students to examine race representations in movies and advertising. She tries to help her students identify what exactly constitutes cultural transformation and how it can be achieved.

Kimberle has never married and doesn't want to get married. Yet she notes that many black professional women who do want to marry face real challenges, and that professional black women, as a group, have among the lowest rates of reproduction in the United States. She reports that a constant conversation among her friends who are looking for their Prince Charming is their belief that black men don't feel comfortable with women like them and that not many non-black men are willing to cross the racial barriers.

On advice to other women, Kimberle emphatically states: "Don't allow the expectations of other people to squeeze the life out of your dreams." Adding, "I have always been motivated by my gut and what I feel passionate about, even though I sometimes paid for it. I knew early in my life that I just wasn't willing to keep my mouth shut." She goes on to say, "Everywhere you go, you may have to elbow your way in. But, being authentic opens you to your deepest power. Meanwhile, move to your own inner music. You might just have to create a tune that suits you better than the one that everyone else is humming and that's just fine. I have a friend who always reminds me to 'do you.' This is proof positive that the simplest advice if often the best."

Charisse Strawberry-Fuller

*"I took my mess and
turned it into
my message.
I took the test
God gave me and
made it my testimony."*

serve on the Board of Directors for the Bay Area chapter of the National
Council for Alcoholism and Other Drug Addictions. Our Executive
Director, Arthur Bosse, and President, Brigette Lank, kept insisting that I
had to meet this amazing woman to include in this book. Numerous times
they asked if I had made contact with Charisse Strawberry. Finally, they
helped me get an appointment with her. I saw her across a room before we
had been introduced. "You'll know who she is immediately," Brigette had
said. "How will I know her?" I wanted to know. "Well, she's quite tall and
absolutely gorgeous! Everyone in the room will turn and look at her when
she enters the room. You can't miss her." I didn't disbelieve Brigette, with
Arthur nodding agreement in the background, but I thought they were
exaggerating. Not at all! It was absolutely true. As she entered a large conference room where I was attending a meeting, all eyes were trained on her.

And she was very, very strikingly beautiful, actually regal in her bearing.

When I met with her later, she was as lovely in sharing her life story with me as she was in her appearance. It turned out that she had been a high school and college athlete in the same county where I was raised. Though she is much younger than me, we shared similar experiences about being raised in "The OC" before it was the glitzy place of TV fame. Our experience was of a place of endless orange groves, strawberry and bean fields, and the glorious, sandy beaches where we spent our summers.

Charisse Strawberry is the oldest child and only girl born to her parents. She was raised in Southern California in an interracial family where her father was African American and her mother was Caucasian of partly Norwegian descent.

Charisse's father was a successful professional basketball player, having played first at The University of Utah, and then for the ABA and NBA. He was a disciplinarian, she says, and she was closer to him while growing up, than to her mother.

Charisse's parents were very young when they married and began having children. When Charisse was fourteen, they divorced. It was a very rough time, and Charisse went to live with her father and her paternal grandmother, "Nana," who had a strong influence on her.

When Charisse was with her mother, people would ask if she was adopted. Her parent's attitude about being an interracial family was very strong. "You have the best of both worlds," they would tell her. As a result, she says she can readily identify with both worlds. She had friends from all sorts of backgrounds.

Charisse attended Esperanza High School in Fullerton, California. She was a good student, but really stood out in sports. She played varsity volleyball and basketball as a freshman, and was an All-City and All-County player in California Interscholastic Federation (CIF) finals. Indeed, as of this writing, she continues to hold her high school record for rebounds. Though Charisse was social in high school, she says that sports kept her focused and busy. Her father was strict and she was not allowed to do what some of her friends were allowed to do, like wearing make-up, having pierced ears, or dating until she was sixteen.

Charisse was recruited to play sports by many schools, but accepted a volleyball scholarship to attend California State University at Fullerton. She says that she just didn't feel ready to leave home, nor did she want to leave her brother, Miles, who was eight years younger and a bit like her baby.

Charisse left the volleyball team after her sophomore year. She didn't like the program as it was configured and she says she felt a bit lost.

By this time, Charisse was living independently. While attending a friend's party, a charming man cut in on a dance to dance with her. She noticed that he was a bit arrogant, but in time she came to appreciate his big heart and easygoing manner. She didn't know at that first meeting that this was the well-known baseball player, Darryl Strawberry.

Charisse says that her father's protectiveness had left her somewhat naïve about this whole other world she was about to enter. She was young and her father had played professional sports in a whole different era, so his impressions of professional athletes were colored by his own experience.

Their romance was a whirlwind and Charisse was swept off of her feet. They dated for a year and a half, became engaged and then married in a small ceremony. Charisse's parents liked Darryl and approved of the marriage.

Darryl had been previously married and had other children. There was easy acceptance all around. What Charisse didn't know was that Darryl had a significant drug problem. It was rather hidden from her inasmuch as he apparently didn't use drugs during baseball season.

They had begun having children and lived in-between New York and California. Jordan was born first, followed a year later by Jade.

When Darryl's addiction came to her attention, she truly didn't understand it because her own life was untouched by alcoholism or addiction.

Darryl entered The Betty Ford Center for treatment in 1994 after an intervention took place. The Dodgers were notified and Charisse called her pastor and her parents. She attended the family program at The Betty Ford Center and truly believed that all would be well and they would resume their lives normally.

It was recommended that Charisse attend her own 12-Step Program. "I understood nothing of the concept," she says now. And she refused.

As time went on and Darryl's addiction continued to resurface, Charisse became desperate. She says that she had to find some sanity and serenity. She began to attend Al-Anon, a 12-Step Program for people whose lives had been touched by someone else's alcoholism and/or addiction. "I saw women in those meetings who were able to detach from the addicted person in their lives in a loving way. It was amazing and I couldn't imagine it. I was advised to sit in the Al-Anon meetings for a while and just listen. That's what I did and I came to see that this is a devastating family disease. Darryl mostly only used drugs in the off-season and I came to dread the off-season."

What ensued were several years of ups and downs with the devastation of addiction. When Darryl's health insurance plan said they would no longer pay for his treatment, Charisse couldn't believe it. She says it really took her a long time to get the concept of the intractable nature of the disease, and to accept her situation.

"I'm a hard-headed woman. I wanted to fix my family. It was so difficult to watch someone I loved suffer from addiction. My powerlessness in this situation was very troubling to me." Charisse goes on to say that the fact that she and Darryl were in the public eye made the entire situation more difficult. She felt a need to protect Darryl, a conflict of loyalty that causes many people close to addicts to remain quiet. This desire to protect Darryl's reputation and her own concerns about exposure caused Charisse to feel quite isolated. It also contributed to what she says was her biggest inner conflict - to be open and outspoken or to continue to keep quiet, thereby enabling him to remain secretly addicted. When his problems became public knowledge, it was somewhat of a relief to her. Charisse could share more authentically and be honest. What she says now, having been a faithful member of Al-Anon for over thirteen years is that she can now see her own issues of control, and how this contributed to the problem.

Darryl continued to relapse time and again. He was also diagnosed with colon cancer. He was suspended from professional sports for a year, and was treated for addiction again, as well as for cancer.

When Charisse was pregnant with her third child, Darryl had a reoccurrence of cancer. He was at home and angry. When he was court-ordered to further treatment for addiction, Charisse found herself alone. She found solace in church and her deep faith.

Darryl had violated his treatment protocol and was ordered to more treatment, where he began a relationship with another woman. Charisse says that going through all of this in the public eye was horrific and beyond embarrassing. When Darryl went to jail again, she decided she was done.

The Strawberry's were living in Tampa, Florida. While visiting in New York, Charisse met a woman named Adele Smithers, whom she refers to as "the mother of recovery." They made a connection and Charisse was looking for something meaningful to do with her life. She wanted to use her notoriety to bring awareness and compassion to families struggling with alcoholism and addiction. And so, Adele Smithers provided the seed money for Charisse to start a Tampa, Florida chapter of The National Council of Alcoholism and Other Drug Dependencies. "I took my mess and turned it into my message. I took the test God gave me and turned it into my testimony," she says now.

Charisse created a job for herself and worked out of her home at first. Her home telephone number was on the business cards and stationery. She had a baby and two older children to manage and she had to be resourceful and creative.

"I tried to reconcile with my husband," she says, "but I just couldn't take it anymore. It was a very tough decision and I made it after a lot of prayer. I just couldn't do the work for both of us anymore."

Charisse surrounded herself with supportive people. She learned more about patience, perseverance, and prayer. "My grandmother came to Florida constantly.... all through the drama, she helped. She was the backbone for me," she says gratefully.

Charisse has been divorced for several years now. She has a full life, working and raising her children.

She has a number of things to say to women who have an alcoholic or otherwise addicted family member. She emphasizes that one can't and shouldn't have to handle the problem alone. She says to remain positive and surround yourself with positive people. "The secret is terrible! Don't keep it in the dark, because it will not make it better. Addiction does not discriminate."

"Women need to pursue what makes them happy," she advises. "Put God first, then your children, and then yourself. So, don't miss out on opportunities that come your way. I put my life on hold for a lot of years being so concerned and caught up with someone else's problem."

Charisse is quick to emphasize that although she is not facing the challenges of living in poverty, as are many African American women, she recognizes that her term as a single mother trying to raise her children alone, was difficult and sad. Though the children's father is supportive and they enjoy a good relationship, he does not live close by, and therefore this is a work in progress.

"Addiction in a woman's life can destroy her self-esteem," she says. " I wondered if I would have another relationship."

Charisse found the answer to that question recently. It seems that a wonderful man came into her life in the form of Corey Fuller. He not only wanted her, he wanted to be a stepfather to her children, and they seemed willing to accept him in that role. Charisse and Corey married on August 8, 2008. They decided on that date (08/08/08) as a theme for the new beginnings in their lives.

The marriage involved a move to a new city and leaving behind her position on a daily basis at the NCADD in Tampa, though she continues to volunteer with fundraising and advocacy, as well as maintaining connections to friends and colleagues.

Adding to the theme of "new beginnings" is the birth of their son. "My prayers were answered," Charisse says. "I prayed for a partner who would love me, and my children, and that is what I got. It is a wonderful experience and I am enjoying this gorgeous baby boy and my new life with my husband!"

Charisse says that she is aware of evolving and changing. Her children and her husband are her greatest joy. In addition, her passion continues to be expressed in her work consulting for The National Council for Alcoholism another Drug Dependencies, bringing alcoholism and addiction into the public awareness without stigma. "I want addiction to be respected as a disease, just like cancer," she says. "I intend to continue my public speaking about the ways in which addiction impacts families." Though Charisse recently spoke to a crowd of over 350 people, she also likes to speak to small groups, where there is opportunity for questions to be answered in a more intimate setting. "I try to be transparent about my own experience," she says. "I really want people to understand that addiction is not a moral issue."

We owe gratitude to Charisse Strawberry-Fuller for surviving her test and making it her testimony, and thereby providing resources and support for others facing similar challenges.

CHAPTER 6

The Creatives

*If there wasn't something called acting, they would
probably hospitalize people like me. The giddiness and the
joy of life is the moving and grooving, and the exploration.*
— Whoopi Goldberg

Creativity is often defined as the process of bringing into being
something that is novel and useful.

The Creative spirit in African American women is legendary
and has its roots in the ancestral tradition of figuring out how to make
do with very little in the way of material goods, and how to live joyfully
through music, athletic competition, and the arts. This creativity is exemplified in survival skills such as sewing and cooking, and extends to its
expression in artistic pursuits such as music, theatre, dance, and sports.

Creative people tend to be nonconforming, independent, intrinsically
motivated, open to new experiences, and risk takers. In addition, intelligence, tolerance of ambiguity, self-confidence, and flexibility in thinking
are other attributes of the creative person. Further research suggests that a
positive mood increases both motivation and creativity.

Every one of the women I interviewed expressed her creativity in a wide
variety of ways. For some, it was the pure ingenuity of accomplishing what
she had set about to do. For others, creativity in some form had become

their means of making a living. Many of the women spoke of their mothers, grandmothers, aunts, and even great-grandmothers as the creative geniuses of the family, managing to make ends meet with few resources at their disposal. They spoke to me of the sense of style that was expressed in the way these relatives dressed, or of how older women in their communities had produced dresses for them to take to college from the cotton sacks that had held flour.

Research on creativity indicates that mood is a powerful inducer of creativity, and that both positive and negative mood states can be a catalyst for the creative spirit.

The following stories are wonderful examples of creativity in action.

Luisah Teish

"Expose yourself to the diversity that is on this planet so you can choose and connect. Always look for where you can contribute and attract your kindred to you."

My mentor, Angeles Arrien, had mentioned Luisah Teish to me many years ago when I was looking for an African American cultural consultant for some work I was doing. I bought her book, *Jump Up*, and loved her suggestions for seasonal ceremonies and decorations. But, I couldn't find her in the telephone book. I finally paid a private investigator to find her for me!

It is hard to describe Luisah Teish's wonderful, booming voice on the telephone. But, when I called her home to ask about an interview, she answered with a strong and joyful, "Alafia!" which roughly means, "May all be well with you and may you be at peace with your neighbor." This was the beginning of many such greetings.

Teish, as she prefers to be called, has proved to be a marvelous friend and confidant. She came to my 60th birthday party to tell and dramatize a wonderful African story, and she had my thirty guests up dancing and singing to accompany the telling. Such fun!

When I discovered that she did oracle readings using a casting of cowry shells, I signed up immediately. It was an amazing experience, including a glass of water that spontaneously shattered, leading Teish to insist that I scoop up the water and put it all over my neck and scalp, to wash away the doubts I had been having.

Later, she suggested that we travel to the ocean, where she erected a little tent, complete with chairs, pillows, and her tools of transformation. She washed my hair with a mixture of river water, honey, and Efun, a chalky substance mined from river bottoms in Africa. It was a sticky mess, which was then rinsed out with ocean water. BRRRR! My clean hair was wrapped in white cloth to "set" the transformation, and I pulled three stones from the ocean to leave in my room that night to ground the experience. I had been instructed to leave an offering Mandala for Mother Ocean, consisting of cornmeal, molasses, seven pennies, and a melon. I made a beautiful design as a sign of my gratitude, and we made our way home.

I owe a great debt of gratitude to Teish for all her help in the writing of this book. Her comments and support have been invaluable. Best of all, she is the kind of woman who is so comfortable to be with, that it is clear one could ask her anything and she would not take offense. In cross-cultural conversations, this is invaluable, because it allows for the freedom to be authentic without worrying about giving offense. Teish will tell me if I am in error or on shaky ground. And she will do it in a way that I feel supported rather than chastised. Safety with another person is a valuable thing!

Luisah Teish is a writer, storyteller and ritual designer. She is the author of several works of creative non-fiction, poetry and plays. Her most notable work is *Jambalaya: The Natural Woman's Book of Personal Charms and Practical Rituals*, which was published in 1985 and has since become a women's spirituality classic. She travels around the world gathering myths and folktales from elders and rendering those stories into contemporary language. She teaches the transformative arts at all educational levels and she designs personal rituals and public ceremonies.

These interests and talents are grounded in her childhood. Teish describes her growing up as a combination of mystery and misery. She explains that in New Orleans everything has folklore behind it. Teish spent the early days of her childhood in her paternal grandmother's house, the former home of Mam'zelle Marie LaVeau, the Voodoo Queen. She remembers that there were family picnics on the levee with stories of swamp creatures that came out at night. The children were spoken to in proverbs and the stories that were told sounded as though they had happened just yesterday and just around the corner. It wasn't until years later that Teish realized that these were classic stories of the oral tradition.

Teish says that her mother is the ground of her being. "She is a wonderful example of an African American woman's ability to make something out of nothing. She has courage beyond reason, a hair-trigger temper, and a flirtatious sense of humor. She knew how to work hard and laugh loud and 'find a way out of no way'."

Teish really valued how the women of the community stuck together. She believes that they couldn't have survived without the help and support they offered one another with children, gardens, and protecting each other "from all types of foolishness." All this was accomplished without the help of the local government or law enforcement. Witnessing the strength of these women shaped Teish's identity as a political activist, and as a feminist. Her experiences of growing up in this community of women contributed to the narrative of *Jambalaya*.

Teish, recalls that her father was a rather tragic figure in several ways. Although he was a talented singer, and musician, he suffered socially and emotionally from the effects of racism. His interest in mythology and his dream of becoming an architect were overshadowed by the demands of the times. He worked as a longshoreman before black men were allowed into the union and was instrumental in bringing about that change.

Also, in his work as a longshoreman, he experienced some sort of toxic exposure that resulted in his suffering with hiccups for twenty-one years. As a result of this and many other experiences, Teish became an environmental justice activist.

Her father personified the type of macho behavior that disempowered men often act out. Though Teish's mother was always trying to engage him, he couldn't invest his heart in relationship and was largely alienated from his children as a result. His contribution to family life was the money he earned. This attitude changed in the years before his death.

Teish says that this early experience with her father has left her with a "vulture's eye" on relationships with men. She watches closely to see if what they say matches what they do. "There are wonderful men in the community who have been pillars. I honor their spirits; but, there are too few of them," she says with emphasis and adds that the wounded men, such as her father, need to heal themselves and stand up beside the women. "The salvation of the whole planet depends on this rebalancing." She thinks there should be a ritual for those men who refuse to change and grow. "They should be put in the compost heap!"

Also, Teish was drawn by the mystery of television. She didn't like the "Amos and Andy" type shows, which portrayed black people in only the most negative light. Rather television allowed her to see the juxtapositions of rich and poor, leisure-class people and workhorses, sophisticates and country folks.

"You have to understand that living in the black, segregated south was akin to living in another country, in another century. For example, we had really guarded courtship rituals. I knew a boy who lived down the street. One day he came to our fence and called to me that he was willing to help me with my math homework because he knew I was having trouble with it. My father met him at the door with a pistol in his hand. Courtship in my family meant you could sit on the porch with your grandmother and the visiting boy. On top of that, my father was one of eighteen children. I had fifty-one cousins on that side of the family alone. It seemed that everybody in town was somehow kin to me and watching what I did."

So, in 1964 Teish left New Orleans and went to live with relatives in a very small black community in Palm Springs, California. She experienced culture shock.

"Some of the kids threw rocks at me just to hear me cuss with my New Orleans southern accent. They asked stupid and insulting questions. They thought I was a slave on a plantation or something. But there was another big problem. I had come from a socially and sexually repressive environment to a place where I was the only virgin in town and word got around about that. The local boys came on to me in all sorts of creative ways. One of them told me he had a heart condition and his doctor told him the only cure was sex. So much bullshit!"

Teish has a big smile and a twinkle in her eye when she says she grew up "between the finger-fucking fifties and the wild and wooly sixties!"

It wasn't long before Teish moved to Los Angeles where her aunt worked as a maid for celebrities. Her adolescence in Los Angeles had some interesting contradictions. She loved school and her teachers and the whole process of learning. At the same time, she was intrigued by the Los Angeles street gangs and was briefly a member of the female version of the Gladiators, which was called the Del Viqueens. "We were tough and it's amazing I survived it," she says now.

Teish gives praise and thanks to two of her teachers at Manual Arts High School in the inner city of Los Angeles for inspiring her. "My physical education teacher told me if I kept dribbling the basketball while standing on my toes, I'd be sent to the dance teacher." Ms. Joan Bailey, the dance teacher, pulled Teish aside after school on a Friday. She told her that she wanted her to stay after school an extra half hour every day so that she could work with her. "I believe you could be a professional dancer," she told Teish. By the following Monday, Joan Bailey was dead. A car accident had taken her life. But, the conversation they had was the impetus for Teish to take a personal oath to be the best dancer she could be.

The other teacher was Miss Joyce Combs, who taught journalism. "She turned my head around and helped me make good choices," Teish explains. "I was hanging out with one of these bad boys and Miss Combs told me I could go with him and become trash on the street, or stay with her and become a famous writer. I stayed with her. Teachers never know how far their influence goes."

Teish graduated from high school in 1966. Miss Combs helped her get a job at Marymount College teaching dance and supervising fifteen to seventeen year-olds. She was only eighteen, but they thought she was older. Meanwhile, she had won a full scholarship to Pacific University, a United Church of Christ school in Forest Grove, Oregon. There were eleven black students and some Hawaiians in this school of 1100 students.

"I was shaped by the Civil Rights movement," Teish says. "I was a member of The Black Student Union when a friend and classmate asked me if I was into justice. She wanted to show me something and took me to nearby farms where migrant workers were picking filbert nuts. The conditions were so bad that I had a flashback to slavery on the plantations. I went back to school and told others we had to do something. I wrote an article and was able to get two houses and eleven beds donated. A women's group in Los Angeles called Las Madrecitas did a clothing drive and sent clothes."

"When the student body elected a male and female student as 'Son and Daughter of the University,' I was elected 'Daughter.' I wore a Grecian gown and African trade beads in my hair. The 'Son' was the president of the Young Republicans. I guess I've always had a strained relationship with Republicans." She rolls her eyes and smiles.

"In my Human Anatomy class, I asked the professor to explain the physiological function of the birth control pill. I was told that this could not be discussed, that the pill was not used at Pacific University, and that abstinence was the only way. I was told that the only way sex could be discussed was with my father's permission. In an anatomy class??? I couldn't stay there. Conservative Christian fundamentalism still turns my stomach!"

"So I transferred to Reed College in Portland which was the seat of intellectual achievement and social eccentricity at that time. I participated in an insurrection called 'Operation Chitlins' – taking over the administration building and negotiating for black studies. I was one of the negotiators assigned to speak to the media. Reed College was far more receptive to new ideas than the other schools were, so we won our Black Studies department. But in my World Dramatic Literature class, the literature was only about Europeans. I said, 'Could we please redefine where the world is?'"

Reed College had a good dance department with lots of experimental theater and performances. Several people suggested that Teish should apply to The Dunham School because of her interest in African dance. Katherine Dunham, "The First Lady of Black Dance," gave Teish a scholarship to be a teacher-trainee at her school in East St. Louis, Illinois. She says she had to "re-wire" her dancing brain, which was more attuned to ballet and modern dance. She learned the Dunham technique and was inspired to create choreography. After dancing with the Dunham School, Teish became the choreographer for the Black Artists Group, in St. Louis, Missouri, and the Artistic Director of The Omowali Dance and Drum Ensemble in 1970. This was one of the most creative periods of her life. In one year, the ensemble grew from three dancers with one piece of choreography to thirty dancers and twenty-two pieces of choreography. She taught multi-generational classes, three times a week, three hours each for fifty cents per person. They pioneered what is now referred to as "authentic movement" and "cultural activism." Teish was at the center of controversy for appearing bare-breasted in a retelling of the story of Adam and Eve. Another time, a spectator tried to make a citizen's arrest when she wore a costume made of an American flag. It was "the revolution" personified.

In the mid-seventies, Teish moved to Oakland to work for the public schools as a "cultural enrichment specialist." She found folktales, music and dances representing each child's ethnic background and taught these in the classrooms. "I'm good at opening up new territories," she says.

During this time, she had also had a pregnancy that ended in the death of the baby. So, this period embodied both creativity, as well as tragedy.

In 1974, Teish broke a very important rule for dancers. She was running late for a dance rehearsal and did not take the time to warm up. Rushing to keep up with the others, her timing was off and she hit a wall and injured her back. It was serious. "Acupuncture and alternative medicine saved my life," she says now. "The acupuncturist suggested that I look at the spiritual component of my life. I began to use dance as a meditation." Twenty years later, another accident largely ended Teish's dancing days, though she says that on a good day, "I can still cut a step or two."

The late '70s were a time of great turmoil and Teish sought spiritual guidance from a priest of the Yoruba tradition. The priest said the prayers to open heaven and earth and read the cowrie shells. In her reading she received the following message:

"You are a child of love, and not only that,

you are a favored child," the elder said.

"The finest jewelry is tempered in the hottest fire,

and then it is plunged into the coldest water before it is polished.

It's polishing time."

Teish continued to practice the tradition informally and took formal initiation (Kariocha) in 1982. Her life has not been the same since.

In 1980, Teish married David Wilson, a musician and writer. She says her husband (now known as Awo Falokun Fatunmbi) was a brilliant and creative man. They supported one another through difficult economic times, and achieved their goals of publishing, traveling, and addressing world problems. But, after twenty-one years of marriage, the differences in their temperaments led to divorce.

She published a little book of poems in 1980 called *What Don't Kill Is Fattening*. This was followed by *Jambalaya* in 1985. *Jambalaya* has become a women's spirituality classic and is used by women's groups and in college classes to this day. *Carnival of the Spirit: Seasonal Celebrations and Rites of Passage* followed *Jambalaya* in 1995, which describes multicultural rituals and traditions. The third book *Jump Up: Good Times Throughout the Seasons With Celebrations from Around the World*, published in 2001, contains Teish's travel notes and illustrations. She has several works in progress and expects to finish some of them soon.

She established a spiritual temple, Ile Orunmila Oshun (the House of Destiny and Love) in 1983. The temple holds monthly services and provides community education on a variety of spiritual systems. "It is a house of learning and love, honoring the ancestors and spirit of the world," she says. In addition, she continues her work writing and teaching in many venues. The Daughters of the Gelefun (the cloth of power) is a two-year women's spirituality education and ritual program, available online and in real time.

"I am what is called a modern day eccentric," Teish says with pride. "An eccentric is one who operates from a different center and that's me. I've discovered there are hundreds of thousands like me, who operate from that different center."

Though a world traveler, at this writing, Teish has lived in the Bay Area (Oakland) for more than thirty-six years.

"I would advise other women to do what they can to expose themselves to the diversity that is on this planet so they can choose and connect. Always look for where you can contribute and attract your kindred to you. Having a community around you is so valuable. Human culture has reached critical mass. We cannot waste anybody's intelligence."

"To the woman who has difficult pressures, ask for dreams for guidance from your ancestors. When you wake up, face the wind and call for mentors and people who will help you. Open your eyes and connect because you are valuable."

Jasmine Guy

"Beware of negative thinking. Self-defeating thoughts and overdone humility become self-doubt. Chase that away."

Sekyiwa Shakur gave me the book Jasmine Guy wrote, *Afeni Shakur: Evolution of a Revolutionary.* I count Afeni as a friend and couldn't wait to read this book about her life. It was a wonderful story and I admired Afeni's courage in being so forthcoming and honest in it's telling. But, I especially enjoyed Jasmine's very readable writing style, and admired the fact that she is obviously so multi-talented. Making the leap from performance artist to author indicates considerable versatility.

I had admired Jasmine's role as an actor for many years. Her talent was obvious and she was very beautiful to me. So when it was suggested that I contact her for an interview, I looked forward to the opportunity.

My husband had spotted Jasmine at Sekyiwa Shakur's wedding and pointed her out to me. She was busy chasing her little daughter. And, though lovely, as always, her personal presentation was low-key. She was friendly and unassuming and it was easy for me to talk to her.

Jasmine Guy is the eldest of two daughters born into a bi-racial family in Boston, Massachusetts. Her father had wanted to be a concert pianist, but became a Baptist minister instead and was pastor of the historic Friendship Baptist Church in Atlanta, Georgia for thirty-five years. Friendship Baptist Church served as an early home for Morehouse and Spelman Colleges. Her mother was a high school English teacher. Obviously, this was a family where education and learning were valued.

In elementary school, Jasmine began attending the Spelman College Dance School for Children. She loved dancing and credits her teacher, Miss Ann, with giving her "just enough love and attention to feel special." She expresses gratitude to a number of early mentors in her dance schools, for nurturing her talent. By ninth grade, she was attending North Atlanta Performing Arts High School. During this time she auditioned for the Alvin Ailey Dance Company when it was in town, and won a summer scholarship to this famous group.

All during Jasmine's growing up, her parents were foster parents for babies. They provided short-term care for over thirty babies who were awaiting adoption. Jasmine says that she loved always having babies in the house. She recounts a particularly disturbing aspect of this service in which one baby remained in their home for a year, because his thirteen-year-old mother would not relinquish him for adoption. At the end of that year, Jasmine's parents arranged for his placement elsewhere, as they were not prepared to do long-term care. Jasmine was devastated. She had considered this baby her brother and could not understand why her family couldn't keep him. His own mother never did relinquish him and when Jasmine searched for and found him later on, he had suffered a painful life. She says it has been hard for her to accept the powerlessness and randomness of it all. Jasmine has an affinity for babies and young children that she attributes to these early experiences. She is godmother to many children as a result.

When Jasmine's parents divorced it was very difficult for her to adjust to the separation of her family. "It just made sense when we were all together," she says. "I'm such a product of the two of them. But, being with just one or the other feels so different." Her pain about the divorce is evident when she says that at one point she believed, as many children do, that the divorce might have come as a result of something she had done; in this case, her decision to leave home and go to New York to pursue a career in dance. But, of course, that was not so.

Jasmine says that her parents have always been proud of her. They valued her intellect over her looks, and she says that her beauty was downplayed. In fact, her mother insisted that she withdraw from the "Miss Ninth Grade" contest, because she did not like the emphasis on Jasmine's appearance.

Her parents tried to balance the considerable praise and attention she was receiving in school. For example, when she received an "A++" on a high school composition, her dad pooh-poohed it, saying that there was no such thing as an "A++." As a result of this sort of "balancing," Jasmine says that self-doubt is her challenge. "I am constantly countering myself in my mind," she says.

Jasmine went to New York to continue dancing with the Alvin Ailey Dance Company at seventeen. She had been invited into a junior company and was able to make a living as a dancer. When she was twenty-one,

Debbie Allen, the famous choreographer, called Alvin Ailey and asked that all their dancers be sent to Los Angeles to audition for the NBC series, *Fame*. Jasmine auditioned with hundreds of dancers and was chosen for the part. She says that it was the first time she had seen life outside the world of dance. But, after four months in Hollywood, Jasmine was courageous enough to speak up about her desire to leave and return to Alvin Ailey. She told Debbie Allen that although she was making $750 a week doing *Fame*, and would return to AlvinAiley for $75 a week, she felt as though she was being treated like an extra. She had no contract and she believed she should receive credits and residuals. The producer wouldn't budge and so she returned to New York. "I didn't want to be a concert dancer. I wanted to be an Ailey dancer. I eventually performed every classic Ailey piece, and I left having fulfilled what I started out to do," she says now with pride.

When Jasmine returned to Hollywood, she auditioned for a part as a prostitute. The casting director said that she was "not really black enough." Prejudice happens in all sorts of ways, doesn't it? But, she found work with Spike Lee on *School Days* and had parts in several soap operas. Between 1987 and 1993, she won six consecutive NAACP "Image Awards" for her role as Whitley Gilbert on, *A Different World*. She says she had a "love/hate" relationship with her character Whitley.

Jasmine is one of those rare performers who is equally at home dancing, acting, and singing. "My gift is being multi-faceted," she says. Though dance is clearly her first love, in 1990, her debut music album introduced three *Billboard Top 100* hits.

Her stage credits include *The Wiz*, *Leader of the Pack*, *Grease*, and *Chicago*, to name just a few. She has appeared in numerous television shows, such as *The Fresh Prince of Bel Air*, *Melrose Place*, and *Touched by an Angel*.

In addition to Jasmine's many artistic accomplishments, in 2004, she collaborated with Afeni Shakur in writing the latter's biography—*Evolution of a Revolutionary*. It was her first literary attempt, and the two were successful in bringing the story to life.

Jasmine is forthcoming in describing her biracial experience. She says she had always felt different in her community in Atlanta, where her classmates were mostly African American. When she got to New York at seventeen, she saw more people who looked like her and she felt at home. But, she has certainly experienced prejudice from both racial groups.

Her own adaptation was to learn never to cry or to complain. "I had to suck it up." This was her way of adapting, but also led to feelings of self-doubt and low self-esteem. She says that she felt as though happiness and contentment were eluding her and that this just didn't make sense. Jasmine made several attempts at psychotherapy, only to back away if the therapist got too close to her core issues. "I would manipulate the situation and then decide it was a waste of time," she says. But, finally she found a therapist she trusted and began her own healing work.

"I had to work on my own self-perception. I want to be connected to what is reality and truth," she says with great emotion. "I have had a lot of negative thinking and self-defeating thoughts, which needed correction in order for me to be happier and more content."

Jasmine is well aware of the multi-generational and ancestral trauma faced by all African Americans. "For us, we're layered in our damage. There is work to be done as a whole for black women." She emphasized that this does not imply a victim stance, but a mandate to do the healing work required to plant new seeds for the next generation. "So, beware of negative thinking," she warns. "Self-defeating thoughts and overdone humility become self-doubt. Chase that away."

When asked about her own reaction to her obvious beauty, Jasmine says it's a chore. "Beauty is such a pain in the ass, especially because being in the dance world makes a person too much of a perfectionist. And then, you can never really win because there will always be someone there to criticize you… Its frustrating!"

Nowadays, Jasmine says her greatest joy is in raising her daughter, Imani. "Children are truly of God. Sometimes I look at Imani and see myself. Most times I see that she is her own person, artistic, perceptive, wondrous, adventurous. I just enjoy her company."

Though Jasmine makes light of her image as a beautiful woman, downplaying it much the way her parents did when she was growing up, her beauty has had its impact on the sensibilities of the general public through her long presence in the performing arts and in the media as an actress and film and television star.

Valarie Pettiford

"No matter what your spiritual beliefs are, use them. Find comfort in the them."

One of my patients mentioned to her uncle, a Hollywood agent, that I was writing a book about African American women. He was quite enthusiastic and said he would like to submit several names for possible inclusion. I was delighted to hear his suggestions and called both women immediately.

Valarie Pettiford agreed to the interview and I flew to Los Angeles to meet her. We met in a restaurant in Studio City and I had my usual nervous stomach, which was, as usual, needless.

Valarie is vivacious and cute! She had her hair piled up on top of her head and was wearing the kind of sundress I only wish I could wear. There is a hint of New York in her speech.

Valarie is easy to get to know and seemed to be completely open right from the beginning of our time together. When she related an anecdote about a teacher giving her a discouraging message that still haunts her, I could relate, and shared a similar incident in my own history. We agreed that while criticism can be helpful in building our character and skills, a woman should pay attention to the spirit in which this criticism is offered. Both of us had had the experience of being criticized in ways that attacked our character and were unfounded. But, these so-called "witch messages" were powerful and destructive.

I came away from my time with Valarie amazed at her obvious talent and creative genius. Her energy and enthusiasm are contagious and I felt energized from our time together, rather than tired from the intensity of the experience.

Valarie Pettiford is the younger of two daughters born to her parents. She first lived in the South Bronx, and the family moved to Queens in New York when she was two. "It was a wonderful life," she says. "I could walk to school, the houses all had backyards and it just seemed safe."

Valarie says that her father was an amazing man who loved life to the fullest. He had great style and had the suits he wore to work as a car sales-man for Oldsmobile tailored at Barney's department store. And, in addition to his "cool cat" good looks, he was a devoted family man with plenty of common sense and wisdom, which he freely dispersed to the local kids who came to him for advice. She fondly notes: "He taught me to be a thankful, grateful person, and to treat everyone with kindness and respect."

Valarie goes on to say that she did not realize how hard her father had worked to give her and her sister everything they needed. The dance lessons, pointe shoes, and costumes that she wanted to pursue her goal of being a bal-lerina were an ongoing expense that he never once complained about.

Valarie's mother was a housewife, which was exactly what she wanted to be. Valarie describes her as gorgeous, with a beautiful singing voice and says she is full of life and love. Her mother also had a great sense of style. There were yearly photos at Easter with the family dressed in what Valarie describes as "classy, fancy outfits, like Jackie Kennedy," which included hats and gloves. Her mother was always in the center, and mother and daughters are shown with carefully posed feet—"Beveled," Valarie says.

Since some of her mother's extended family were world travelers, the Pettiford girls had doll collections, with dolls from all over the world. They were also told the stories of these travels, and there was a great appreciation for music and the arts. The girls were taken into Manhattan to see Broadway shows, and their home was filled with music. Valarie's parents said that when she was born, she "came out dancing." She entered The Bernice Johnson Dance School and Company when she was eleven. By age twelve, she was selected to be in an elite group within the school, teaching, choreographing, and performing for annual recitals at Carnegie Hall and Avery Fisher Hall. During this same period, Valarie and her group were performing all over New York. She says they even performed on the street and on tabletops. She learned how to sew costumes, how to manage the lighting and all aspects of theater productions. In addition, she was acquiring a fine work ethic that has served her well. She emphasizes again that her father was managing to pay for all these experiences, including tuition, costumes, and other supplies. He never made an issue of it.

Valarie is quick to emphasize that her sister, Atonia, is to this day, her idol. "She taught me how to give a great interview, which got me my first agent," Valarie explains. "She took me everywhere with her and didn't seem to mind having her little sister along. She has always believed in me and has given me the best advice in all facets of my life. What would I have done without her?"

She speaks about her charmed family life in her one-woman shows.

Valarie eventually entered Performing Arts High School as a ballet student. But, she switched to modern dance when she experienced the work of a wonderful teacher, Penny Frank. "She was an incredible, beautiful woman," Valerie says now, and clearly a great influence on the young girl determined to be a professional dancer.

When Valarie was sixteen, she auditioned for the movie, *The Wiz*. She was offered a part as one of the principal dancers. She had to leave the Performing Arts High School to accept the part, as the school did not allow students to leave for extended periods. She transferred to the Professional Children's School for the remainder of her school years. She and one other dancer were the youngest cast members of *The Wiz* and it was her film debut.

Valarie says she learned valuable lessons while working on *The Wiz* and with Bernice Johnson, which had nothing to do with dancing, per se. She learned to have respect and consideration for her co-workers and to hang up her clothes. She learned to manage with very little in the way of special treatment. To this day, she says she is not a demanding performer. "Just give me tea, honey and a spoon and I can make it work," she says.

Harking back to her formative years, Valarie recalls that her family had only one television, and she would have to compete with her father when football games aired at the same time as Hollywood musicals. She claims that she always won out and especially loved anything starring Cyd Charisse or Ginger Rogers. Her dad had to buy another television for himself.

Though she noticed that there didn't seem to be any African American dancers on television or in the movies, except for *Stormy Weather* or the occasional featured black dancer, it didn't effect her aspirations. She had not been much aware of prejudice or the "color line" as she grew up, except when visiting her grandmother and extended family in North Carolina. There, she had noticed the white store owners looking at her and her cousins with disdain. She was only nine at the time and wondered what it was all about and why they didn't like her.

Valarie did begin to notice that in the ballet world there were few or no African American dancers. She was relieved when she met Judith Jameson at The Alvin Ailey Dance Company and The Dance Theatre of Harlem, and saw so many beautiful, black dancers all in one place. "I knew then that there was something I could do," she says.

"Crossing the color line in the performing arts is still very difficult," Valarie says. "It is a challenge to audition for roles as an actor knowing I am unlikely to get the part due to being African American. If you watch your favorite mainstream television show, you might see one black woman on it, seldom two. There may be a black man. That's a fact and I just have to suck it up and keep going."

Valarie quotes a mentor of hers in her film career, Susanne DePasse, who advised her, "Don't try to go over the mountain. Go around it."

"I get sick and tired of having to brush it off," she says. "It is discouraging to know that although I have a resume that is enviable and that people would kill for, I'll only ever be considered in an all-black version of *Gypsy* or *Cat on a Hot Tin Roof*. Those kinds of roles just don't go to African Americans."

Indeed, Valarie has a magnificent resume. She has huge versatility in all styles of dance and a gorgeous voice featured on her solo album, *Hear My Soul*. She was nominated for a Tony Award for her featured performance in the musical, *Fosse*. And, in fact, her collaborations with the famed choreographer, Bob Fosse, prior to his death, are among her proudest accomplishments.

Valarie has received numerous awards for her television, film and stage roles. Among them are three NAACP Image Awards for her portrayal of Big Dee Dee Thorne on the TV series, *Half and Half*. Even so, she says, the difficulties she faces as an African American performer persist.

How does she cope with the limitations and challenges? "I focus on how blessed I've been," she says evenly. "I don't get caught up in what I didn't get."

At this point, Valarie recalls a disturbing message that haunts her to this day. "I had a teacher when I was fourteen or fifteen years old," she relates. "She said to me, 'You just think you're all that! But, what you really are is wild and out of control.' It broke my heart and I still sometimes wonder if she was right." Most women face fears of some sort of incompetence it seems.

Remembering her joy at being chosen to sing "All That Jazz" at the Kennedy Center honoring her friend, Chita Rivera, hopefully reminds Valerie that she really is "all that." "I have really been blessed to work with so many incredible people," she says citing a long list of performers and entertainment professionals.

Valarie is now separated from her husband of many years. She says that when her father died, she realized that she did not want to be married anymore. "At the end of the day, I was just not giving my husband what he needed," she says. "We had tried unsuccessfully to have children.

The mental, emotional, physical and financial demands of that effort were traumatic. It was the beginning of the end. My husband handled it all with grace and dignity. He is still my best friend," she says.

Though Valarie's parents were spiritual people, they adhered to no particular religion. As a child visiting her North Carolina relatives, she loved attending the local Baptist Sunday School with her cousins. But recently, as Valarie has been challenged to redefine herself subsequent to the end of her marriage, she has found comfort in The Living Waters Church, leading her to advise women, "No matter what your spiritual beliefs are, use them. Find comfort in them."

In addition, Valarie is adamant about encouraging all women to "find something you love to do and do it to the fullest. Enjoy every minute of it. And, no matter what people say, do it!"

Cheryl Boone Isaacs

*"Just get a job!
You will learn
more that way.
Whatever you are
doing, put your whole
heart into it."*

I asked Jasmine Guy to suggest another woman for the chapter on "The
Creatives." She suggested Cheryl Boone Isaacs. As I waited for Cheryl in
a little restaurant in Los Angeles, I tried to imagine what she might look
like. I had not seen a picture of her and had no idea what to expect. Unlike
other writers who do a lot of research on the people they interview, I try
not to know too much about the person I'm about to meet, so that I can
hear their story directly from them and form my own impressions.

Cheryl strikes me as a dynamo! She is a small woman, impeccably dressed
in a casual outfit. She has a huge, warm smile. Her energy emanates from
her in a way that feels magnetic to me. I can imagine that Cheryl approaches
every project or challenge with enormous enthusiasm and creativity.

As we enjoyed our breakfast together, Cheryl told me the story of her life in the abbreviated form that an interview allows. But, the impression that I took away is that she is bubbling over with enthusiasm for life.

At the end of our time together, she leaned forward across the table, and with a big smile and a little giggle, she said, "Well, how'd I do?" "Fabulous!" I say, and I mean it.

Cheryl Boone Isaacs says that when her mother died in 1980, her father had a big adjustment, because he had not spent a single night of his adult life by himself. Her parents were that close. They had four children, and Cheryl was the baby. Her father worked at the post office and her mom was mostly a homemaker, though she did do some work in a department store.

Cheryl says that she thinks of her growing up years in Springfield, Massachusetts, as rather idyllic. She felt secure, loved, and close to her other family members. There was always music playing and lots of dancing, and her Aunt Viola, who seemed just like the movie character, "Auntie Mame," visited often and added to the overall feeling of delight.

Cheryl emphasizes the fact that all members of the family routinely did chores that were not assigned by traditional sex roles. "If the laundry needed to be done, my dad was as likely to do it as my mother," she says. "Twice a year we took everything out of cupboards, closets, and just everything in the house, and washed it, whether it needed it or not."

"I can remember my mother calling us to the television set in the 50's, to see a "colored" person on *The Ed Sullivan Show*. It was a novelty and a cause for great excitement!"

Cheryl lived in a neighborhood with a mix of people, but mostly African American. "I do not like that term, *African American*," she says. "We are unbelievably unique. We're a blend of many cultures and backgrounds, just like most other Americans. But, there is a cultural connection among us." Neither of us could think of a better term though, so we continued.

"But, our family mostly associated with other African American families. Even so, when a man in our neighborhood married a German woman, no one said anything about it one way or the other. I just don't think there were these more rigid distinctions of race, class, or intellectual abilities. It seemed to me that we were all just there together in a rather mixed neighborhood."

"I went from this rather protected environment to a junior high school where there were hard-core African American kids. It was shocking to me! When bussing occurred, I chose not to participate, which turned out to be a mistake, because I had not realized the differences in the rigor of the mostly white schools compared to the ones in our neighborhood. In elementary and junior high school, I had been a top student. When it came time for high school, there were five high schools to choose from: a Catholic high school, Trade High School, which was a vocational track, Commerce High School, which was a business track, Technical, which was an engineering and science track, and Classical, which was the college preparatory track.

"When I went to meet with my school counselor to decide which high school to attend, I said that my choice was 'Classical'. The counselor, who was a woman, said, 'No'. She said that I should go to Commerce. That was her recommendation. I went home crying. This was my first taste of overt racism."

Cheryl goes on to say that when she went to Classical, it was predominantly white and Jewish. She began to see that she had received an inferior education in her previous schools. And, she worried that she wasn't so smart after all.

Nevertheless, she worked hard academically to catch up and performed with the marching band as a majorette. "I had the boots, the hat with the tassel, the uniform, the whole thing," she says with a laugh. In addition, Cheryl's classmates voted her the girl with the "best smile," "most popular," and "best personality." Believe me, these attributes are still evident as we meet and talk about her life. She is full of smiles, warmth, and personality!

In 1965, Cheryl's older sister moved to California, met a man, and prepared to get married. Cheryl got in the car with her parents, and drove the famous Route 66 to attend her sister's wedding. It was July, and she saw how gorgeous Southern California was with its fresh air, sunshine, and loads of flowers in bloom. She decided to stay, and though her sister wanted her to attend college at UCLA, Cheryl says that it was just too big a school for her and she decided on Whittier College instead, where she was a political science major, with a minor in economics and religion. "I loved my course of study," she says. "My friends don't always like what I have to say now regarding politics, because I'm so far left, I'm almost right!"

Cheryl spent the junior year of college in Copenhagen, Denmark. While she had been one of a few African American students at Whittier College, in Copenhagen there was only one other student who looked like her. "I lived with a Danish family and they thought I was just fascinating," she says. "I was viewed as something different, but not in a racist way, but more just out of curiosity. I loved Copenhagen and cried when I had to come back to the States," she says. "I didn't want to come back to the violence and unrest that was happening here in 1969."

When Cheryl graduated from Whittier, she considered working in foreign affairs, but she realized that she would need a Master's degree to be really successful in that area, and she just didn't want to do it. She wanted to get into the workforce, and so she took a job at Robinson's Department Store in a six-month training program, with the hope of being a buyer. But, what she discovered was that it took years to become a buyer and the pay was not very good. Cheryl says that she knew that she needed to make more money, and because she had a friend who was a flight attendant, she thought to apply to and was hired by Pan American Airlines. As a result of her work for Pan Am, as it was called, Cheryl traveled all over the world: to the Caribbean, the Middle East and Europe, South America, Asia, Australia, and New Zealand. The travel was an amazing education in itself. It was also an experience in some very overt racism! She heard things from white passengers, such as, "I like my coffee like I like my women ... hot and black." And, in first class, "I'll order for my wife. She doesn't talk to the help." Cheryl managed these comments with equanimity.

When Pan Am began cutting bases in 1973, Cheryl decided to leave her job and worked at Cost Plus as a buyer for a few years.

Then she heard about a position with Advocates for Women in San Francisco, helping women to enter and re-enter the work force. She worked with low income black and Latina women through the CETA program. She says it was great to see women being able to enter blue-collar men's jobs, such as climbing telephone poles, etc. It represented true empowerment for these women to have decent jobs that paid a living wage.

"But, I wondered, where am I going?" she says. I decided to come back to Los Angeles and try to get a job in the film business.

Cheryl's brother, Ashley Boone, was a major pioneer in Hollywood. He had numerous positions in the film business. Among them was his copresidency of 20th Century Fox, where he was also President of Marketing and Distribution.

"He was really great," Cheryl says. "He took me to so many events that were spectacular; like to Shea Stadium to see The Beatles, and to see Quincy Jones, Sydney Poitier, and so many others. He had the kind of work I aspired to," she says. "But, it was the age old thing of, 'There's only room for one of us (African Americans).' We talked and argued and he really would not help me, although Ashley Boone's name did give me some entree. It took me three months to get a job and I was getting hysterical because it was taking so long. I was eventually hired by Columbia Pictures to do publicity for the film, *Close Encounters of the Third Kind.*"

Eventually, Cheryl landed a job with Melvin Simon Productions as publicity and advertising coordinator, later becoming Vice President of Publicity and Advertising Worldwide. "My boss, Jonas Rosenfield, was an icon in the field. He was in his late 50's by then, and working as his assistant was like being in graduate school. Having him as my boss was wonderful!"

This led to a job offer from The Ladd Company, a division of Warner Brothers, where Cheryl worked with Alan Ladd, Jr. on such movies as, *The Right Stuff,* as director of advertising and publicity.

Independent companies were starting to fade, so when Cheryl was offered a job at Paramount Pictures, she took a huge pay cut and a demotion to West Coast Division Director, just to have more job security. She was with them from 1984 to 1997, eventually rising to be Executive Vice president of Worldwide Publicity.

In 1997, Cheryl was offered a top position as president of theatrical marketing at New Line Cinema, developing and executing marketing campaigns for such movies as *The Wedding Singer*, *Austin Powers*, *The Spy Who Shagged Me*, and *Rush Hour*. She was the highest-ranking African American in a studio!

In terms of her personal life, in 1981, Cheryl met Stanley Isaacs. He is a writer, a producer, and a director. They married in 1982. "After thirteen years, Stanley and I wanted to start a family. When you embark on that road, it is a huge commitment," she says. "We adopted Cooper in 1995. He is a child of mixed parentage, and reflects our own ethnicities."

"When Cooper was four, I realized that I was working so hard that I was hardly ever home to put him to bed. Stanley was working hard, too, and so I decided to stay home for two years and just be with Cooper. It was a good decision."

Nowadays, Cheryl has her own consulting firm, CBI Enterprises. Her office is near her home. She has been a respected film-marketing executive for over twenty-five years. She was the first African American woman to run a studio-marketing department, overseeing creative advertising, publicity, media buying, co-op advertising, product placement and market research. She was also the first African American woman elected to the Board of Governors of The Academy of Motion Pictures Arts and Sciences, and the first African American woman named to the Board of The Motion Picture and Television Fund. In 1997 and 1998, Cheryl was profiled in the Hollywood Reporter's Special Issue "Women in Entertainment, The Power 50." As a Governor at The Academy of Motion Picture Arts and Sciences, she is only the third African American to hold this position. She explains that the public relations branch elected her. It is an office that one is nominated for and then an election is held. It is her sixteenth year in this position, and she is proud to say that she has never campaigned, but people just voted for her anyway. She has served in other capacities on the board, including vice-president and treasurer, and more recently as secretary.

"There are fourteen branches of The Academy," she says. "I have been a governor for eighteen years. First, I had been Chairman of the Public Relations Coordinating Committee, doing marketing and publicity for *The Oscars*. Then, I was Chairman of the Governor's Ball. Now I am President of The Academy Foundation, which is the cultural and educational arm of The Academy. We give out Student Academy Awards, screenwriting fellowships, and do cultural and educational events."

In addition to her entertainment career, Cheryl has been adjunct professor at the prestigious University of Southern California School of Cinema and Television, teaching classes in Motion Picture Marketing.

"I think the hardest thing for young people is figuring out what they want to do with their life," Cheryl says. "My advice is to think about how you want to spend your day - indoors, outdoors, with people, alone. What kind of people do you want around you and what kind of support?"

"But, most importantly," she says, "Just get a job. You learn more that way. Whatever you are doing, put your whole heart and soul into it. And, don't be in a hurry. Be sure to save time for friends and family!"

Lola Love

"My prejudice is ignorance. Get all the education you can, and I'm not just talking about school!"

I t turns out that Lola Love lives in an area of Los Angeles where I used to teach school. I enjoyed driving in my old neighborhood, where I had lived and worked as a newlywed, some thirty-nine years earlier. I love being in areas where there are mature trees and landscapes, and there is a feeling of a sense of community that has been present there for a long time.

Lola greeted me at her front door and we visited in her comfortable living room. She, as with so many of the women I included in this chapter, positively exudes energy, and a sense of adventure and fun. Her enthusiasm and *joie d'vivre* was evident in the relaxed, but stylish way she was dressed, as well as her exuberant manner.

Lola invited me to Victoria Rowell's High Tea at the Beverly Hills Hotel. She has been intimately involved in this philanthropic effort for some time. She made sure that I knew to wear a hat. "You'd feel naked without one," she said.

When my daughter-in-law and I arrived at that elegant event, there was Lola to greet us and direct us to our lovely table. She was wearing a gorgeous apricot colored hat with flowers, and an equally gorgeous dress. She had made sure that we had wonderful table companions, and was there again to take my money when I bought a hat at the hat auction.

The best way that I can describe Lola is that she has "personality plus!" She laughs easily and it's clear that she can be silly or serious. In a book she showed me about the life of James Brown, with whom she traveled as a dancer and back-up singer, he refers to her as "something else." Yes, indeed.

Lola Love is the second of six girls born to her parents, Mattie and Charlie Holman, in The Bronx River Projects, a public housing project in New York City. Her father was a quiet man who worked hard and brought his entire paycheck home to his family. He worked to support his family as a gas station attendant, and finally as a custodial engineer at Albert Einstein Hospital until his retirement. He was a World War II veteran, who returned home after the war a fearful and obedient man who had witnessed racial injustice within the armed service. He had been raised in the south in the early 1900's and appeared to be quite content with his lot in life living in the projects.

Lola's mother, on the other hand, was a vital force in the lives of her daughters. She never saw the projects as a way of life, but as a way station to home ownership. To this end, she worked hard as a beautician and nurse's aid. She was energetic and resourceful, straightening all the girl's hair at the same time and drying it with the vacuum cleaner! (This was before blow dryers.)She was a stickler for learning, encouraging all her daughters to strive for a good education. She would tell her girls it wasn't enough to be good, being a girl you had to be the best! In addition, Lola's mother taught her girls that if any man ever hit you, they would also kill you! Lola laughs as she recalls her father hitting her once as a young adult. Lola's father never disciplined the girls. The task of punishing or reprimanding the children was her mother's, because they were girls. She wouldn't allow a man to put a hand on them, not even their father. So when her father struck her in the face, she tried to kill him. She stabbed him with the scissors she had in her hand! Her father never ever hit her again. Lola's mother was very protective of her girls, never allowing them to sleep over at their friend's homes. When Lola asked her mother why the Holman girls weren't allowed to spend the night at their friend's homes, her mother calmly said, "Because some people walk in their sleep." Mattie's daughters were never molested.

Lola remembers that her parents fought a lot and she decided early on that marriage and children would have to wait a long time in her case. She wanted to "go places," and because she could sing and dance from a very young age, she set her sights on a performance career. Even though someone commented to her that, "with that behind, you'll never make it in dance," she paid no attention.

The girls in Lola's family were all quite talented and it was Sophronia, Lola's oldest sister who discovered the High School of Performing Arts and wanted to attend the famous high school in New York City. Obviously, it was not easy to be admitted to such a prestigious school. A review of past academic records and an audition were required for application. However, Sophronia gained entrance, and then helped Lola prepare for her audition by writing an amazing monologue for her, which would assure her admittance two years later. Sophronia was very gifted as an actress, but resented that Lola was following her to the High School of Performing Arts, and made it very clear to her mother that she did not want Lola to embarrass her in any way. This competition, and/or resentment between the sisters was difficult. Lola was multi-talented and received the bigger parts in productions, increasing the competitive feelings. Then her sister became pregnant just as they had both been tapped for parts in their first movie, *Up the Down Staircase*. Lola was seen in this, her movie debut, but her sister had to drop out of the production due to her pregnancy.

Lola's mother never talked negatively about anyone's child living in the projects, because she said, "I have daughters, and any one of them can go off and do something that would cause much stimulated conversation, like being pregnant before you're married."

Patricia, Lola's next younger sister, was gifted and a brilliant cellist. She, too, had become pregnant and had a baby in junior high school. Even so, their mother lobbied hard to help her gain entrance to the High School of Performing Arts and succeeded in getting her admitted. But, before long, she had become pregnant again, making it impossible for her to attend. It was sad and Lola affirmed to herself again that for her, children and marriage would have to wait a very long time, if ever.

Lola was the first in her family to graduate from high school and then college without being married or having children. She actually became an inspiration for her other two younger sisters, Carol and Monique, who eventually would graduate from high school child free.

While still in high school, Lola was part of The Urban Arts Corps, which was a professional acting company under the direction of the famous Vinnette Carroll. Lola performed with such artists as Hope Clark, Debbie

Allen, Trina Parks, Michael Peters, Talley Beatty, Otis Sallid and a host of other talented performers. She was rehearsing late into the night and sometimes getting home just in time to get to classes at school. Her mother allowed this because she could see Lola's talent and believed that this training could lead to other opportunities.

Lola's mother insisted that she go to college. The only school she applied to, Hofstra University in Hempstead, New York on Long Island, accepted her and awarded her a full four-year academic scholarship. In 1969 Hofsta University was a small, private school with a student body largely made up of Jewish and Italian American students. Lola entered as a physical education major, switched to a history major, then a theater major, but eventually ended up in the speech therapy department. She began her experience at Hofstra in a summer program called NOAH, which stood for "Negro Opportunities at Hofstra". The name was eventually changed to "New Opportunities at Hofstra," and it was meant to acclimate underprivileged students from all nationalities to college life.

Dating or having any kind of social life at Hofstra was very difficult because of the make-up of the student body. There were few blacks there and students did not socialize much across the color line.

During her years at Hofstra, Lola was still very focused on performance. One of her friends said, "You didn't come here to learn. You came to get out!" Actually, she was there to do both. But, performing was number one. She graduated in 1973 and got a job as a vocational education counselor in The Bronx River Projects. She had met a number of gang members from a gang called the Black Spades there. They were known for terrorizing the neighborhood. In her counseling role, she was contacted by August

Darnell, of *Kid Creole and the Coconuts* fame. He was making a film called *Good Morning Mr. Sunshine.* August wanted Lola to be his co-star in the film and she agreed. They both attended Hofstra University and had done many film projects together. But when he found out that she was working with the notorious Black Spades, he asked if she could get them to come over and be in a court scene in the production. Since Lola's job was to get students who were not in school back into school and into job training, she was able to get some of the Black Spades to participate in the making of the film as part of her job performance. Meanwhile, Lola's manager, Tony Major, introduced her to the famous, Mama Lou Parks, who was looking for a dancer to join singer, James Brown, on tour. She auditioned for Mama Lou Parks and was asked how well she could take direction. She said she could and would, and was hired.

Lola was on the road with James Brown, the "Godfather of Soul," for ten years as a singer and dancer. She appeared on *Soul Train, In Concert, Midnight Special*, and numerous other music variety shows. "Mr. Brown was an interesting man," she says now. "When I met him, he said to me, 'I wanna make you my woman. I'll put you in a hotel room and I'll keep the key. No one goes in or out but me, except maybe your mama.' I said, 'Make me a star and you have a deal.' Mr. Brown looked at me in disbelief and laughed and said, 'You're something else!'" No female had ever challenged him and he left her entirely alone. From then on, he called her his "little sis." She goes on to say, "He came to visit my mother when she was sick with cancer, and he gave her a bundle of cash. He made my mom very happy in her painful days with breast cancer. Mr. Brown could be kind that way, but, unfortunately, he didn't take care of his band with that kind of compassion."

Lola was part of the James Brown entourage when the famous "Rumble in the Jungle" took place in Zaire in 1974. Muhammad Ali was to fight George Foreman. They traveled with The Pointer Sisters, Lloyd Price, Don King, Etta James, among many others, on a private jet. It was quite an adventure for Lola, who was just out of college! The women in the group were not supposed to leave the premises of their hotel, but Lola couldn't resist going everywhere she could with the South African trumpeter, Hugh Masekela. Everyone said she would get fired, but she didn't. Her dance partner was annoyed with her because she wouldn't sleep with James Brown. He tried to get her fired, and replaced with another dancer who would probably accept Mr. Brown's advances, but she prevailed and didn't get fired. Mr. Brown said, "Miss Love is my best dancer ever!"

"I had no interest in having a relationship with anyone on the road, especially James Brown," Lola says now. "But, overall, the experience was great! I was on tour in Japan, all over Europe, and Africa. I saw a good part of the world and experienced new cultures that were fascinating. This was truly an education that was priceless.

Mr. Brown never stayed in the same hotel as the band, choosing better places for himself. It was particularly hard traveling in the South because of the racism. When I once tried to eat at a restaurant that was not part of a chain, like Denny's or something, I was sold rotten meat. That's just how it was, and I'm talking about in the 1980's."

In 1977, Lola had a baby fathered by a talented jazz drummer, who played with Nina Simone and many jazz greats. He didn't want to get married and he had no money to support a family. She had been somewhat influenced to have this baby by her mother's pleas, "Have one, Lola. Just one. You'll really appreciate having a child later on." Her mother died one month after her son, Kenn, was born. Lola says, "Kenny was the best thing that ever happened to me. I am so grateful that I had the wisdom to listen to my mother and had a child." Kenn was a baby with lots of health challenges. His allergies were so severe that they would abscess if he scratched them, and his asthma and eczema took them both to the hospital many times. His health issues affected his growth rate and he was very small for his age.

When Kenn was two and a half, Lola met the man she would later marry. He owned a popular recording studio in New York City and he seemed crazy about her. If she named a wine she liked, he had a case shipped to her address. When he asked her what she especially liked to eat, she said "lobster." He had a feast of lobster sent over immediately. He wanted her to move in with him, but Lola told him he would have to marry her if he wanted them to live together. They were married at the United Nations chapel in the summer of 1980. Lola says that her husband was the first person to make her feel beautiful and special. "He provided me with any and everything I wanted and put me on a pedestal," she says. "I thought I was his very best friend. I had seen how stuck my mother was in what appeared to me to be an unhappy marriage with six children. I really didn't want that, so when I made a choice to marry my husband, I thought I had made a decision that would be good for all of us."

Lola was married for twenty-seven years. But, over time, they moved in different directions. "It was a non-traditional marriage in every way", she says. "I realized that he didn't really want a wife; he wanted an arm piece and a ready-made family. He turned out to be a bully. My son's father was a musician and my husband was well off financially. He tried to force me to take Kenn's father to court for child support, but it was not my ambition, intention or desire to get involved in the American judicial system for child support. Instead, I went to work for New York City's Board of Education as a Speech Therapist for nine years. So, my paycheck provided more than some state mandated child support check. My husband turned out to be a screamer, and he was very controlling. Be careful of those bearing gifts!"

Lola's son, Kenn, began modeling and making commercials by the time he was eight years old. He was a gifted child and was reading by the time he was two and a half years old, playing piano by ear, as well as playing the drums. She made sure that Kenn was in programs that stimulated him, and did not repress his extraordinary and inquisitive mind.

Lola had returned to school at Hunter College to get her Master's degree in communications sciences. She was working all day as the Speech and Language Coordinator for District I in the New York City Schools, and going to school in the evenings. Kenn was left in the care of his stepfather. "I came home from school one night, to find Kenn sitting in his room in the dark as a punishment for something or other. When I asked him why he was sitting in the dark, he said he didn't know. Then I asked my husband why was Kenn sitting in the dark, and he would say, 'ask Kenn.' This kind of drama was not good for any of us. My days were long and often I didn't get home until late at night. I became annoyed and concerned with my husband and his style of discipline.

Eventually, my husband pleaded with me to quit my job and be his business partner. My son, Kenn, had also expressed that he missed me, because he did not see me much due to my long hours away from home. I agreed for everyone's benefit.

Lola became Vice President and co-owner of their music production company, which was one of the largest all digital multimedia production facilities between New York and Boston, with offices on both coasts. Unfortunately, there was internal discord in the business and Lola spent a good deal of time smoothing over issues with employees. Lola says she was literally "the clean-up woman." In spite of that, she was also able to explore her talents as a music producer and songwriter. She and her husband co-produced the #1 hit, "Over Like a Fat Rat," for Fonda Rae (currently sampled on the triple platinum CD by SWV). She became an artist on Island Records with *Wax the Van* (one of the top ten records of the year according to *The Face* magazine). Her voice and music continue to live on in sample form, most notably on Bango by The Todd Terry Project and music by the dance group DeeLite. Her publishing companies Lola-La and LoLo Music hold publishing rights for, among others, "The Theme From *The Super*" and *The Montel Williams Show*, as well as over 200 titles on The Muzak Network. Lola's commercial credits include the Pringles jingle ("Once You Pop") as well as music for numerous television shows.

In her personal life, Lola had begun spending a lot of time in Los Angeles with Kenn, who was beginning his own entertainment career. Her husband began to be irritated with everything she did. Eventually, when she went home to Connecticut, her housekeeper confided to her that there had been another woman living in her house in her absence. Lola never confronted her husband; however, he suspected that she knew and began harassing and threatening her. He said that if she left him, she would get

$200 a week and nothing more. "That's all you're worth," he said. "I was devastated and said that I guessed I needed to get my act together and get out of this hell," Lola says. "I can be hard and tough, but I don't ever want to deliberately hurt anyone. So I negotiated the housekeeper's exit and quickly made my exit too."

Lola reached out to friends who advised her and helped her to obtain a divorce. She moved to Los Angeles permanently and began working as an entertainment consultant. Lola had been a talent manager for many years; she was the CEO of LHB Management, representing a select group of very talented children and young adults in television and film. Now, Lola is an in-demand motivational speaker, lecturer, teacher, and consultant. She helps parents understand the workings of the entertainment industry as it pertains to their children's careers. She, also, conducts workshops that help young people build self-esteem and self-confidence.

Lola says that, in general, one of the most difficult obstacles for her has been the distrustfulness, resentment and jealousy of other women. "I have noticed over the years, that women are much harder on each other. Women are more critical, suspicious, and accusatory of each other, than men are. We should be helping and supporting each other." She goes on to say, "I think one reason for this may be that so many young girls don't have self-respect. Respecting yourself and truly loving who you are, is the foundation of self-discovery. Another important ingredient is maintaining a healthy lifestyle early in life. Exercising and eating healthily when you are young will aide you when you are older. There is no excuse today, saying that you did not know what was good for you or bad for you when you were younger, because the World Wide Web is available to all. Do the research now! Eat to live, not live to eat." Stressing the importance of being independent, she says, "You must know yourself and love yourself before you can be in any kind of relationship. Do not define yourself by the man or partner that you are with."

Lola has experienced prejudice as an African American woman on many levels. "I'm the darkest one in my family. I say this because I was told this over and over again as a young child. As a child, I remember being told to stay out of the sun and many times I couldn't go out until the afternoon when there was shade over eighty percent of the area I would play in. When in college, I had a Jamaican boyfriend who I really thought I was in love with. However, he clearly told me that we could never be married because I was too dark and his family would never approve of the marriage. It was hurtful of course, and it took a long time for me to develop a healthy self-image. I also have observed that white people appear to be more comfortable with lighter skinned blacks than darker ones. I clearly remember being told when I was younger to smile more so I wouldn't look so menacing to white people. Black folks on the other hand would say things like, she's too black, too dark, ugly, etc., and I have been an eyewitness to prejudice by both whites and blacks.

"My own prejudice is ignorance," Lola says. " I would advise girls and women to get all the education they can, and I don't just mean school. There are many ways to continue learning."

If my mother were alive today, she would be very proud of all of her daughters. We embraced her love and passion for knowledge, by doing what she instilled in us, getting an education. All five of us attended schools of higher education. We have Bachelors of Arts and Master's degrees. We are successful in our chosen careers and have raised our children. Some of us are now enjoying our grandchildren. My youngest sister, Lynda, who has Downs Syndrome, is the star of the whole clan. She received "The Best Actress Award" at her annual themed birthday party.

Lola goes on to say that she is very opinionated and proud of that fact. She worries about the competitiveness among girls in the area of clothing and would like to see all schools, public and private, require uniforms. "Then it is no longer about the clothes you have on, or what the latest styles are, but about YOU." Having been a performer and managing others, Lola says she knows that when you choose what you wear; you choose how people will react to you. "Clothes are like costumes," she says. " You begin to act the part. Your clothing actually dictates to others what your role is. For example, when you see a person in a police uniform, you know what their role is. The same is true for fireman, nurse, doctor, etc. So if you dress like you are a streetwalker, etc., you will be treated as such." This statement may appear, on the surface, to contradict her previous one. But, Lola is emphasizing that girls and women often forget their own value and instead place more value on how they look, to attract the attention they think they want or need. She wants girls to know who they are and value that, rather than placing the most emphasis on their clothes or other superficial trappings.

Lola attends and is a member of The Agape Spiritual Center, led by Rev. Michael Beckwith in Culver City, CA. She is not fond of tradition and says, "The word *religion*, used in a non-spiritual way, makes my hair stand on end! Tradition, to me, means keeping the *status quo*, not being open to new ideas, change or growth. The word *religion* does not mean spiritual understanding to me. Instead, the word, time and time again demonstrates exclusion and condemnation." But, Lola finds solace and support in her spiritual center, and says that she has learned the concept of "no blame." By this she means that she has learned to blame no one for her life circumstances. She takes personal responsibility for her choices and her life. And, above all, she is determined to live in the present, to be positive, and shine brightly as she moves forward in the Light!

CHAPTER 7

The Academics

Do not call for black power or green power.
Call for brainpower.

— Barbara Jordan

An Academic is a woman who has "used the brains God gave her," as her grandmother might have said. She has distinguished herself through excelling in school and intellectual pursuits of all kinds. She is committed to life-long learning in its many forms. Every woman I interviewed for this book has embraced life-long learning of one sort or another. While they have a variety of interests and achievements, what they have in common are very curious minds and the stamina to persevere in their pursuit of educational opportunities.

It is important to emphasize that often, African American women have paid a high price to achieve academically. It is really not so long ago that school segregation was the law of the land, and "separate but equal" meant inherently unequal. Many of the women I interviewed grew up in the segregated South and had to set high goals for themselves at a very young age in order to receive a higher education.

If an intellectually gifted woman attended an inner city school, as many of the women I interviewed did, she may have received an inferior education and there might have been the mistaken notion that being smart and achieving academically equaled "trying to be white." This may have caused her to have to operate outside the social structure of her peer group and be the subject of ridicule or, at the least, loneliness. She certainly had to be able to delay gratification in order to accomplish her dreams. Additionally, many of the academically talented women I interviewed wondered if their achievement made them intimidating to men, and therefore, unattractive to potential mates.

African American women who are Academics often face the double discrimination of being female as well as a racial minority. If they are recognized for their accomplishments through job promotions or gaining entrance to college or graduate programs, there are always those who wonder if they received these honors and opportunities through affirmative action. In other words, maybe she isn't really "that smart."

Nevertheless, these Academics persevered in their own unique ways. Their stories are dramatic and they have ended up in positions of great responsibility and power.

Col. Yvonne Cagle, M.D.

"Aspire to Inspire."

I had waved to Yvonne Cagle from curbside in my hometown of Novato, CA, when she rode by in a fancy convertible in the annual Fourth of July parade. Her smile was radiant as she greeted the crowd on both sides of the street.

And then, some years later, I applauded her inspirational speech at my son, Simon's, high school graduation. She had graduated from the same high school years before, and had returned as the guest of honor and main speaker for the ceremony. She was dressed in her NASA astronaut's uniform and she was impressive!

When I called Yvonne for an interview, she was friendly and willing. I met her in the parking lot of a Safeway grocery store, south of San Francisco and we walked to an area outdoors where we could talk.

Yvonne said later that she took one look at me and wished she hadn't agreed to the interview. She thought I wouldn't understand her experience. But, as we spent the next two and a half hours talking, it turned out that we had more in common than either of us could have imagined. Over the months that followed, we had many reasons to get together for talks and mutual support. We discovered that we both loved listening to James Cleveland lead his choir in singing gospel music.

Yvonne was one of the first people to review the outline for this book and offer her suggestions and support. She has been an inspiration.

Yvonne Cagle came to California from the East Coast with her parents and five siblings in a burgundy Chrysler Imperial. Five of the children were stuffed into a back seat without seatbelts. The children took turns sitting by the windows. Yvonne would roll the window down when it was her turn, to let the wind blow in her face. She comes from a military family that was orderly and disciplined. The family operated as a team with duties delegated down the line of children and everyone knowing their responsibilities. Punishments for infractions were swift and for Yvonne, the threat of, "You're grounded," was the most difficult because she loved to be outdoors. Hamilton Air Force Base became home for the Cagle's, where her father was an X-ray technician and her mother maintained the Air Force Base flight records. By the time Yvonne was twelve, she was watching the airplanes take off from the base and dreaming of going higher and farther than any of them.

In addition to her love of the outdoors, Yvonne was an excellent student. Her parents valued education and remained in California after her father retired so that their children had the opportunity to attend good schools. Yvonne used her spare time in high school to volunteer in various health care oriented programs, because she knew from a young age that she wanted to be a doctor. She volunteered at numerous places including their local hospital and the Red Cross, to learn what she could about the world of medicine. As a true academic, Yvonne used high school as a testing ground, taking every opportunity to develop her intellectual acumen. She was in student government and president of the California Scholarship Federation, but being out in the community was what she loved most.

After high school, Yvonne attended California State University at San-Francisco. She could not afford to live on campus. She didn't own a car and could not afford to ride the express bus to San Francisco on a daily basis. So, she spent three hours riding the commute bus from her home to the campus, every day; then, school all day and the three-hour commute home. At the end of the day, she was dehydrated, hungry and exhausted. She left in the dark in the morning and returned home in the dark. She was fearful walking to and from the bus stop in the dark and learned creative maneuvers to keep herself safe. She found ways to study on the bus. Yvonne says that taking that bus every day and being at San Francisco State was culturally broadening: "The world came to my doorstep. I began to realize that I wanted to take my doorstep to the world in service. I couldn't wait."

Yvonne's father earned extra money to support his family by working at the county coroner's office as deputy coroner, assisting with autopsies. By her freshman year in college, she had been granted an internship at the coroner's office assisting with autopsies. She admits that this was an unusual weekend activity for a teenager, but says she loved pouring over the coroner's medical books, and that she was intensely interested in the workings of the human body.

But, Yvonne was growing exhausted from her grueling schedule and long commutes. She was becoming increasingly discouraged. It was just so hard. About three months into her school year, she began to notice a pre-teen girl boarding the bus, wearing a parochial school uniform. Yvonne wondered why a young girl was getting on the bus so early in the morning and in the dark. Was the girl as fearful and wary of it all as Yvonne was? It didn't seem so. Yvonne says that this girl was perfectly poised. She noticed how well groomed and "together" she seemed. "She didn't have an 'attitude,' but sat quietly and patiently." Yvonne was very impressed with and inspired by the girl's composure. After awhile, Yvonne began to depend on observing this girl's poise and attitude. Day after day, they rode the bus together, never speaking, but making eye contact on a daily basis. "Psychologically, I needed her to get on the bus. It was just part of my morning routine and ritual," she explains.

One day, the girl didn't get on the bus. When one day became several, Yvonne became concerned and wondered if she was sick. She stumbled onto a newspaper article about a tragedy. She was shaken to her core to realize that the tragedy reported in the paper was about the murder of the young girl from the bus, robbed of life by senseless violence. Only then did she recognize that this was the very same young girl whose autopsy she had just witnessed as part of her internship.

Yvonne, speaking of her anguish to no one, attended the young girl's funeral seeking silent closure. But, to this day, reconciliation eludes her. "The hardest part," she says with emotion filling her voice, "was doing that commute without that young girl. I would start each day of classes with rage and unimaginable grief. But that rage gave me a drumbeat of energy to push forward. I was determined to be that chance in life that she was so woefully denied."

Yvonne says that she is really a "right-brained person." She loves art and literature. "I just can't learn in a left-brained way; and here I am, a biochemistry major. It's one of the hardest majors there is and I had to translate everything from my artistic, adventurous right brain to left-brain functioning. Sometimes it would take several pages of work to get to the solution of a biochemistry problem. Though having this major helped me, the study of science illuminated by art, I opened my cherished companion, *The World Atlas*, to discover dimensions and prisms of thought and understanding heretofore unimagined."

Having persevered, when it came to medical school, she had to choose between Harvard University and The University of Washington, Seattle. She chose the latter because she wanted the opportunity to practice medicine in remote areas, which The University of Washington provided. She loved medical school and had the opportunity to provide services in underserved areas of Alaska and Idaho. She flew into remote Alaskan islands to deliver babies and worked on Indian reservations.

Prior to medical school, Yvonne joined the Air Force, in part to honor her father and partly because she had really enjoyed military life as a child. She knew that the Air Force would help her go to medical school in exchange for the honor of serving her country after her graduation. Three years into her Air Force career, she decided on a flight rotation. Her dreams were coming true inasmuch as she was practicing medicine and flying in jets – fighter jets at that. She loved being a flight surgeon. Yvonne got to the point of being able to identify aircraft by their sound alone. At the end of her four-year obligation, she signed on for a career as an Air Force flight surgeon.

Yvonne was unsure about how she, as a young, black female flight surgeon might be received. But, she believes that many of the men confided things to her that they might not have revealed to another man.

I asked Yvonne how she had decided to become an astronaut. She said that two things led her to it. While on Air Force rotation in England, she was watching the news when the first black, female astronaut M.D., Mae Jemison's picture came on. "I thought to myself, 'that could be me,'" she says. Yvonne learned that she had many of the same qualifications as Dr. Jemison. "Mae demonstrated to me that my insatiable thirst for understanding humans in high altitude, hyper-dynamic flight was still unquenched," Yvonne says. She knew now that she wanted to ride the space shuttle. To her delight, Yvonne's application to NASA for astronaut training was accepted.

Nowadays, Yvonne continues her research on what happens to the human body in space. She investigates the effects of macro to micro gravity on the body. She says that her professional obsession is how to minimize suffering and maximize quality of life for all people. She hopes to ride the shuttle on a future science mission.

Yvonne has much to say on the subject of what will help African American women achieve their rightful places in society as a whole. She emphasizes the need for more nurturing and bonding amongst them. She says she is discouraged by the fact that often women (not just black women) are vicious in their attacks on one another. She believes this comes from self-hate and sagging self-esteem. Yvonne says she has met many high achieving black women who are tempted to leave their chosen fields because they experience being a target for attack by other women. "Let's don't shove each other off of the ladder. Share the limelight and pull each other along. We must get more representation on selection committees," she says. "If we don't have qualified diversity at the highest levels, then we, as a society will be deprived of achieving our full potential." She has focused on qualifications, confidence and competence for her own career development. In fact she says, "Aspire to inspire."

Yvonne is a deeply spiritual woman affirming, "I give it up to the Lord every day. You are never as great, strong, or accomplished as you think you are. There is a Higher Power, however you may want to describe it, and that Power holds our destiny in its hand. So, give it up to that Power. We'll never be smart enough to figure life out on our own."

"I am fascinated with physiology and I love that there is a Creator who choreographed our body in such a way that our heart beats in synchrony with every breath we take every second of every day. We are a miracle and a mission in discovery."

Finally, Yvonne has enormous humility. "Every time I have an accomplishment, I remember what Ida B. Wells was able to do, the risks she took. Look at what she accomplished." She reminds me that in the mid-1800s, Ida B. Wells was not only noted for her anti-lynching crusade, but also as an early proponent of women's rights. She says that for every woman represented in this book, there are so many other untold stories "of majesty and value." "Ask the black cleaning woman about her story," she suggests. "Open the dialogue and see what you might learn."

Loretta Devine

*"You can never
give up on yourself!
Sometimes we get tired
and we want to give up.
But, remember,
the magic can happen
at any moment."*

Hollywood agent, David Galligan gave me my introduction to the amazingly talented, Loretta Devine. "She would be a great addition to your book," he said. He was right!

Although I didn't recognize her name at first, as soon as I looked at her vast resume, I realized how many times I had seen her perform on television and in the movies. "She's a triple threat!" David had said, referring to her ability to sing, dance, and act, an unusual combination of talent.

What David didn't tell me about Loretta was that she is an accomplished Academic, with a Master's degree from Brandeis University, and an Honorary Doctorate from her alma mater, The University of Houston. She taught at Brown University while beginning her dramatic career. So, the world of higher learning is quite familiar to her.

The other thing that struck me about Loretta is the obvious joy she feels about life itself. If you call Loretta's cell phone, as I have done periodically, you are greeted with Loretta's infectious positive attitude as she invites you to leave a message and says, "I'm in the world!"

Loretta Devine was very young when her parents separated. Her father was a crane operator in Houston, Texas, where Loretta was raised. She can remember going to his house when she was so small that she could stand under the dining room table. "He was a tall, dark, drink of water," she says. Her mother says that he came to pick Loretta up a lot.

At that time, she and her four sisters and one brother lived with her mother, who owned a beauty shop. After school, Loretta went to the beauty shop to baby-sit her younger brother and sister. She did whatever chores her mother might have for her to do, like sweeping and cleaning. Loretta's mother had learned how to operate a small business from her own mother, "Big Mama," as she was called. Big Mama had her own corner store in Texas. Loretta says that Big Mama was the head of everything in the family. Big Mama and Loretta's mother managed the home and all the children, and even managed to buy property, as well. Since there was no adult male in the family, the girls learned to be independent. Loretta was doing book-keeping for her grandma's store when she was still in grade school. She kept track of how many of this or that product was on hand, how much each item cost, and what needed to be ordered.

Loretta attended George Washington Carver High School, which was segregated but had a few white teachers by the time she graduated.

She had a small group of girlfriends and was definitely not in the popular crowd. She was a shy teenager, but her drama teacher saw talent in her and began entering her in a number of extra-curricular activities, such as dramatic interpretation contests with other high schools, spelling bees, and debate teams at several different universities. She often won these contests.

At the same time, another of her talents was much sought after at The Star Bethel Missionary Baptist Church choir, where she was known for singing the obbligato part of music, the highest notes that no one else could reach. The choir director would point to her and she would sing to the heavens as high as she could. Who could have predicted that these high notes would bring her money on Broadway and help get her hired for the Broadway shows? Loretta could belt out music above High C, and that was a talent!

Loretta was in the high school marching band, trying to learn to play the trombone that had been given to her mother by one of the beauty shop customers.

By the time the end of her senior year arrived, three different boys had invited this shy girl to three different proms from different schools. Her mother chaperoned all of them by driving Loretta and her various dates to and from the proms.

Loretta recalls one of the last episodes of her high school drama endeavors in Dramatic Interpretation. The event took place at Texas Southern University and her name was not included on the list of finalists for the senior drama competition. Loretta believed that she was the best one there. She had heard all the other contestants and she just knew no one was better! She refused to go home a loser, so she took the list of finalists home and secretly re-typed it with her name included somewhere in the middle. The next day she re-posted the list and waited to see what would happen. She was so afraid that they would stop her and tell her she was not supposed to be on the list, but no one did. She got what she wanted, a chance to compete! That night she won the entire competition and she learned a valuable lesson: NEVER GIVE UP!

Loretta remembers overhearing her high school drama teacher, Johnnie Hudspeth, asking another teacher, "What do you do with a student with a lot of talent, but she's ugly?" That stuck with Loretta and when they went to the next university to compete, they put lots of light make-up and a big wig on her. Loretta lost her confidence and she did not win. Ms. Hudspeth was one of Loretta's favorite teachers. She believed in her talent. Loretta says that because Ms. Hudspeth believed in her talent, she believed in herself. "But, I've never felt beautiful," she says. "Talent has gotten me everything. I still don't consider myself beautiful, though many people have told me that I am, so maybe its true. But, for me, talent is far more important than beauty. I can paint on beauty, but when I act or sing, that is all mine. Its what I have worked on all my life." Over the years, Loretta has learned to do her own hair and make-up, so she says that the illusion of beauty is always at hand.

Loretta says that wonderful women have helped her all along the way. These women, to whom she refers as angels, have been positioned in different places throughout her life. She laughs when she says that these angels have come in all races and sizes.

One of these angels was Loretta's boss while she worked her way through The University of Houston at the Medical Center. This white angel, Helen Patterson, helped Loretta stop struggling because she believed in her. She introduced her to an angel in a wheelchair, Tina Allen, who worked in The University of Houston's finance department and helped Loretta with scholarships and loans. As a result, Loretta was able to move into the campus dormitories and she says that her life was changed for the good forever.

Loretta joined Alpha Kappa Alpha sorority while at the university and loved the camaraderie of other women, like Debra Frye and Candy Harris, who have remained life long friends. She kept up her singing, dancing, and acting and actually broke her leg trying out for the cheerleading squad. Her enthusiasm was obvious to all!

Barbara Marshall was the black angel who taught Loretta many things about theatre and life, in general. Loretta is quick to credit many other supporters throughout her life. She mentions her Sunday School teacher, her sisters, her Aunt Bea and Uncle Ervin, her mother and grandmother, her pastor, father, professors, and even her students, who she considers angels in her life; loving her and having faith in her. She says that all this love and faith meant, "I just had to amount to something. I had to bring pride to those who helped me by believing in me."

After college, Loretta taught at Hester House, which was an alternative school program for youth who were not in regular school. She later became one of the founders of The Black Arts Center, where she taught, directed, acted and created theatre. She acted in many of Houston's community theatres.

After years of hard work, Loretta decided that she needed to do more and be more. She decided to continue her training in graduate school and she applied to Brandeis University in Waltham, Massachusetts for their Master's program. She had a rather amazing start in this program! Due to a series of late and cancelled flights, Loretta ended up having her audition for her application to this prestigious University in the Atlanta airport. The piece she auditioned with was Sonia Sanchez's, Sister Sonji. On her knees in the terminal, she begged the head of the theatre department, Charles Moore, who was to audition her, not to leave her without hearing her piece.

"People thought this young Black girl on the floor was sincere. Professor Moore turned beet red; he was so embarrassed. But it worked! She got into Brandeis and he told the story of that experience over and over. "I couldn't be stopped!" she says now.

Though she completed her Master's of Fine Arts at Brandeis, Loretta says they didn't quite know what to do with her there. They were doing plays like *Hedda Gabler*, and diversity was not "in" in Boston, so there wasn't much call for a Loretta Devine. She played maids and witches, and by her final year they had figured out how to utilize her talent, but she was ready to move on. She went straight to New York and auditioned for *For Colored Girls Who Commit Suicide When the Rainbow is Not Enough*. She got the part! But, she was still doing a small part in a production at Brandeis and was not allowed to leave with a good grade if she did not finish. She stayed and got her degree; but she was on fire for New York. Though she had worked as a dormitory director while at Brandeis to help pay for her tuition, she left with her degree and a huge loan debt.

Loretta was offered a job at Brown University immediately after gradu-ation and she worked in theatre there with George Bass and the play-wright, P.J. Gibson. When she finally got to New York, *For Colored Girls* had become a hit without her and she went to work at Gimbel's selling cos-metics. She would go to auditions on her lunch breaks and after work. She was finally cast in a show at LA MAMA, Ellen Stuarts's theatre deep in the village. Loretta would cry every time something didn't work. If she didn't get a job she had tried for or if things had gone badly at work, her tears came easily. Ellen Stuart, the director would admonish her in her heavy French accent, "You must not do dis, babe!" Miss Stuart helped Loretta get her first big audition for *Hair*, which was on Broadway; but, first, Loretta had to promise not to cry if she didn't get the part. She got it!

She worked endlessly for all the Black theatre companies. She worked for Hazel Bryant and Woodie King, among others. She was living off the income from mostly part-time work, unemployment checks, and the little bit that the theatre paid her. She had to take classes to keep current with her acting, dancing, and vocal skills. It was all very expensive. "I don't know how I did it, but I did," she says now. "I auditioned with Tom Eyen and Henry Krieger for a show that eventually put me on the map. It was called 'Project Nine' for a long time, but was eventually called *Dreamgirls*. After four hard workshops that were each six-weeks long, 'Lorell' was the character I created. She has stood the test of time, and the movie *Dreamgirls* is the proof of that."

Loretta says that she was really afraid of what would happen to her after *Dreamgirls*. "There was nothing to go to. The show moved on without us," she says. "With each revival, Los Angeles, London, and on and on, there was a new crop of girls. I got a job at Radio City Music Hall right before the end, but the end was coming fast. I heard about a new Fosse show, but I couldn't get an audition. No one would recommend me. They had decided that I was not the right type. I was doing my club act at one of the small midtown clubs, when out of the blue, Bob Fosse was in the back of the room watching me. I got the Broadway job, *Big Deal*. I was the right type after all and he knew it!"

Big Deal ended up closing very fast. Loretta could not believe that the world did not love it, but it got panned and she was left out of the Tony awards. She was devastated. "I was offered a role playing a maid in a little show with Carol Channing, or *The Colored Museum*, down at the New

York Shakespeare Festival. I lost sleep over this one. One was a huge production and the other was very small. I didn't want to play a maid again. I wanted Carol Channing's role. So, I took *The Colored Museum* and prayed that it would be the right choice for me. That show took me from New York to London to Los Angeles. It was the right choice!"

Loretta's first major movie role was with Sidney Poitier in *Little Nikita*. Her first regular television role was as 'Stevie,' the dorm director in *A Different World*. Her career was definitely launched! Loretta has now appeared in over fifty movies: from *Waiting to Exhale* to the much discussed movie, *Crash*, to *This Christmas*. She has received four NAACP Image Awards and seven nominations. She can be seen on television in various roles, including her recurring role as 'Adele' on *Grey's Anatomy*.

Loretta's alma mater, The University of Houston, has honored her with an honorary Doctor of Humane Letters degree. Even so, Loretta says, "I've worked at this career my entire life and still have not been discovered. I am proud to be a working actress, but you look in *Forbes* magazine and there are no Black actresses making millions of dollars a show. Perhaps a handful are really making it, but there is so much talent that is untouched and unknown. It is unfair and sad. Everyone wants to work and be appreciated. Everyone wants to make enough to give back."

Loretta encourages women to do the very best they can with the gifts they have been given. "We each have incredible gifts," she says. "Sometimes we get tired and we want to give up. Or, we just can't seem to get something right, and so we think, 'I'm just going to give up today.' So, remember, the magic can happen at any moment. The dream can happen. Fear is such a part of our culture. Try not to live in fear."

Joycelyn Elders, M.D.

"To whom much is given, much is required. If you give to people in need, you'll get it back double."

I had searched and searched for a way to contact our former Surgeon General, Dr. Joycelyn Elders. I found her telephone number on the Internet, but I was afraid to call her. It seemed presumptuous of me to call such a distinguished person without an introduction. And then I remembered that my friends, Dr. Rick and Rev. Susan Smith lived in Little Rock and I thought that maybe, just maybe they knew Dr. Elders.

When I called Rick, he said that Dr. Elders had been one of his professors in medical school, and that he still saw her around the University from time to time. He mentioned how hard working she was and that he had recently seen her in the airport, sleeping in between flights. He agreed that I could give his name as an entrance.

Well, I don't think I needed to be the least bit concerned! Dr. Elders is as friendly and welcoming as can be. She asked when I would be in Little Rock and invited me to come to her home outside of town. When I got there, I noticed that we have the exact same Victorian chairs in our living rooms. We even have the same upholstery material on them! Her friend and colleague, Dr. Barbara Kilgore, was with her, and as the interview progressed, Barbara would remind Dr. Elders of this or that experience or incident that she thought important. Dr. Elders gave me a copy of the book she wrote telling her life story, which I subsequently read with great interest.

I visited with Dr. Elders again a year later, when I was in Little Rock for the dedication of The Arkansas House of Prayer, an exquisite building devoted to silence and meditation. She had forgotten that I was coming first thing in the morning and wasn't ready when I arrived. Opening the door in her bathrobe with a big smile on her face, she invited me to go into her kitchen and make some coffee while she made herself presentable. As I followed her invitation, I thought, "I'm rummaging around in the Surgeon General's kitchen! I can't believe it!" And then I thought about the timelessness of women meeting in each other's kitchens, and what comfort there is about that. As always, Dr. Elders was welcoming and easy to talk to. We had our picture taken together and I visited for a bit with her husband, Oliver. They both said that they had assumed that as they got older (both are in their late 70's), life would slow down. But, in fact, just the opposite has happened. They now find themselves busier than ever. Oliver said that it seems that the last chapters of life must be similar to the last quarter of a basketball game, where what happens is critical to the outcome of the game.

Dr. Elders was born in the tiny town of Shaal, Arkansas, population ninety-nine. She is the eldest of eight children born to her parents. She was called Minnie then, and her family called her Mint. Her parents were farmers, raising cotton, corn and hay, among other things. She says that growing up on a farm meant hard work to survive, but also, Sunday dinners with lots of aunts, uncles and two sets of grandparents.

In addition to growing crops, her father hunted raccoons in the winter in order to sell their fur to buy Christmas presents. They also had hogs and cattle.

"Mint" went to school in a one-room schoolhouse. When she started kindergarten, she already knew her numbers and her alphabet. Eulastine Brown was her teacher in this segregated school and she recalls her mother saying, "If you want to get out of the cotton patch, you have to get something in your head."

For high school, Joycelyn traveled thirteen miles to attend the Howard County Training School. She imagined that if she could just finish high school, she might get a job at Dillard's Department Store as a salesgirl. This was an interesting aspiration, as there were no black clerks in department stores in Arkansas at that time. But, it is a good illustration of how Joycelyn began her life's journey imagining doing "the impossible."

While her home economics teacher was training the girls to become maids, Joycelyn was worrying that her country schools might be inferior. So, she stayed up late at night reading everything she could find. Since there was no electricity, she would make a tent out of a quilt and light the space with a kerosene lamp, so as not to bother the rest of the family. It's a wonder she didn't catch the house on fire!

Joycelyn says that being the oldest child in her family taught her leadership, discipline, and responsibility. If her mother went to work in the fields, then she took over the household and younger children. If she was sent to the fields, she was to see to it that the hired hands did their work.

As a young teenager, Joycelyn accompanied her parents to Richmond, California so that her mother could work in the shipyards as a welder during World War II, while her father was in the Navy. Her parents hoped to earn enough money to buy a farm. Joycelyn was tested at school for grade placement and because she was moved ahead in school in California, upon her return to Howard County Training School, she was able to graduate at age fifteen.

Joycelyn says that she knew she did not want to be like her mother or have a life like her mother's. "She had given her whole life to her children. Her prayer was to see her children raised," she said.

So, on the night of high school graduation, when she received a college scholarship from The United Methodist Women of Philander Smith College, she saw her opportunity for something different.

Joycelyn's family was so poor that they did not have $3.34 for bus fare to Little Rock, where she was to attend college. Her brothers and sisters picked cotton to earn the bus money for her, and neighbors helped by making her clothes. She boarded the bus for Philander Smith College knowing no one there and having never been to Little Rock. Her grandmother had encouraged her by saying, "Go on honey. I got enough younguns' to hold you up."

When she arrived, there was no record of her admission or scholarship and so she sat down on the steps and began to cry. Fortunately, the president of the college found her and reassured her that he would intervene. He sent her to the dormitories to find a room, and since her scholarship only covered tuition, Joycelyn cleaned the halls and bathrooms to earn her room and board. She continued working as a domestic to support herself, while carrying full academic loads with majors in biology and chemistry. By going to summer school every summer, Joycelyn graduated at eighteen years of age!

Joycelyn had known for some time that she wanted to become a doctor. She told me that this was odd, since in all her growing up, she had never actually seen a doctor. But, she says that often in her life she has been at the right place at the right time and it was one of those times when she joined the U. S. Army after college. She knew about the GI bill and she wanted it so that she could go to medical school. The Korean War was happening and physical therapists were needed to treat injured soldiers. She was trained as a physical therapist and served three years as the only black woman in her group.

After completing her Army obligation, Joycelyn applied for medical school at the University of Arkansas, which did not admit African American students to its undergraduate schools. Three black students were admitted to her class, two men and Joycelyn. Although she was not allowed in the cafeteria, and had to use the "colored" bathrooms, she was well received by her fellow students. "I was just one of the guys," she says.

Joycelyn married Oliver Elders, her husband of over forty-nine years, during medical school. He has always been a staunch supporter of her education and career. At one point in her training, he even sent her to Minnesota for a year to pursue an opportunity in pediatric surgery, while he stayed behind. But, she decided that she preferred general pediatrics to surgery and returned to Arkansas to become a pediatrician, and to be with Oliver.

Joycelyn had excellent grades and a superb work ethic. When she was chosen from amongst her peers to be chief resident, it was a very major event. She was a woman, and a black woman at that, attending medical school at a segregated university, in an era when few women of any ethnicity were admitted to medical school. The chairman of her department had really wanted her to win. "He convinced those young white men that they would not let me fail," she says. It was such a big event that CBS did a special program piece on it, and *Ebony* magazine did a layout. And so, Joycelyn Elders became a pediatrician. She remained on the faculty of the University, where she teaches and conducts research to this day.

She is emphatic when she states, "We always walk around and say what we've done, but I'll tell you, we've stood on a lot of shoulders to get where we are."

When asked about her marriage to Oliver, she says she definitely married the right person. She describes him as tolerant and supportive of whatever she has needed to do to further her career.

The Elders have two sons, who are now in their forties. She says that she worked in the lab doing great research during both pregnancies, and grew African violets, too. She gives credit to her dear friend and colleague, Dr. Barbara Kilgore, for helping to maintain such a good atmosphere in their lab all these years.

During the years Joycelyn was raising her boys, she would go to bed after dinner and then get up at 3:00 a.m. to be alone and write grants and papers. She is still in the habit of rising at 3:00 a.m. to write.

Oliver Elders is a celebrity in his own right. He was a high school teacher and renowned basketball coach, who has been installed in the National High School Coaches Hall of Fame. Joycelyn took her boys to all of Oliver's basketball events, and even sustained some nerve damage to her hands from applauding so much at the games!

Joycelyn was appointed Director of the Health Department of the State of Arkansas by, then Governor, Bill Clinton. She was able to maintain her tenured professorship at the University during the six years she served in this capacity. She had already begun giving inspirational speeches at graduations and in classrooms.

Hillary Clinton invited her to serve on the governor's Commission on the Status of Women. These appointments were the beginning of her active political life. When Bill Clinton became president, he tapped her to be Surgeon General of the United States of America. Again, she made sure to secure her position at the University before leaving for Washington, D.C., and Oliver was able to find work there.

Of her work as Surgeon General, Dr. Elders says, "I enjoyed it. I made it the kind of job I wanted it to be. I really wanted to make sure that we improved education and health for adolescents. I wanted to reduce the rate of teenage pregnancy and have the resources to prevent sexually transmitted diseases." Believing that children need comprehensive healthcare education beginning in kindergarten, Dr. Elders supported Bill Clinton's Health Care Reform, which was ultimately defeated. She says that right-wing fundamentalists believed she had too much power. "I was not about abortion," she declares. "The best way to prevent abortion is to prevent pregnancy in the first place." Dr. Elders worked to increase immunization of children, reduce obesity, and reduce the incidence of drug use, tobacco use, and violence. She was in favor of education in the use of condoms to reduce teen pregnancy and the spread of sexually transmitted disease. When there were complaints, Dr. Elders was surprised, but would not budge. "I wouldn't have changed my stance and sacrificed our young people for ideology. I believed I was correct and needed to stand by my conviction," she says emphatically.

At a conference having to do with AIDS prevention, Dr. Elders responded to a casual question regarding whether or not she thought advocating masturbation might reduce the spread of AIDS. The question came as a surprise and she says she didn't give too much thought to her affirmative reply because, as she says, "When most men and half the women masturbate, what's the big deal?"

It set off a tempest that resulted in her being fired as Surgeon General. She refused to believe that Bill Clinton would fire her and demanded that he tell her personally, which he did. "It really mattered to me and I was upset," she says. "But after I thought about it, I realized that he had to do what he had to do." He later apologized for this in his book.

When she checked on her job status at the University, she learned that she would need to return in a matter of days to keep her health insurance. Though her husband had resigned his job to accompany her to Washington, D.C., he said, "Shug, why don't we just go home."

Since then, Dr. Elders has continued her work at the University. She's been on the speaker's circuit, talking about issues related to healthcare, education and aging. She believes strongly that health care is a human right, and that every sick person should have the right to see a doctor. She laments the fact that our country has not used its resources well in this regard, emphasizing emergency care rather than prevention.

Dr. Elders had much to say when asked about her advice for young women. "First of all," she said, "we must be in control of our own bodies. If you can't control your reproduction, you can't control your life." She went on to say, "Common sense is the sense that we have to keep those other five senses from acting the fool." In addition, Dr. Elders said, "You have to set a goal, and then don't give up just because it's not a straight line to the finish. Don't give up! Stick to it! Keep your eye on your prize. Decide what you want to do and stick to it."

Dr. Elders emphasized her belief that if a woman keeps trying, even when life is hard, somewhere along the way, someone will help her. In addition, she says she has a strong faith in God. "I don't wear my religion on my shoulder. But, I know He expects me to use the resources I've got to help His children."

She quotes a familiar Bible verse, "To whom much is given, much is required," and goes on to say, "If you give to people in need, you'll get it back double."

Aurelia Harris, Ph.D.

*"If you don't know
who you are,
you can't succeed
or help anyone else.
Know yourself—
your strengths and
your weaknesses.
Get honest."*

When I interviewed Lovie McGee in Albuquerque, New Mexico, she asked me if I had met "the doctor" in town. I said that I had not, but that I had her name and was going to call her. Lovie offered to make the call and see if Dr. Aurelia Harris was available. She was.

The tenor of her interview was much the way I pictured her approach to life, practical and to the point, with no frills. She was matter of fact in presenting her life story, as if what she had accomplished was really quite ordinary and not that remarkable. Well, it is remarkable!

I was so struck by her parents' encouragement when she was accepted to graduate school in Michigan, which is a very long ways from Florida, where she was raised. My own mother was nearly frantic when I moved fifty miles away to go to college, worrying about my safety and ability to navigate a whole new world. But, Aurelia moved far, far away, to a completely unknown place. And her mother encouraged it! In fact, I was amazed at all the risks Aurelia has taken in her professional life. She seems unfazed and not all that impressed with her own courage.

A year after our first meeting, I met her and Lovie McGee in a restaurant in Albuquerque for dinner. Aurelia was telling me that when you are only two percent of the population, as African Americans are in Albuquerque, the disadvantage is that everyone knows you and you just can't be anonymous. With that, people two tables away called out to her in greeting. They had recognized her from church. "See what I mean?" she said.

Aurelia Harris, Ph.D. was fifty years old at the time of this interview. She is the middle child of parents who were themselves educated and who valued education for their children.

Aurelia describes her early family life as middle-class and rather mundane. She says, "There wasn't much exciting happening...the usual round of church activities, school, and piano lessons." Though her parents often spoke of their difficult experiences with Southern segregation during their own lives, Aurelia says she was not particularly conscious of the racism around her. She attended Catholic schools, which, though segregated, provided a bit of a protective environment in St. Petersburg, Florida where she grew up. It was "just understood" that all three children in the family would attend college, and they did.

Aurelia received her Bachelor's degree in accounting from Southern University, a historically African American school in Baton Rouge, Louisiana. She had become active in Delta Sigma Theta sorority as an undergraduate, an affiliation she has maintained, and where she has served as president of the Albuquerque, New Mexico chapter.

Not satisfied to be an accountant, Aurelia applied to and was accepted at The University of Florida at Gainesville, with a Rockefeller Scholarship for Academic Achievement. She received a Master's degree in Food and Resource Economics from that institution. She taught for three and a half years at The University of Arkansas at Pine Bluff and then was recruited by Michigan State University where she received a fellowship for a Ph.D. in Agricultural and Natural Resource Economics. When I asked her how in the world a city girl had ended up working for the U.S. Department of Agriculture in agricultural economics, she simply stated that lots of city students were interested in agriculture and rural areas as a function of a desire to try something new. Her parents were fully supportive of their daughter's spirit of adventure and actively encouraged her explorations. Though I was amazed, she didn't seem to view this as anything special. "I was using information I gathered bit by bit," she says. "I would see someone whose life looked good to me and try to emulate them."

Aurelia has worked in several arms of the Department of Agriculture: 1) as a researcher, and 2) for the National Forest Systems Management of National Forest Lands, working in State and Private forestry. State and Private Forestry is the division of the agency that deals with economic development of areas adjacent to National Forests, where logging has ceased or been greatly reduced.

It was in Albuquerque, New Mexico, during her most recent assignment, that Aurelia began to be involved in issues of civil rights. As you may have guessed, traditionally, there have not been many African Americans of either sex working in the area of agricultural economics. The department wanted someone to be the African American Special Emphasis Program Manager and Aurelia agreed to do the job. Her work has evolved into her present position as Equal Opportunity Program Manager, coordinating all programs for the Southwest Region having to do with African Americans, such as career fairs, recruitment, outreach and African American educational activities.

It has been in these specialized capacities that Aurelia has become more personally aware of racism. She tells two poignant stories as examples of this.

"In the last twenty years, I have been traveling to colleges with four white, male colleagues. We go to a particular area and do outreach and recruitment at colleges and universities in the vicinity. One day in Huntsville, Alabama, we stopped at a gas station to ask directions to Alabama A&M. The attendant said, 'You mean that nigger school up on the hill?' My colleagues were horrified and apologetic. I told them not to take it too seriously. You just say to yourself that that person doesn't know any better and you develop a thicker skin." She says emphatically, "You cannot let yourself be held back by these things. You have to take control of your own destiny."

Sometimes the racism is less overt. In Jackson, Mississippi, the group headed into a restaurant for lunch. One of the men informed the hostess that there were five in their group. The hostess said, "You mean four?" "No," she was told, "there are five." Again, she said, "I think you mean four." Finally, the man counted out loud as he pointed to the four white men and Aurelia, "One, two, three, four, five," he said. And finally, they were seated. Was she invisible standing in the midst of four white men? Or, could the hostess not conceive of the notion that an African American woman would be having lunch with this group of professional looking men? We'll never know. But, Aurelia is quick to point out that less obvious forms of racism persist, such as the naïve assumption that traditionally African American colleges and universities provide an inherently inferior education, which is untrue. She points out that working with rural populations can be challenging for minorities because in rural areas, people have less contact with changes in the larger culture and often, less experience working with diverse people. She says the same is true for all women working in the traditionally male arena of agriculture. But, with her usual, casual attitude, she states, "It's always been this way for me (the only woman and only African American), and I wouldn't know what to do if it was different."

Aurelia has valuable advice for African American women—all women, really. She says, "Don't ever let anyone tell you what job you can have, or what or who you need to be. Determine that for yourself. Know who you are and act accordingly. You have to be strong in life. If you don't know yourself, you cannot succeed. Know your strengths and your weaknesses. Weaknesses are nothing to be ashamed of. Use your talents and get people with the talents you don't have to fill in for you."

When I asked her how she got to know herself, she said that it was just a little at a time, through trial and error. She emphasized, "Get honest with yourself and then visualize doing well. It takes work. So, don't be lazy. Everyone has to struggle."

Aurelia is the mother of one daughter, a college student, of whom she is very proud. Her daughter began school in Fort Collins, Colorado, where less than one percent of the population is African American, and more recently, in Albuquerque, where only two percent of the population are African American. This gives the word, "minority" real meaning. "We've had no trouble being in such a minority status. People seem to be fine with us (African Americans) if there are just one or two. It's when there are lots of us that the dominant population gets uncomfortable, it seems."

Aurelia learned the value of volunteering from her parents. Through her sorority, Delta Sigma Theta, she volunteered as a tutor during college. She works in her church, and is on panels for the United Way of Central New Mexico, deciding how monies received are allocated. This involves doing site visits to the various organizations requesting funds. Her sorority chapter sponsors Girls and Pearls, matching eight to ten year-old girls with a seasoned community leader for the purpose of providing mentoring and encouraging the girls to strive for success.

Aurelia is on the boards of three area non-profits and is the Chairwoman of the Advisory Board of the Mayor's Office on Volunteering and Engagement. She is the President of the Albuquerque Alumnae Chapter of Delta Sigma Theta Sorority, Inc.and Chairperson of the New Mexico EEO and Diversity Council.

When her mother said, "Aurelia, you should do something different with your life," she took the chance and the challenge. Her intellect and enthusiasm are obvious and worthy of emulating.

Yvonne Lawson-Thomas, R.N., M.D.

"The biggest thing in my life was from my little old, illiterate black grandmother. 'Sweetheart,' she said, 'being good is easier than being bad, and if you pretend long enough it becomes part of you'."

had completed all the interviews for this book when Yvonne Cagle, one of The Academics called me and encouraged me to do one more. "You have to meet this woman," she said emphatically. Yvonne went on to say that she had gone to the medical clinic at Travis Air Force Base in Fairfield, CA with a minor complaint. A friendly and energetic nurse, with a slight patois accent in her voice ushered her into the examining room. As the two Yvonne's talked, they discovered that both were physicians. Why Yvonne Lawson-Thomas was working, as a nurse is a story I will soon tell.

I called Dr. Lawson-Thomas to see if I could arrange to meet her in March of 2009. She was agreeable and asked if it would be all right to send me a poem she had written to honor emergency response workers, who save so many lives, and who are often over-looked when credit is given. As I was to learn, Dr. Lawson-Thomas gives credit and honor to everyone except herself. "I've never done anything of great importance," she says with real sincerity in her voice. If that is the case, how is it that in 2002 The American Medical Association honored her with their prestigious Humanitarian Award and Lifetime membership?

Yvonne, as she quickly asked me to call her, is a prolific and published poet, as it turns out. She sews, paints, and engages in all sorts of creative pursuits. In fact, creativity seems to just pour out of her. I had no sooner returned home from our day together, involving a trip to Domaine Chandon in the Napa Valley wine country, for a lovely lunch and champagne, when another one of Yvonne's poems arrived by email. For the thirty-first time, I told my husband that I had met "the most amazing woman of all!"

Yvonne Lawson-Thomas is the only woman interviewed who was not born in the United States. She is Jamaican by birth and from Kingston. She tells me that she is biracial, with an English father and a Jamaican mother. Her mother's ancestors were Incan, Ethiopian, Spanish, and Irish, and hailed from the Canary Islands off the coast of Africa. She is the personification of diversity and multiculturalism.

Yvonne is seventy-one years old and the product of a rape. She did not know her biological mother until she was ten years old, when her father married the woman he had assaulted. She had believed that her mother was a woman who was actually her aunt. Her father was a very powerful man in Jamaica and her mother an impoverished, but very beautiful factory worker, who was referred to as 'The Flamingo.' When the fact of this lengthy deception came to light, Yvonne began to act out. "I did her a real disservice," Yvonne says now. "I looked down on her because our family was upper class and she was not. I didn't understand her situation." Since

Yvonne's mother was a talented seamstress who sewed for the aristocracy, it is likely that much of Yvonne's creativity was inherited from her mother.

Yvonne says that she lived an affluent life, but didn't realize that it was any different from anyone else, because she was so sequestered at home. Her father's need for high security meant that outsiders came to them and not the other way around. Even the cobbler came to the house to measure their feet for the custom made shoes he created for them. "I had no idea that you there was such a thing as a shoe store with different shoes to chose from, or a dress shop. Everything was custom made for us and I just didn't know anything different."

Yvonne always had a curious mind. When she was only four she asked the cobbler how it was that he could stitch the leather for the shoes and the thread didn't break. He explained that he used waxed thread. Not long after that, a Golden Retriever jumped over a fence in Yvonne's back yard and cut open his stomach on the sharp fence stakes. Yvonne asked a servant for waxed thread and a needle and actually sewed up the dog's wound. Hard to believe, but true. It was a preview of things to come. "I was always a doctor and a mother, even when I was a little girl," she explains. "I would say, 'When I am a big girl, I will take care of all the children of the world.'"

Because her father was so difficult and cruel, Yvonne's aunt suggested that she go to boarding school in England when she was sixteen. She agreed to go and traveled from Kingston, Jamaica to New York Harbor all alone. From there she boarded the Queen Mary for an Atlantic voyage and landed in Liverpool. She attended Colchester Essex, which was a nursing school, where she continued to get herself in trouble. Yvonne says she was a problem child and laughs as she tells about dropping an Alka Seltzer in one of the nun's chamber pots. "Her pee effervesced!" she giggles. Another time she sneaked out the dining room window to take a walk late at night. While she was out, the silverware for breakfast was placed on the serving table under the open window and when Yvonne tried to crawl back in, all the silverware clattered to the floor. She dashed back outside and entered the basement boiler room, where she knew there was a trap door leading back into the house. When she emerged from that trap door covered in soot, into a sitting room, Sister Pichocka was standing there waiting for her.

So far from home, Yvonne felt terribly alone and unhappy. When other students went home for vacations, she remained at the school. She even remained at school while recuperating from appendicitis. She continued to be incorrigible, but she graduated in 1959. Later, one of her supervisors said to her, "You are an excellent nurse, but you are rude and act indignant and belligerent." Yvonne doesn't deny it.

Finishing school in Switzerland came next and Yvonne makes the point that her life had been so privileged that she never did her own laundry until she was eighteen years old. But, she had begun to feel guilty about her privileged status as soon as she understood it. "I felt guilty that I had come from a rich family, that I was smart, and had a good education. I just felt guilty all the time and for everything."

Yvonne believes that to some degree, her guilt led her to marry a military man from an underprivileged background. He was an American soldier and her family opposed the marriage. Yvonne made a decision at that point to legally change her name to the name she is known by today, and had a new birth certificate issued. It took her over a year to obtain a visa in her new name because her father refused to sign the necessary documents.

To Yvonne's great disappointment, hers was not a happy marriage. Her husband seemed to be intimidated by her intellect and her upper class mentality. Every Friday night, after working all week, Yvonne would clean the house and bake. Her husband's friends would come over and make fun of her accent. She was the butt of many jokes and jibes. She was despondent and attempted suicide by taking forty pills.

It is here that Yvonne speaks of one of her "visions." "My husband discovered me and got me to a hospital. I was unconscious but I can tell you everything about that room," she says. "I watched from a place in the corner of the ceiling as a nurse put a breathing tube down my throat and turned on the ventilator. I heard someone say, 'her ph is 7.17, which is not compatible with life.' When I was placed in a hospital room, a small man came to see me. He said that he was Dr. Cole, and his name on his white coat confirmed it. I can visualize him today. He looked at my chart and took my hand and I was crying. He said that God made our lives in a tapestry. Then he corrected himself and said that it was not a tapestry, but a jigsaw puzzle, where we have to find ways to fit the pieces together to make a whole picture. He said that we are all placed on this earth for a purpose, and though we may take many detours, God will bring us back. He said that if we ask God long enough, we'd get what we want, but that there will be a price. Then he left. After awhile, Dr. King, my attending physician came in to extubate me. I told him that I wanted Dr. Cole to come back. He said that they didn't have a Dr. Cole or any other doctor in this area. I was insistent and so was he. We were both puzzled that my records had disappeared."

My husband said to anyone who would listen, "Yvonne is so stupid! Did you know that she tried to kill herself?"

Yvonne became a United States citizen over her family's objections and followed her new husband to numerous assignments, Dover, Delaware, Boise, Idaho, Miami and Tampa, Florida to name just a few.

She had to be certified as a registered nurse in the United States and pieced together her education by taking classes wherever her husband was stationed. She finished her R.N. at The University of Southern California and The University of Minnesota, and followed that with a Master's degree in public health from La Universidad Central del Este in Santo Domingo, Dominican Republic. By this time, Yvonne had given birth to three children, two girls and then a boy. She had left them with her husband from time to time to complete this part of her education.

As she traveled to different assignments with her husband, Yvonne would find work. While working as a nurse in the neonate intensive care unit at The University of Massachusetts hospital, she assisted in the appendectomy of a two-pound baby. She spoke up to the attending physician when he was screaming orders at everyone. She told him in no uncertain terms to tone it down. When she returned to her unit, she was promoted. She overheard a fellow nurse say that this had happened because "that nigger was having an affair with one of the doctors." "If you want to see how a nigger acts, I'll push you out that window and they'll have to scrape you off the pavement," Yvonne announced loudly. She talked tough, but she was in despair and retired to a darkened room in the hospital that was used as a place for staff to rest. She sat in the darkened room looking out at the night sky and said out loud, "I'm too black to be white and too white to be black. When will I be happy?" She goes on to explain that she felt that no one had ever loved her. Out of the darkness, a voice said, "Yvonne, you should go to medical school." It was Dr. Leonard, who had been resting on a cot in the back of the room. She hadn't known he was there. Dr. Leonard continued his encouragement and eventually gave her $58,000 to help pay for her medical school education.

"Despite my accomplishments and my tough exterior, I had low self-esteem and was insecure. I thought that if I was a doctor, everyone would see that I was worth something," Yvonne explains. She was accepted to medical school at Ross University in New Jersey in 1981. Ross has campuses in the Caribbean, which appealed to her since it was familiar and she began her training. As had been her experience, her husband continued to try to undermine her efforts. When friends would ask what she did in her spare time, her husband would complain that she always had her head in a book. He said that by the time she finished school it would be time to collect Social Security. He claimed that she had "high-falutin" ideas." She didn't let it stop her.

After one of these instances of verbal humiliation in front of family and friends, her daughter followed her into the kitchen and said, "I think you should leave him." Yvonne quotes one of her grandmother's proverbs, "The fox gets his tail caught in a trap, which lops it off. Then he tries to get everyone else to get their tails cut off, too." She knew she did not want to have her "tail" lopped off to save someone else's self-esteem.

Yvonne says that she entered her marriage quite emotionally dependent. But, when her husband did a tour of duty overseas, she had become quite self-sufficient. He just could not adjust to the change in her and had escalated his verbal abuse.

Soon thereafter, Yvonne gathered her children and told them that they must never, ever believe anyone who said she didn't love them but she was leaving and would come back for them when she could.

She set out for California from Mt. Home AFB in Idaho with fifty dollars in her pocket and wearing a fleece parka in the dead of winter. She had no snow tires on her car. As she drove along at night, her car skidded out of control and down an embankment near a frozen lake. The car glided to a stop at the slushy water's edge. A few more inches and she would have plunged into the freezing waters. A man driving a tractor saw what had happened and pulled her back onto the road. She gave him $15 for his trouble. He told her that she should turn around and go back where she had come from before something terrible happened. "I told him that I knew what was in front of me and what was behind me and that I wasn't going back," she says firmly.

"I just kept going. When I got to Reno, NV, I paid $10 for chains for my car. The police were closing the pass into California due to road conditions, but I sneaked onto the road when they weren't looking. I got to Sacramento with $15 in my pocket. A friend who was an intern at the University of California at Davis sent a medical student over to me to deliver keys to his apartment, where I was finally able to rest. But, I quickly moved to a woman's residence. I had left my husband to find out who I was and what I wanted to do with my life; not to get involved with someone else."

Yvonne's friend gave her a small amount of money to get to San Francisco. She filled her gas tank and had $5 remaining. She contacted the A-1 Nursing Agency and told them her situation. She bought herself a half a loaf of bread, sat on a bench and prayed. Yvonne found an advertisement for a rental in the newspaper that day. She told the woman who answered her call that she just knew that if the woman met her, she would let her stay on the promise of money she would earn nursing. The woman met her and simply put her up for the time it took to wait for her job to come through, and the first paycheck to arrive.

In time, Yvonne found an attorney and began divorce proceedings. Her husband claimed that she had abandoned her children, who were six, five and three at the time. He said she would never get them back.

"I threatened to tell everyone, including his commanding officer, that when he would go overseas he would leave us with no money. He eventually sent the children to me."

I was living in an apartment that did not allow children. I worked for three months, sixteen hours a day in the burn unit at San Francisco General Hospital, so that I could move from that apartment.

It is here that I gasp in disbelief. I live in the San Francisco Bay Area and I know very well what it means to work in the burn unit at General. It's some of the most grueling and heart-wrenching work there is.

Yvonne had sneaked her children into the apartment and told them they had to be quiet. She was at S.F. General for four years and took in sewing in her "spare" time to make extra money to support herself and the children. She received no child support.

As far as medical school was concerned, "I took the long way around," she says. Her husband had come to California and begged her to reconcile. "I thought maybe it was unfinished, so I tried to return to him." But, it was not to be.

However, Yvonne was able to take her pre-med training at the University of Minnesota. She took her entrance exams and was accepted to medical school. She began at The University of Santo Domingo and then transferred to the United States. She did her residency in Minnesota, becoming a cardiologist and then a trauma surgeon.

Yvonne began traveling with Interplast M.D.'s, performing needed surgeries in third world countries. Although she had become a U.S. citizen, her many years spent in the Caribbean led her to create a foundation in 1991 dedicated to changing health conditions in the Caribbean Basin. Many island nations, as well as Central American countries have been blessed to receive her gifts of donated medical supplies and training for local physicians and nurses and emergency response personnel. "Power is not in the closed fist," she says evenly. "It is in an open hand. My anger is about the complacency of our society. I think more people should spend time helping others in one way or another."

Yvonne has had a remarkable career as a physician, all the while raising three well-adjusted and accomplished children. But, when her third child was born, she developed pulmonary carcoidosis. She lost her hair and was treated with steroids. Over the years, several other significant medical challenges were treated with steroids. Ultimately, the treatment with steroids interfered with her eyesight. She was gradually losing her sight and had significantly blurred vision. She had to have lens implants. Her eyelids began to droop. "I tell you what," she says with a sideways glance, "I see better with my eyes closed anyway." But, that was the end of her medical career. "I couldn't see," she says now, "but I packed a lot of boxes and shipped a lot of stuff for the Caribbean Basin during that time."

Yvonne says that she became quite depressed by her situation; all those years of training, all those sleepless nights and time away from her children and for what? "One of my daughters came to me and said, 'You better shit or get off the pot.' It was indelicate, but she was right. I decided to re-activate my nursing license and be a nurse again. I was always like a roll-ing stone," she says. "I was either looking for something or running from something. I had become a doctor for the wrong reasons anyway. Being a doctor does not define who I am. I want people to see me, Yvonne, and not jump to conclusions."

In 2002, Yvonne was awarded The American Medical Association Humanitarian Award for her work bringing emergency medical response training and supplies to various countries in the Caribbean Basin. She received a lifetime membership in the AMA as an honorarium. She still seems surprised at this turn of events.

Yvonne has valuable advice for all women. "Learn to be selfish and learn to be autonomous," she says emphatically. "There is nothing wrong with being selfish to develop your own identity. If you are selfless, as so many people recommend, you take on other people's personalities." And then, "Learn autonomy. Chart your own course. Be a leader, not a follower."

Nowadays, Yvonne can be found most days in the clinic at Travis AFB in Fairfield, CA. She says that though she had never voted in her life, she voted for Barack Obama in the 2008 election. "I want an audience with Michelle Obama," she says evenly. "I want to tell her how important it is for our soldiers to have mandatory debriefing and treatment for grief and post-traumatic stress disorder. I am also very concerned about obtaining treatment for the many women in the military who have been sexually harassed and even raped by their fellow soldiers. This is a problem that is not talked about very much, and I want to talk about it!"

And so it goes with Yvonne Lawson-Thomas, R.N., M.D. She is onto her next creative plan to do what she has done most of her life – serve others.

In closing, it was interesting to me that Yvonne never mentioned to me that Chappie James, the first African American Four Star General was her daughter's Godfather. I had learned this piece of information before the interview. When I asked her if this was true, she answered affirmatively, but with that same characteristic humility that so exemplifies her. It is just not in her nature to brag.

CHAPTER 8

In the Eye of the Beholder:
The Beauties

*"The kind of beauty I want most is the
hard-to-get kind that comes from within —
strength, courage, and dignity."*

— Ruby Dee

What does it mean to be seen as beautiful, even considered glamorous, when one belongs to a racial minority whose appearance has historically been made into caricature or assumed to be unattractive? According to psychologist, Dr. Kumea Shorter-Gooden, "Beauty is an arena where racism and sexism intersect with a vengeance." If beauty is defined as light skin and eyes, with small features, what does this say about how African American women might view themselves and define their attractiveness? Dr. Shorter-Gooden goes on to say that often when people of all ethnicities are asked who their contemporary icons of Black female beauty are, they give responses reflecting famous women who have facial features, skin color and hairstyles that resemble Euro-American looks. "Rarely is the Black beauty icon a dark-skinned, broad-nosed woman who wears her dark, kinky-curly hair in an unprocessed hairstyle," she continues.

It is an enormous undertaking to challenge and change the predominant way in which a culture views the physical aspects of its members and determines what is considered attractive.

Grandmothers have long said, "Pretty is as pretty does," and of course that is true. However, every little girl and every woman, no matter her ethnicity, hopes to be viewed as attractive.

African American women have had to work at defining beauty on their own terms and press that definition into the consciousness of the general public. This is no small task when the stereotypes have been so deeply ingrained. It's easy enough to say, "Black is beautiful." But, having that statement translate into the mindset of an entire society is quite a task.

In addition to broadening the definitions of beauty and attractiveness for our society as a whole, there is the issue of internalized racism, which created a sort of caste system within the African American community itself, in which lighter skinned women (and men, for that matter) were preferred. Many women interviewed for this book spoke of the effects of this hierarchy of perceived desirability within the African American community as having created obstacles for them to overcome in the internal world of their view of themselves, including identity and self-esteem, as well as in the outer world of job possibilities and general desirability.

The Beauties have helped American society to broaden its definition of physical attractiveness. This strength may seem superficial, but when research indicates that people who are considered physically attractive tend to be hired for jobs more easily, not to speak of their increased desirability as romantic partners, among other things, it is obvious that enhancing and appreciating overall beauty and personal style is very important.

Beauty and style can also project very political overtones. Hair styles, for example, among African American women can serve as metaphors for deeper racial issues that are often hard to speak of in this country: issues like internalized racial superiority or internalized racial inferiority can be evident in what hairstyles are considered, not just acceptable, but glamorous and stylish. So, the Beauties can be a catalyst for changes in attitude that are deep seated and not easily shifted.

Beauties are women who actively enhance their appearance without apology and demonstrate how to value and pursue the joy of feeling attractive. They know that receiving attention and compliments for their appearance is a legitimate way of being affirmed, and they are creative about their particular style. There isn't just one definition of beauty for them, but many. Being uniquely attractive is more important to them than fitting a stereotypical framework. This is a great gift to all women, regardless of ethnicity, because it tends to allow for more perceived acceptability of a wider variety of body type, hairstyle, and overall appearance. This may be one reason fewer African American teenage girls are diagnosed with eating disorders than is true for teenage girls in general.

The women I interviewed frequently did not see themselves as particularly beautiful, but I surely did. When asked which strength most personified her, not one claimed this characteristic. Maybe it seems unattractive to affirm that one is attractive! Nevertheless, every woman I interviewed could easily be placed in this category, though they would probably deny it and many did.

Since research indicates that a great percentage of our first impression of another person has to do with their appearance, it is important not to underestimate the power of personal presentation.

But, since none of the thirty-one women I interviewed would claim this strength, I would ultimately choose for them. I considered leaving this chapter with no representatives and decided against it because I thought it was important to give a variety of examples. I worried about choosing a woman with light skin. Would I be accused of falling prey to the very thing that had been done by people of both races? I worried about doing the opposite and being in reaction to the racism and internalized racism of our society. But, the truth is African American women are very much the product of a complex and mixed heritage, which includes many ethnicities and many varieties of outward appearance. It is this variety that is a cultural strength. And so, I chose four women to exemplify this very important category. You, the reader, will have your own ideas about what makes a person attractive to you. But, I think you will see that each of the women in this chapter have a personal style that sets her apart and is noteworthy. In addition, each is generous and exemplifies the inner beauty, that hard-to-get kind that Ruby Dee speaks of. It is my belief that their appearance as well as their brilliance in their particular field has been a contribution to the status of women, as a whole.

Finally, stereotypes do not change over night. One of my early psychology supervisors said to me, "Sonnee, you cannot legislate caring." I believe that the same might be said about changing perceptions. Changes in perception cannot be legislated. But, the women represented in this chapter have contributed, each in her own way, to the celebration of African American women's appearance, in addition to their other accomplishments. I hope they are pleased by their inclusion in this chapter.

Gloria Bouknight

"We all have that quiet, little voice inside us that we often suppress. It should be our guiding star."

I was teaching a weekend class at Miraval, the lovely wellness spa in Tucson, AZ, popularized by Oprah Winfrey. I kept seeing a gorgeous African American woman here and there at the resort. She was very tall and thin, and very dark. Her looks were exotic to my eye, and I just couldn't stop looking at her.

One morning, I ran into her in the gift shop. "You are so beautiful!" I exclaimed. "I hope you enjoy your beauty." With that, the woman started to cry and said that she had really needed to hear something nice. Her name was Gloria Bouknight, and she went on to say that her husband was dying of cancer, and she had been taking care of him during his long illness. She had come to the resort for a break before returning to Connecticut to continue his care. I was going home to Northern California, and it seemed unlikely that we would meet again.

Gloria and I had several long chats during the remainder of our stay at Miraval and agreed to keep in touch. We called one another from time to time just to visit, and over a period of months we developed a sweet friendship.

I brought my family to Gloria's for a visit when we passed near her home on a family vacation. We all spent the night and had a great time getting to know each other.

After I interviewed Gloria, she asked if she could give me some fashion advice. "Of course!" I said having no idea what was to occur. "The hairstyle has to go," she said. "Very '80s. You're really out of date. And, your wardrobe needs re-doing, too." Now, I really liked my curly hair and my boutique style clothes. So I protested a bit, but not too much.

Gloria researched the "right" place for me to have my makeover in San Francisco. She made the appointment with the "perfect" stylist. When I arrived at the up-scale salon, I was told that my fashion consultant had just spent a half hour on the telephone with them, giving instructions as to how I was to look. And so, I emerged completely transformed. The makeover was completed some months later when Gloria insisted that she help me with a new wardrobe. She taught me about the concept of fashion versus style as we shopped. And so, I not only made a wonderful new friend, I got the benefit of her creative eye and gentle and not so gentle guidance. Gloria has become a close friend. We have shared many fun times, serious talks, and meaningful experiences. Her story is a magical one and she is magical!

Gloria Bouknight, runway model, featured on the cover of numerous magazines, and now a fashion forecaster and merchandizing consultant, was born the fourth of thirteen children, on Irmo Island, off the coast of South Carolina in the Sea Islands. Her father was a mosaic artist from Cameroon, Africa. Her mother was Kiahwah and Blackfoot Indian and African American.

There was no running water, nor many paved roads on Irmo. Glorious, as she was called then, was delivered by a midwife in her grandmother's home. There were no doctors or dentists; so herbs, ritual, and ceremony were the modalities of healing.

When the midwife, Miss Mamie, arrived, during the last minutes of her mother's labor, Gloria was born. Miss Mamie took the baby onto the front porch of the home, held her up to the sky, where the sun was bright and rising, and said, "Oh, what a glorious day!" And that is how she got her name—Glorious. Everyone calls her Gloria. Her father returned to his native country with his sons and Gloria's mother married another man, and went on to have nine more children, including three sets of twins. As a result, Gloria went to live with her grandmother. She says that this was where she learned all of her spiritual principles. "I come from a culture of storytellers," she says and she tells the following story.

"One day, when I was five years old, I was walking home from church with my grandmother. She had been 'testifying' in church about what God had done for her. I asked how she knew there was a God. She took my arms and wrapped them around a huge tree trunk and said, 'Now, you are touching God.' Then, she had me lie down on the ground and look at the sky. 'Now, you are seeing God,' she said. Then, we walked to the creek and she had me put my hands in the cool water. 'Now, you are feeling God!' she exclaimed. After that, she said, 'Now, you have touched, seen and felt God.'"

She also taught Gloria about the natural world. By today's standards, she would be considered eccentric, and even then she was a bit different. She taught her granddaughter about nature; the habits of animals, where to find edible plants and berries, where to find healing herbs, and which plants not to touch because they were poisonous. Her grandmother's advice was to spend time in nature, especially during times of difficulty or turmoil.

Gloria says that when she is confused or upset, she finds a place in nature to sit or walk, and that this practice has helped her at significant junctures of her life. "If I hadn't had my God in me, I don't know what would have happened," she says emphatically. "I often affirm a quote from the Bible, 'This is the day the Lord has made. I will rejoice and be glad in it.'"

Because there were no hotel accommodations on the mainland for the black musicians and entertainers, many notables, such as Howlin' Wolf, Muddy Waters, and James Brown boarded in her grandmother's house or with neighbors during their local stints. They would sit out in the yard singing and playing their instruments. But, they were of little note to young Gloria, because it was her Uncle Muss and Uncle Tail who taught her to play music on the organ, the Jew's harp, and the harmonica. It was a financially impoverished, but culturally rich environment.

When Gloria was nine, her grandmother moved away to take care of a sick relative. Gloria returned to her mother's home, where she says that she felt like the darkest, ugliest thing there. It was a difficult time in stark contrast to her peaceful time with her grandmother.

As with most women I interviewed, there were people whose influence on their lives proved life changing. In Gloria's case, she recalls a fifth grade teacher, Miss Morgan. On the first day of school, she asked her class, "What did you do over the summer?" Although Gloria had done nothing out of the ordinary, she made up a big story about her father and brothers returning from Africa. When the other children were giggling and making noises expressing disbelief, Miss Morgan said sternly, "Excuse me! We are listening to Gloria. She is telling what she did." "She helped me tell it and she filled in some blanks for me. She knew it was made up, but she preserved my dignity. She made everyone applaud and she hugged me," Gloria says.

Two years before that, her third grade teacher, Miss Hagle assigned her to deliver the report cards for promotion to fourth grade to the fourth grade teacher, Mrs. Cole. It was the first time Gloria had ever been chosen for anything. If we know that Gloria's stepfather was "beyond cruelty" and that her step-grandmother had told her never to stand by her brothers and sisters because she was too ugly and dark, then we can understand what it meant to her when Miss Hagle said, "Take these report cards to Mrs. Cole. She looks like you." And she hugged Gloria when she said it. It meant that being dark like Mrs. Cole was acceptable.

Gloria says she grew up hearing her grandmother and great-grandmother's stories. Her great-grandmother, Betsy, was Native American and never spoke her own name. She had watched her own mother be captured by slavers, put in a wagon and taken away, never to be seen again.

Gloria was taught to lock herself in the house at night to be safe from drunk, white men. "I thought white people were the devil and I was taught never to speak to them and to run if I saw a white man coming," she says. "I had no interaction with white people until I left home. I saw the lynching of a young boy and my friend, Betsy's house set on fire. My mother did clean house for a white woman but that was it. I worked hard to stay invisible."

When she was twelve, her mother sent her to New York to work as a live-in maid for a white family. Imagine! She traveled from South Carolina to New York with $5 and a chicken sandwich. She had never been around white people before and had been taught not to speak to them. She did not speak Standard English. When she arrived in New York, she had no idea how to get to her job. A bathroom attendant kept her safe and took her to the Red Cross and put her on the NE Railroad to her destination. Her employer paid her $30 a week plus room and board. Gloria sent this money home. On days off, she would go with other maids to Harlem and she says she was in awe of the people she saw wearing fancy clothes. She tasted her first Pepsi and would wait outside the bars for the others because she was too young to go in. The woman Gloria worked for was kind and gave her the first birthday present she had ever received, a money tree with fifty $1 bills tied to it!

Gloria emphasizes that she was a naïve, sheltered child, with little or no experience of the outside world and it was overwhelming. It is here, she says, that she began "living in my head." By this she means that she lived in fantasy much of the time. But some things were real. Both of her sons were born while she was a teenager. She no longer could work as a live-in. She got a job tagging clothes in the garment district, and then several jobs as a maid or waitress. It is probably an understatement to say that life was hard with two growing boys to take care of. She says of that time that she always felt ugly. She was tall, 5'10", and skinny, 114 pounds, and very dark. Her survival often required lying and pretending. She says today that many people were kind to her over those years and she didn't always repay them with kindness. So, now she tries to repay those debts by passing on kindness to others.

After her first son was born and Gloria could no longer work as a live-in maid, she entered a home for unwed mothers. They cared for her baby while she found an apartment and a job nearby and the two of them moved in. She dashed home on breaks and at lunch to care for the baby and when a co-worker figured out what Gloria was doing, she offered her a place to live.

In time she had a second son and she moved her little family to Los Angeles. On a bus in that city, on the way to a job interview to be a maid or a waitress, a woman said to her, "You are so beautiful. You should be a model." Gloria was eighteen and still did not talk to people much, especially white people. But, she took the woman's card and called her in desperation because she had no money for food or rent. It was a fortuitous phone call. She had been told she was ugly her entire life. But, she was chosen for the "Black is Beautiful" spread for a major magazine and over night she became "Sable Knight" from Nigeria. "My survival was lying and pretending and I lived in my fantasy world," she says today. "I was this tall, skinny woman with hair as big as the moon."

Sometimes she had trouble keeping her story straight. During one appearance on Johnny Carson's *Tonight Show*, she forgot that she was supposed to be from Nigeria and said she was from South Carolina. Johnny covered for her by saying, "Yeah, me too." They laughed about it at the break.

As Sable Knight, she lived for a time at the Playboy Mansion. She says she did well as a runway model because, "I liked to walk." She worked in Europe and lived in Rome for five years because she was considered too dark to model in the United States. Her boys were always with her and she loved her new life. She appeared on numerous magazine covers.

"I didn't really have choices," she says now. "Things were chosen for me, in a way. My own choice would have been to create a village for unwanted children, unwanted dogs, and elderly people with nowhere to go."

Gloria was married for many years to a man much older than herself, who is now deceased. She says that he was her best friend and a man of great integrity and kindness. Although they separated after many years of marriage, Gloria took care of him in her home, during his terminal illness.

She made a decision to stop modeling in 1997 and attended The Fashion Institute of Technology to study merchandising and buying, and began her career as a fashion forecaster and merchandiser. When I asked her how she knows what the coming fashions will be, she says that she is informed by the cycles of nature and by the mood that is engendered by world events.

But, she makes a clear distinction between fashion and style. "Fashion is about what is currently selling in stores. Style is something inside of you that radiates and lets the world know who you are. It is a statement about yourself and that is a big difference," Gloria emphasizes.

These days, Gloria finds time, while working in the fashion business, to visit women's jails and other institutions, dragging a mannequin and a suitcase of clothes along. She teaches the women how to dress for job interviews and other occasions, how to identify their own style and conduct themselves properly. Gloria was required to attend etiquette school when she was a model, and she realizes the importance of the lessons she learned there. So, she teaches these skills to the women she comes in contact with.

When asked about any advice she might have for other women, Gloria says, "Believe absolutely in yourself and not necessarily what people tell you. Accept yourself and value yourself. We all have that quiet, little voice inside us that we often suppress. It should be our guiding star. We are all here on a spiritual journey, so learn your lessons."

Gloria also makes the point that travel is broadening and enlightening. She says that her first trip to Africa was just such an experience. "I got on Air Afrique Airlines at Kennedy Airport. Both pilots and all the attendants were black; they had chests and butts. When I got off in Dakar, West Africa, it was the most healing thing that could happen. It was not Tarzan and Jane, and no shacks. It was a beautiful, efficient city, and everyone was jet black. For the first time in my life, I was in the majority; and, it was all beautiful! The illusion I had been taught of Africa, as strictly a place of disease and famine was not true. A guide at the museum said, 'American blacks do not know who they are.'" Gloria has obviously discovered who she is. The years of illusion and pretense are in the distant past. She is beautiful in every sense of the word... and always was.

Laura Murphy

"A mighty few will make the difference. Be one of them!"

I told my friend, Marci Shimoff, about the book I was writing. "You HAVE to interview Laura Murphy!" she said. I had never heard of Laura Murphy, and said so, but Marci was insistent. She went to her address book to get the telephone number for me and encouraged me to call Laura right away. "She is one of the most powerful women in Washington, D.C.," Marci emphasized. And so, when I called Laura and asked if I could come to visit her for the interview, it was a wonderful surprise to have her invite me to her home.

The first thing that struck me about Laura when I met her was her beauty and her grace. There is graciousness about Laura that is so evident in her personal presentation and the content of her conversation. This brilliant, tough, and politically astute woman is perfectly dressed, with every hair in place. She wears magnificent jewelry that she has made herself. Her face is soft and her manner is generous. She is elegant! She also loves beauty, which is evident in her surroundings.

On another occasion, when I met her in a hotel coffee shop, people turned to watch her walk across the room to our table. She draws that kind of attention. When she spoke in our interview, of her work with Shirley Chisolm, the first African American woman elected to Congress, as personifying femininity, I thought, "I don't know about Ms. Chisolm, but you, Laura, personify femininity." And, so, though Laura could certainly be included in any of the other chapters of this book, this one seemed just right.

Laura Murphy's home in Washington, D.C. is breathtakingly beautiful. She has decorated it herself without the help of an interior designer. The living room displays original paintings by Laura Wheeling Warren, among other artists, and Laura says that this house and its contents are a testament to possibilities, and a work ethic that does not include or tolerate corruption.

Laura is the youngest of five children born to her parents, and these five represent three generations of college-educated people in her family. Her father, a lawyer in private practice in Baltimore, became the longest serving judge in the state of Maryland's history.

She describes her mother as essentially a "free-spirit," who experienced what Laura describes as "the crushing oppression of a traditional marriage." It was a family of very high expectations for all the children, especially the boys. But, even though Laura's father was a learned man, steeped in politics and the law, he could also be found watching cartoons with his children.

The entire family sat down to dinner at 6:00 p.m. every evening. You could set your watch by it. This was a family who was not only educated, but also used to a gentile lifestyle.

Laura's father returned from wartime service in North Africa only to be made to ride in a segregated military train. He strafed under the knowledge that although he had an excellent education and social grace, he still could not move freely in his own country. His mother advised him to apply to law school and he gained entrance to The University of Maryland because Thurgood Marshall sued to gain his entrance.

So, it was against this backdrop of high expectations and a politically involved family that Laura evolved. By the time Laura was seven, she was handing out campaign literature in various runs for office, mostly by members of her family. Within her immediate family, there have been fourteen runs for political office.

Laura's paternal uncle, George B. Murphy, Jr., was a wonderful mentor. He had traveled the world with actor and Renaissance man, Paul Robeson, whom her father had defended in front of the House Committee on Un-American Activities, and shared many of these experiences with his little niece.

He also knew Lorraine Hansberry and many women in the labor movement. He was a fiery orator and there were many arguments about politics that would sometimes go until 2:00 a.m. around the Murphy's dining room table.

When she was eight, her Uncle George would ask, "Now, Laura, have you read *The New York Times* today?" When she would reply, "No," he would say, "Well, I'm going on a trip for two weeks and we'll discuss the headlines when I return."

"He talked to me as though I was someone important," she says. "He was interested in what I had to say and he was empowering."

Laura's father's family had started *The Afro-American Newspaper* and many members of the family have served on the board of directors at one time or another. When her Uncle George tried to unionize the workers, he got kicked out of the family business; but Laura didn't miss the fact that controversy often occurs when one stands by his or her convictions.

Laura was accepted to and began attending Wellesley College before she graduated from high school. In fact, she didn't receive her high school diploma until the end of her freshman year in college. She had attended high school in a largely middle-class, Jewish neighborhood where she was met with negative attitudes toward her. She says of this experience that it was a real education about class, and how cruel Americans could be to their fellow countrymen, black and white.

Laura says that she loved "the vibe" at Wellesley. It was very green in the area west of Boston, and it reminded her of her parent's vacation home in the country. Ten percent of her class was African American and she quickly became active in the Civil Rights movement. Though she began as a political science major, she changed to history because she found the political science curriculum out of touch with reality and too academic. Being a history major was her "salvation" as so much about current events was explained by studying the imperialism and colonization practices of the British and French.

In the summer between her junior and senior years in college, Laura was invited to serve an internship in Washington, D.C. in the office of Congressman Parren Mitchell, the first African American elected to Congress from the state of Maryland, and a founding member of The Congressional Black Caucus. This was the beginning of her professional career working in the political arena.

Upon graduating from college, Laura officially went to work for Parren Mitchell (D, MD) in Washington, D.C. As a teenager she had worked hard for his groundbreaking election as the first African American federally elected official from the state of Maryland. At the age of twenty, she was the youngest legislative assistant in Congress. She left after a year, in part because Congressman Mitchell said that he didn't believe single women should receive the same pay as married men who had to support families even if they performed the same duties.

Shortly thereafter, Laura went to work as a legislative assistant for Representative Shirley Chisolm, who was dedicated to the growing movement of "equal pay for equal work." "Representative Chisolm had a staff filled with young, dynamic and intelligent women working for her. We called ourselves 'The Chisettes.' It was exciting and empowering." Laura goes on to say: "Shirley Chisolm epitomized femininity and charisma. She was a wonderful mentor for me."

In 1979, Laura was recruited by The American Civil Liberties Union's Washington, D.C. office, where she was a lobbyist for women's and civil rights. Her work on these issues, especially the Voting Rights Act Extension of 1982, started a life long commitment to working on "difference-making" strategies to help enact federal legislation before Congress. She worked in a coalition of civil rights leaders, many of whom later went on to become heads of national civil rights organizations.

Ever present was Laura's father's concern that she might become a "spinster." Although she had an active social life, she had been single for seven years since college. Her sister had married years earlier and Laura's family worried that she might never marry and have children. And so, Laura married a good man, with a good job, from a good family, and moved with him to Los Angeles, where she raised money for the ACLU and did project management for Mixner/Scott, Inc., a public relations firm.

In 1985, Willie Brown was Speaker of the California Assembly and he asked Laura to come to work for him as Chief of Staff of his Los Angeles office. Laura took the job, which brought her into the middle of the California political scene. She hosted numerous political fundraisers out of her home and raised considerable sums of money for the Speaker in her spare time. It was an exciting time in Laura's career, but her marriage was falling apart, and she and her husband separated.

Laura went back to Washington, D.C. to attend a retirement party for Parren Mitchell. While there, she met an intriguing man who had been widowed for several years. They shared a love of politics and of African American political and economic achievement. He chaired the finance committee for Jesse Jackson's 1988 presidential campaign, and, Laura briefly worked as the director of fundraising for the Jackson campaign. Their close relationship in politics took a romantic turn and they ended up marrying in 1987 and had a son, her only child. They moved to Chicago and Laura took up political fundraising almost full time, working for such candidates as L. Douglas Wilder, the first black governor of Virginia, Atlanta Mayor, Maynard Jackson, D.C. Mayor, Sharon Pratt Dixon, U.S. Senator Paul Simon, State Comptroller, Roland Burris, and many others.

Her new husband was a ground breaking African American entrepreneur. Years before they met, he had acquired a great deal of money after he sued to win the ownership rights to the CBS television affiliate in Boston. During their marriage, Laura watched him engineer deals to purchase the Denver Nuggets basketball team and an NBC affiliate radio station. She was married for five years, but made the decision to divorce, as the marriage could not survive the strain of such strong personalities.

Laura returned to Washington, D.C. to work for Mayor Sharon Pratt

Kelly as a Senior Tourism consultant. This position allowed her to travel extensively and to dispel the public characterization of Washington, D.C. as the "murder capital" of the world. She became director of The Office of Tourism and Promotions, expanding all sorts of government contracting opportunities for small and community based businesses, and creating and expanding new markets in the tourist, hotel, and airline industries. Tourism is the largest private industry in Washington, D.C., and the mayor decided that Laura was perfect for the job because of her experience working on sophisticated strategies that included corporate officials and grass roots organizations alike.

Two years into her tenure as tourism director, the ACLU came knocking on her door again, and they implored her to return to the Washington, D.C. office. Her heartstrings were pulled and she agreed to become director of the Washington Legislative Office of The American Civil Liberties Union. She says that she inherited a staff that initially did not want a new boss. She had to rebuild her staff, which eventually went from nineteen to forty-two members.

In her capacity as director, Laura became the national spokesperson on major policy issues including civil liberties, implications of anti-terrorism measures, criminal justice issues, campaign finance reform, personal and financial privacy issues, and constitutional rights.

In 1998, the congressional newsletter, *Roll Call*, named Laura Murphy one of the fifty most influential figures in congressional politics. And when Attorney General Ashcroft stated that the civil liberties community was aiding the enemy, Laura replied, "Free and robust debate is one of the main engines of social and political justice." Of course, she had originally learned this at her parent's dining room table.

Laura was the ACLU's chief lobbyist and strategist on federal issues before Congress, the White House, the Department of Justice and other executive branch agencies. Her work was instrumental in the passage of landmark legislation such as the Family Medical Leave Act, the Help America Vote Act, the Motor Voter Bill, the Religious Freedom Restoration Act, the Religious Land Use and Institutionalized Persons Act and the Freedom of Access to Clinics Act. She has spearheaded awareness of the civil liberties problems in the USA Patriot Act, and led a national effort to engage civil rights leaders in the civil rights implications of criminal justice policy. She has testified frequently before Congress, organized lobbying visits, and appeared frequently in the national media. She created in-house field and media departments at the ACLU and led several effective "odd bedfellows" national coalitions comprised of conservatives and liberals.

During the tragic events of September 11, 2001, she was one of the first spokespersons of any national organization willing to address concerns Americans voiced concerning their safety and their civil liberties after the worst terrorist attack on U.S. soil in history. After numerous interviews on *CNN*, *The Lehrer News Hour* and National Public Radio, as well as being quoted in the *New York Times* and the *Washington Post*, Laura Murphy soon became a sought-after national expert on civil liberties and the USA Patriot Act enacted in haste by Congress and signed into law by the Bush administration. It was her bold leadership that gave power to much of the ACLU's campaign to "Keep America Safe and Free."

When 9/11 happened, Laura had been a single mother for ten years. Work at the ACLU just exploded into endless months of long hours, late conference calls with ACLU colleagues, press conferences, speaking engagements, television and radio appearances, congressional briefings and testimony, and a bigger staff. Her son cooked dinner as often as she did even though he was only in the seventh grade. Much to her sadness he was largely a "latch-key" kid for the first year in the immediate aftermath of the terrorist attacks. At the same time, her parents' health began failing, requiring more of her attention. Her energy was stretched and her family became concerned about her non-existent social life. Soon, her brother's girlfriend, ("T", as she is affectionately known) intervened when she saw Laura at a Thanksgiving dinner at a relative's home. T insisted that Laura meet her boss at the law firm where she worked. Despite the fact that Laura is African American and Bill is white, there seemed to be no cultural or romantic limitations to their mutual attraction.

Everything in that relationship started to go quickly and well, and they ended up moving in together. Nonetheless, their life together encountered many challenges. "Mr. P." as her son calls him, had no sooner moved into her home than her father died at the age of eighty-five. Several months later, her new husband was diagnosed with a non-cancerous brain tumor and had eleven hours of surgery. A month after that, her son's father died. Her brother-in-law was diagnosed with lung cancer. 2003 was a challenging year, to say the least.

In 2004, Laura came to the realization that she needed a rest. She retired from her position at the ACLU in the summer of 2005, because she wanted more time to spend with her husband and son and to breathe outside of the national spotlight. "I was brave enough to say, 'I need a break,' and to think about my life." Laura lost over twenty pounds and indulged her creativity by making high-end jewelry with natural stones, and re-decorating the house.

It was not long before she began mapping out the next chapter of her life. In 2007 she started her own lobbying firm and business has been booming. "I know that I have a whole other career in me, but only God knows the contours of it at this point. All I can say is that I feel fortunate in the amount of good will I have encountered," she says with a smile.

Laura emphasizes that her career as a lobbyist was similar to that of a "saleswoman." Instead of marketing widgets, she was convincing members of Congress to buy the principles that the ACLU was championing. Now as a lobbyist who represents non-profit, as well as corporate clients, the ideas that she is marketing on Capitol Hill are more tangible: jobs, economic support, tax breaks. She has an empowering belief that she can help bring disparate forces together around a common cause. She says she is at her best when she can generate connections among people who would not normally be of the same political party or in the same interest group.

"I am an optimist and I have loved my career," she says with great emotion. "Otherwise, what is the point? I've done what I've done in the face of a society that is sometimes not very affirming of a woman like me and the constituencies that I have lobbied for."

When a recent contender for high political office approached Laura to come to work in his campaign, he said, "We don't know anyone else like you." "That's pretty damn sobering," she says. "I want to be able to say that I created (through mentoring and inspiration) dozens of others like me, who empower the disenfranchised. Rights are only as good as their reach to those deemed underserved or least popular by society."

Laura has wonderful and poignant advice for all women: "A mighty few will make the difference. Be one of the few. Choose words and companions wisely. Pick people who affirm you. Nurture and cultivate reasons to be optimistic. If you cultivate optimism, it will spread; and, it will help you and draw others. Always keep a spark of hope and that optimistic core."

Joyce Elliott

*"Forget about being
a lady;
be a woman!"*

I had gone to Little Rock, Arkansas to visit my friend, Susan Sims Smith. "We heard this amazing woman speak last night and you just have to interview her!" Susan said. "Let's call her up and see if she'll come over tomorrow afternoon for tea." And so we did. And Joyce said, "yes," and came the next day. We sat in an upper room overlooking the Arkansas River, and Joyce told me the story of her life.

She is gorgeous in an exotic (at least to my eye) sort of way. She has huge brown eyes, and an almost shaved head. Her teeth are snow white and she smiles broadly.

Joyce Elliott is enthusiastic and forceful in her advice to women! "Become self-sufficient by becoming educated and self-educated," she says. "Lower your voices, so that they are not dismissed. No screeching, because you will cover over your meaning. But that doesn't mean you speak with bouquets of sweetness. Forget about being a lady; be a woman!"

Adamantly she continues: "Women came into this world the same way as men. Don't expect to not take responsibility. Run for public office. Don't wait for a man to ask you to do it. Being a woman is fabulous! We are different from men, but not less than men." She is so enthusiastic and engaging, that I am thoroughly convinced!

This dynamo woman was born in a tiny, rural town, Willisville, Arkansas, population 206. Her father and mother had four daughters, Joyce being the second child. Her father was a disabled construction worker who had lost an eye playing baseball as a teenager. He was irresponsible and disinterested in his children and played little part in their lives. One thing he did do was to take them all to live in Kalamazoo, Michigan in a duplex with his parents on one side and his family on the other. Joyce lights up as she talks about the joy of life in the North: snow, the Popsicle man, and sidewalks. She says it all seemed so sparkling clean to her, compared to the heat and dust and racism of the South.

One day, after they had lived in Michigan for a while, without warning, the police arrived at her house. Her mother was packing their belongings to leave on a bus for Arkansas...without her father. They went back to Willisville to live with her maternal grandparents, who were not pleased to see them coming because they already had other family members they were caring for. It was sad for Joyce knowing that they were unwanted. She recalls thinking, "I will never be clean again." There was no toilet, no running water, no electricity, and no sidewalks. There were nine people in a four-room house. Because there were no sidewalks and only dirt roads, dust and dirt were everywhere. At times there was not enough food to go around. Eventually, her mother, whom Joyce describes as fun loving, with lots of friends, formed a long-term relationship with another man. Three more children were added to the family.

Joyce says that her escape was school. She loved it and she was good at it, though she failed second grade. But a great teacher, Mrs. Arthurline Bradford, introduced her to the dictionary ... the world of words. Mrs. Bradford had books she shared with Joyce. "I began to believe that I could be educated," she says. Since neither of her parents completed high school, finishing high school became a huge goal. "By the fourth grade, I was at the head of my class. I knew it and I intended to keep it that way." At age twelve, Joyce figured out that if a student graduated from high school first in his or her class, they received a fully paid college scholarship to what is now The University of Arkansas at Pine Bluff. She set this as her goal. She had already decided that she wanted to be a teacher or a broadcaster. She decided that if she became a broadcaster, it would be from a French speaking country, as she was taking French. These dreams fed her determination. Joyce attended segregated schools, until 1966, when a desegregation lawsuit demanded integration. As luck would have it, Joyce was one of the few students chosen to desegregate Willisville High School. She did not want to do this because it interfered with her plan to be first in her class and to get a scholarship. "I just knew my scholarship would be gone!" she says with a wry smile.

As she came into the classroom on the first day of school at Willisville

High, a boy said loudly, "Oh, my God! Open the window. It stinks in here." That was her welcome. There were two girls who were noticeably nice to her. The others were either mean or indifferent.

Shortly after she arrived at Willisville, she was called to see the principal and superintendent. They asked how she had gotten these grades and said she couldn't possibly have gotten such high grades. It was implied that she couldn't possibly be an "A" student, that somehow her official transcript was a fraud.

Joyce was also a very good athlete. Basketball was her sport and when she tried out for the Willisville High School team, the coach said, "You're very good, but we don't have a uniform to fit you." "I was crushed as much by his lack of respect in giving such an incredulous excuse as I was by being denied the opportunity to play," she says. The following two years, she did get to play. The school was small, numbers were few, and Joyce was good – and needed.

At the end of that year, the other black students from her class who had integrated the high school returned to their old school. Joyce was the only one who stayed.

She was determined to go to college. Her Uncle James, who lived in Michigan, offered to buy her a car and fully pay for her education if only she would come to Michigan to attend college. He hated the South and wanted her out. But, Joyce was feeling a higher purpose. On some level, she had begun to understand Mohandas Gandhi's words – "Be the change you want to see." She says, "I had this calling that something had to be done to change things. I chose to attend Southern Arkansas University because there were very few blacks there and it provided an opportunity to make change in my home state, right in my own back yard." She got jobs and loans to get through, for as she had predicted, integrating Willisville High School meant receiving no scholarship. Her uncle kept his word to help only if she left the South.

Joyce majored in Speech and English. She continued taking French. Though she wanted to play basketball in college, that opportunity was not available since Title IX legislation, which would eventually provide for equality of sports access for women, didn't exist at that time. Ironically, Joyce tutored the boys who were on basketball and other scholarships, rather than receiving one herself.

She loved debate and argument and she wanted to understand language and presentation. "I began to realize that teaching was really important. I wanted to teach so that I could be a better teacher than the teachers I had who let me be bullied by the racist bullies."

Joyce was weary from being the "first black" and vowed not to be in that position anymore. She accepted a teaching position in New Boston, Texas. When she arrived, the superintendent said, "I didn't realize you were black from our phone call." She was the first full-time black teacher at the school: "first" again.

Joyce married a man who was also a teacher. They eventually moved to El Dorado, Arkansas, where her husband was the assistant principal at the high school. She was twenty-nine when her son, Elliott, was born. By the time Elliott was three she had divorced. She says that she had tried very hard to be married, but that she and her husband just could not find common ground on too many important issues. They remained amicable and lived in close proximity to raise their son. Today, they are still good friends.

While teaching in Arkansas, Joyce was elected president of the local teacher's union. She says that she had known since she was ten that she would be in politics. She had been galvanized by the Nixon/Kennedy debate and wanted to talk about it in school, but was admonished to tend to her long division instead. As a teacher's union member, Joyce had seen that her mother and others like her had no worker's protections. She became interested in advancing the rights of working people.

In 1984, she was a delegate to the Democratic convention in San Francisco. Walter Mondale was nominated and selected Geraldine Ferraro as his running mate. Joyce comments, "When Mr. Mondale said we would have to raise taxes and then he put a woman on the ticket, well, I never felt so good about a loss. We overcame an attitude of apathy."

In 1999, Joyce ran for a seat in the State of Arkansas House of Representatives. She ran against three men and won in a run-off vote. She was determined to be "the voice of the people who have no voice." She has served three terms and twice ran for her seat unopposed. Early on, a conservative newspaper named her one of the ten best legislators in the state. She has repeatedly earned this honor during each of her terms. "I have truly enjoyed serving," she says. "People say thank-you to me for being so straightforward."

An example of Joyce's sense of integrity is that while serving on the Judiciary Committee in her first term, there was considerable lobbying for a hate crimes bill. Some ministers and others said they would support it, if the wording did not include sexual orientation. Joyce wouldn't do it. She said that she would rather have nothing than to have laws tacitly allowing discrimination. There is still no hate crimes law in Arkansas at the time of this writing.

"I have always stood up for what I thought was right, even if it was unpopular. Nine out of ten times, it has been unpopular."

One of Joyce's former high school students became an intern in the black caucus. He told her, "Ms. Elliott, I cannot tell you what it means to me to see you living what you taught us."

The list of honors accorded Joyce Elliott is a long one. She was named Power Player of the Year – 2006, by *Power Play* magazine and was pictured on their cover. This is a publication for and about black professionals. She was named one of the ten most powerful women in Arkansas and featured on the cover of *Active Years*, and was named by the Business and Professional Women of Arkansas as "A Woman Who Means Business."

Arkansas Times newspaper wrote a lengthy front-page article about her, chronicling her uncanny ability to maintain her integrity while successfully advocating for political positions that are often unpopular.

The League of Latin American Citizens gave her a presidential award for service. The National Council of Christians and Jews honored her in 2006 with their "Humanitarian of the Year" award. Omni, likewise, named her "Humanitarian of the Year" for her work advocating for peace, justice, and environmental protection.

The night before our interview, Joyce had been honored at the Jefferson/Jackson Dinner, which is a premier event of the Democratic Party. She had been named Democratic Woman of 2006!

When newly elected Governor, Mike Beebe, named his transition team, he turned to Joyce. She was one of four and the only woman. "I was honored to be asked to participate in such a daunting task," she says.

Of all these honors, Joyce says, "I have been privileged to serve."

And what of the boy who raised the window at Willisville High School because of the "stench" so long ago? They ended up at the same college. "He came to see me in my dorm room my senior year. I turned around and saw him and thought it was a mistake. He had come to apologize. He said he had been afraid I would replace him as Valedictorian. We wept together – him openly."

Term limits ended Joyce's career in the State House of Representatives December 31, 2007. She ran for and won a seat in the State Senate, but still has an eye on Washington!

While serving in the House of Representatives, Joyce chaired the Education Committee and worked to require Advanced Placement classes at all high schools, rather than what was then only thirty-five percent. She successfully worked to appropriate more money into poor areas to attract good teachers to these locations that have a long heritage of under-funding going back to slavery. She knows what it means to provide quality education, inspiration, and protection to all children, so that they can make a full contribution to their communities.

That realization is reflected in her present work with College Board, where she is the director of State Legislative Outreach for the Southwestern Region. In that capacity, she works with policy makers and other leaders to help insure all students, especially those traditionally underserved, have access to a rigorous curriculum and an opportunity to graduate from high school ready for college. A former teacher of both Advanced Placement (AP) and non-AP classes, she is keenly aware of what those classes mean to a student's preparedness. "Inaccessibility to such rigor is unconscionable," Joyce insists, "so I won't accept such an injustice."

Daphne Maxwell-Reid

*"Don't let your successes
go to your head
or your failures
go to your heart."*

My secret desire in high school and college was to be Homecoming Queen. In my schools, it was the football team who nominated and voted for the girls who would be so honored at the big Homecoming Game and accompanying festivities. At that time, it seemed to me that having all those football players nominate you as their favorite had to be the ultimate endorsement of desirability. But, it never happened for me. Not even close. And so, it was a delight for me to hear the story of Northwestern University's first African American Homecoming Queen, Daphne Maxwell-Reid. And though the whole idea of a Homecoming Queen and other, so-called beauty contests or popularity contests may seem outmoded in this day and age, women who receive this honor are often multi-talented and, of course, quite physically attractive.

And, also, women like Daphne, who broke the barriers of race and racism in areas highly visible to the general public, are to be particularly honored for putting African American women on the "radar" of the general population. This is a contribution not to be overlooked or trivialized.

Daphne Maxwell-Reid was born and raised in a public housing development in New York City. She's a middle child and freely admits that she was her mother's favorite daughter, which is an inside joke she has with her mother. Her father was one of many World War II veterans who left the virulent racism of the South for New York. Daphne says her father, who could have passed for white, never considered it. "He was more concerned about poverty than racism", she says. And, New York City had more opportunity. By the late 1940's, her father had taken a job as a "soda jerk" at Whalen's Drug Store. This was fun for his three children, but Daphne says that at home he was very strict and expected a lot.

Daphne's mother was a seamstress, who took in sewing, as well as making most of her own and her children's clothes. "My mother was the single most wonderful person I have ever met," Daphne says. "She was a devout Presbyterian who was a peace activist in the 1960's & 70's, and very active in many church and community activities."

It was exciting to grow up in New York City at that time. There was a cultural explosion happening. The Lincoln Center for Performing Arts was built nearby and Carnegie Hall was an easy subway ride away. Daphne makes the point that she didn't learn to drive until she left New York and married. There was just no need, as everything was easily accessible.

"We lived a charmed life in poverty," Daphne says. "I had no idea that we were poor. My mother made beautiful clothes for us and she actually was a great homemaker. I really appreciate that."

Because Daphne was very bright, she went to specialized classes for gifted children in the public schools. She was usually the only African American child in her class, or one of only two. Eventually, she entered Bronx High School of Science, which was one of the public high schools for the gifted and talented in New York City. She had lots of after-school activities, such as the All City High School Chorus and The Negro Ensemble Theater, as well as church activities and sewing projects at home. In her senior year of high school, she was elected class president. "It was a great life, but not over-scheduled and rushed, the way it is for so many children today," she says.

Daphne was a National Merit Scholarship winner. Northwestern University in Evanston, IL recruited her. "That's when I found out I was a nigger," she says evenly. "When I arrived at the dorms, the girl who was supposed to be my roommate said, 'I'm not rooming with a nigger.' This was my welcome at college."

Daphne remained at Northwestern for the remainder of her college career, majoring in interior design & architecture.

One of her high school English teachers submitted Daphne's photograph to a magazine editor who was preparing an article on college women for *Seventeen* magazine. This led to a trip to New York and a full-page photograph of her in the magazine, as one of *Seventeen* magazine's "Real" girls. Daphne appeared in the January 1967 issue, wearing an outfit made with a McCall's sewing pattern. The "Real Girl" spread was meant to highlight accomplished teens, and so Daphne was featured along with the Betty Crocker "Bake-Off" winner and a baton-twirling champion, among others. At the same time, Daphne's name and photograph had been entered in the traditional Northwestern University contest for Homecoming Queen.

Anyone attending college during this time period will remember that being in the Homecoming Court, usually comprised of four or five women, was a very big vote of confidence for the woman's beauty and general popularity.

Since there had never before been an African American woman entered in the contest, Daphne didn't give much thought to winning. Much to her surprise, she was one of the final five contestants. She was shocked, she says. As was traditional, the Homecoming festivities involved a parade prior to the official announcement of who among the five would be queen. The day before the parade, Daphne was informed that the green dress she intended to wear was inappropriate. She was told that she must wear white. This was just the beginning of what was to come.

The president of the University was to name the winner of the contest at a large student assembly. When Daphne's name was announced as Northwestern University's homecoming queen for 1967, the auditorium became completely silent. One of the other contestants began to cry. The others were consoling one another. Daphne walked across the stage, curtsied and walked off. The university president had held the crown of flowers over Daphne's head, for a quick picture, never actually placing it on her hair. She attended the homecoming football game the next day to receive her trophy. When the yearbook came out the following spring, there was that very small photograph of her and the president. Her name did not appear. Daphne had the courage to ask the editor of the yearbook why she did not receive the typical full-page photograph and pictorial and information spread accorded to all Homecoming Queens and their courts in years past. "It was not important this year," she was told.

Daphne was the first black Homecoming Queen that Northwestern University ever had. In fact, she was probably one of the first to be accorded this recognition at a major university anywhere in the United States.

But, the obvious disdain with which she was treated caused her to let the Alumnae Association know that when she received future solicitations for money or was asked to speak kindly of her Northwestern University experience, she would respond to neither.

Daphne's "Real Girl" spread had been seen by someone who took it to the Eileen Ford Modeling Agency. The agency expressed interest in her and she was told to lose five pounds and go see a woman named Amy Green. She did both. Amy took Daphne under her wing and mentored her as "one of her girls." It was a real break for her career in modeling.

In 1968, Daphne married her college sweetheart. She says now that they were probably too young, but that they had a lot of fun together in the eleven years of their marriage. He was a teacher and a coach, and she was busy modeling and doing commercials in Chicago.

At work, Amy Green had a variety of pictures taken of Daphne in various settings. Amy wanted to do a "cover-try" with Daphne, submitting her photograph to magazines for their cover. Much to her own surprise, Daphne became the first African American woman on the cover of *Glamour* magazine. She found it out when she walked by a newsstand and there it was!

Daphne learned how to do narrations and expanded her modeling career to speaking. She did a six-week stint as the first female "rock-jock" on Chicago's WLS radio station. The station was negotiating with someone else, and so Daphne was a stand-in and did a great job.

By this time, Daphne and her husband had a son. But, the marriage had deteriorated. She says that her husband was a good father and her son had a firm home base and stability in Chicago with his school and friends.

When she divorced, Daphne made a decision to leave her son in Chicago with his father, while she pursued her career in California. "Everyone was aghast. But, though I made more money than my son's father, I could not offer stability. And I knew it. We had a joint custody agreement; and, I took no alimony."

Robert Conrad discovered Daphne's talent. He gave her a start in television, on his show, *The Duke*. Its story line took place in Chicago and he knew her Northwestern connection. He called her "Queenie," knowing she had been Homecoming Queen there; and, he took a shine to her.

This break was the beginning of Daphne's very successful television career. She appeared in numerous shows, such as, *A Man Called Sloan*, *Hardcastle and McCormack*, *The A Team*, *T.J. Hooker*, and *WKRP in Cincinnati*, just to name a few.

Sadly, the situation with Daphne's former husband had deteriorated, and after five years of separation, she went to Chicago, picked up her son, and brought him back to California. In 1982, Daphne had re-married. So when she brought her son, Chris, to Los Angeles, they became a blended family, which included her new husband, Tim Reid, and his children.

In the late 1980's, Daphne's new husband produced a show called, *Frank's Place*, the first half-hour-long comedy that presented African Americans without caricatures. In addition, it was the first situation comedy without a laugh track. Then he produced thirteen episodes of *Snoops*, depicting a black couple, Nick and Nora, working in Washington D.C. Daphne had a leading role in his life, as well as the television shows.

In 1989, Tim and Daphne bought property in Charlottesville, VA. They moved there to escape some of the ever-present pressures of production in Los Angeles. Together they created a talk show—*The Tim and Daphne Show*—which was shot in Baltimore and ran for seventy-six, one-hour episodes.

In addition, she approached the McCall's sewing pattern company to produce an educational series, teaching people to sew. The *Suddenly You're Sewing with Daphne Maxwell-Reid* four-video kit was the result. When it was featured on the QVC shopping program, 1600 kits were sold in forty-five minutes. The Home Sewing and Craft Industry gave her kit its "Best New Product" award. McCall's "DMR" pattern collection is named for her. In the early '90s, she auditioned to be the replacement for the part of "Aunt Viv" in the television series, *The Fresh Prince of Bel Air*. She got the job and stayed with it until the end, three years later.

Nowadays, Daphne and Tim own and operate a full service film studio located in Petersburg, Virginia. It is called, "New Millennium Studios", and they produce movies, commercials, documentaries, etc.

Daphne has been married to Tim for over twenty-five years now. As of this writing, her son, Chris, was one of only twenty-nine black men to receive a Ph.D. in biochemistry in the entire United States. He is married to a wonderful woman and they have made Daphne a very happy grandmother.

Interestingly, after forty-one years since being mistreated as Homecoming Queen, Northwestern University attempted to right an old wrong. The Black Alumnae Association inducted Daphne into their newly established "Hall of Fame." She and three other former students were the first inductees. *Jet* magazine had made it a cover story in 1967, and the president of the university stated that her experience of so long ago was "a situation that had to be rectified." And so it was in October 2008.

Presently, Daphne is trying her hand at digital photography and is looking forward to her first gallery exhibit. "I am living a wonderful life", Daphne says. "I've had the freedom and the ability to work as I want and travel as I please. I have had great work experiences and loving relationships with family and friends. I couldn't ask for a better life."

When asked about the wisdom she would like to share with other women, Daphne had a number of things to say: "Always dream bigger than you are. Don't let your environment define you. Look for joy!"

"Most importantly, don't let your successes go to your head or your failures go to your heart. Keep that balance and though you may not reach a particular destination, you will have enjoyed the journey.

CHAPTER 9

A Balance of Blessings

A s is probably the case with most of you, I am constantly challenged to live a more balanced life. It is difficult in our fast-paced culture to eat properly, exercise regularly, find the right vocation, manage our family relationships and friendships, and our households, and still find time and energy to "give back" in our communities. I get overwhelmed. Nevertheless, the challenges of our time demand our full energy and intention.

So many times, during the years of writing this book, I have been asked why I had chosen this subject matter. In other words, why was a blond, blue-eyed, white woman writing about African American women? I was asked this question by people of various ethnicities, cultural backgrounds, and by both sexes. I was asked if I was afraid of being criticized for my efforts or my intentions questioned. And so, over and over I explained that I just thought that if a person had overcome a cultural atmosphere of prejudice in which African American women throughout the history of the United States, faced the double jeopardy of being discriminated against because of race and sex, then they must have some valuable insights and wisdom to pass on to each other and to the rest of us. And I was right!

Their insight, perspective, and wisdom comes from their experience of marginalization, combined with their clear determination to not allow this very marginalization to define them and be the end of their story.

Blessings come to us in many ways. There are some blessings we are born with: our particular family, perhaps, or our various abilities and talents. Whatever the case, if we are to thrive, we need to learn to multiply those blessings and share them. I hope that you noticed that every woman featured in this book named other people who had been a blessing to her. Sometimes this came in the form of a criticism, as when Carolyn Hall's mentor told her to go home, wash off her make-up, get rid of the mini skirt, and put on nylons before going to her interview at the bank. Sometimes it came subtly, as when Gloria Bouknight's teacher told her to take some papers to another teacher, who "looks like you," thereby helping her to see herself differently. Helping each other and looking for those helpers is essential.

But, there is another important element here that should not be overlooked. That is that research indicates that cultural diversity, while challenging at times, breeds more creativity. This has been proven in the workplace, and probably extends to our personal lives.

And creativity is surely needed in our country and the entire world, if we are to solve and resolve the challenges facing us all.

And yet, as the old proverb says, "Birds of a feather flock together." Demystifying and embracing people and cultures different from ourselves often goes against the tide of our natural tendencies. It may take some effort and even discomfort to overcome these separations and segregations based on race, religion, or other factors of personal identity. It's not only worth doing for personal growth, but for the well being of our world community.

Finally, each of the strengths I identified in the various women interviewed is valuable for everyone's personal development. The seven strengths represent values that promote health and wholeness. They also illustrate various forms of leadership. Its important to remember that if we overdo our strengths, they can become our weaknesses, and so maintaining balance is essential. Even the most effective leader is subject to "burnout" if she overdoes her strengths. The advice offered by several women interviewed, having to do with self-care is invaluable.

The women featured in this book are a blessing to our larger community, each in her own way. Some are well known and some you have heard about for the first time. Either way, they have contributed to the world's work in meaningful ways and have been generous in their service to their communities.

Finally, it is my hope that after reading the inspirational stories of these thirty-one women, you will be moved to reach out to people unlike yourself, to enjoy your commonalities and be enriched by, as well as challenged by your differences. Expanding our worldview improves our overall functioning. It is in this way that our own gifts and talents are multiplied as we learn from, and are inspired by one another—as these thirty-one women have so richly demonstrated.

Bibliography

Beals, Melba. *Warriors Don't Cry: A Searing Memoir of the Battle to Integrate Little Rock's Central High*. New York: Simon and Schuster, Inc., 1994.

Elders, Joycelyn. *Joycelyn Elders, MD.: From Share Cropper's Daughter to Surgeon General of the United States of America*. New York: Wm. Morrow and Co., Inc., 1996.

George, J.M., and Zhou, J. (2002). "Understanding when bad moods foster creativity and good ones don't: The role of context and clarity of feelings." *Journal of Applied Psychology*, 87(4), 687-697.

Rowell, Victoria. *The Women Who Raised Me*. New York: Harper Collins, 2007.

Shorter-Goodwin, Kumea. "From the Outside In: African American Women, Beauty and Psychotherapy." *The California Psychologist*, January/February 2007, 16-18.

Strawberry, Charisse and Darryl. *Recovering Life*. Pennsylvania: The Plough Publishing House, 1999.

Wattleton, Faye. *Faye Wattleton: Life on the Line*. New York: The Ballantini Publishing Group, 1996.

About the Author

Sonnee Weedn, Ph.D.

Clinical and Forensic Psychologist

D r. Weedn is the mother of two sons and has been married for 42 years. She is a member of a faith community and a long-time spiritual seeker. Her psychology practice in Novato, CA is devoted to helping people to embrace their lives fully and live with gentleness, compassion and integrity toward themselves and others. She does this using a variety of methods suited to the particular individual. Though her practice is a general one, she has specialized in addictions and codependency since 1985. She is a consultant to various legal entities, providing psychological assessment and consultation. Her greatest joy is providing professional training to other therapists and giving retreats of a transformational nature.

Acknowledgements

When I began this project, I had a powerful dream. I dreamed that I was paddling a small raft, far, far out into the ocean. I was "pushing off into the deep." I was told in the dream that although I was in deep water, definitely way over my head, and far away from shore, I was safe.

I want to acknowledge and thank the following people for encouraging me when I periodically lost my bearings and didn't know how to navigate. They provided me with guidance in the "deep waters" and reminded me that I really did know where I was and could find my way.

I am deeply grateful to the women who shared their stories with me. Their time and their patience with me, and the process were invaluable. In addition, several of them recommended others that I should contact. And, so, the project grew.

George McLaird and my friends at The Sausalito Presbyterian Church have contributed greatly to my personal process. Keith Arnold, Albert Sombrero, and Joe MacDonald are true brothers, always supportive and encouraging. Dana Patterson and Tina Powers shared their gifts of intuition to guide me.

Afeni Shakur was encouraging from the beginning. I would hear her voice on my message machine saying, "Hi, beautiful!" It lightened my day.

Marci Shimoff, Rev. Susan Sims Smith and Dr. Richard Smith, Kay Cash-Smith, Susan Johnson, Dr. Michele Saloner, Dr. Brigette Lank, Arthur Bosse, Dr. Kenneth Perlmutter, Dr. Ana Nogales, Martin Shore, Judy Karau, Leda Nix, Denise Mozetti, and Laura Welch: these friends and colleagues offered moral support and encouragement. Some offered names of women to contact. Steve Long helped me find women I was looking for and wasn't able to locate.

Janet Ray, Carolyn Saade, Andrew Dieden, Rhonda Daley, Dedocio Habi, Arundati Simmons, Jan Kingaard, and Benelia Terry were kind enough to read early versions and offer suggestions.

Cynthia Stewart's work and encouragement as my agent, was so helpful, as was that of Lynda Banks.

Thank-you Sherri Powers, J.D., MFT, and Gary M. Hoeber, MFT, for the valuable lessons of "Race Matters."

And finally, thank-you to my mother, Delight Wiseman, for teaching me the values of dignity and respect for all people. She gave me my original lessons in social justice.

Breinigsville, PA USA
17 March 2011
257860BV00005B/2/P

9 780983 277606